THATCHED BUILDINGS
OF DORSET

THATCHED BUILDINGS
OF DORSET

Michael Billett

Photographs by R. D. Megilley – Dorchester Studios

ROBERT HALE · LONDON

Robert Hale Ltd
Clerkenwell House
Clerkenwell Green
London EC1R OHT

British Library Cataloguing in Publication Data
Billett, Michael
  Thatched buildings of Dorset.
  1. Vernacular architecture – England
  – Dorset.   2. Thatched roofs – England
  – Dorset
  I. Title
  721'.5   NA969.D7

ISBN 0-7090-1962-9

Photoset by Rowland Phototypesetting Ltd
Bury St Edmunds, Suffolk
Printed in Great Britain by St Edmundsbury Press
Bury St Edmunds, Suffolk
Bound by Woolnough Bookbinding Ltd

Contents

			Page
Introduction			11
Chapter	*1*	Building Materials	21
Chapter	*2*	Thatching Styles	37
Chapter	*3*	Thatched Manor House Buildings	51
Chapter	*4*	Thatched Pubs	68
Chapter	*5*	Thatched Cottage Orné	91
Chapter	*6*	Thatched Farms and Barns	104
Chapter	*7*	Thatched Villages of Central Dorset	123
Chapter	*8*	Thatched Villages of North Dorset	148
Chapter	*9*	Thatched Villages of South Dorset	161
Chapter	*10*	Thatched Villages of East Dorset	184
Chapter	*11*	Thatched Villages of West Dorset	197
Bibliography			214
Index			215

Photographs

Chapter 3   *Page*
1 Woodsford Castle — 53
2 Hammoon Manor House — 57
3 Toller Whelme Manor House — 59
4 Thatched Range of Toller Fratrum Manor House — 60
5 Thatched Stable Range of Athelhampton House — 63
6 Winterborne Muston Manor House — 64
7 Thatched Barn of Waddon Manor House — 67

Chapter 4
8 Smugglers Inn – Osmington Mills — 70
9 Smiths Arms – Godmanstone — 75
10 Brace of Pheasants – Plush — 78
11 The Fox Inn – Corscombe — 79
12 The Worlds End – Almer, near Morden — 80
13 Wise Man Inn – West Stafford — 83
14 The Old Thatch – Uddens Cross, near Wimborne — 88

Chapter 5
15 Lodge (Cottage Orné) – Holt, near Hinton Martell — 93
16 Lodge (Cottage Orné) – Goathill, near Sherborne — 95
17 Round House (Cottage Orné) – Morden — 96
18 Round Lodge (Cottage Orné) – Compton House, near Sherborne — 97
19 Umbrella Cottage (Cottage Orné) – Lyme Regis — 98
20 Old Came Rectory (Cottage Orné) – Dorchester — 100
21 Regency Cottage (Cottage Orné) – Wool — 102

Chapter 6
22 Moonfleet Farmhouse – Higher Ansty — 107
23 Bovington Farmhouse – Bovington — 111
24 East Farm – Osmington — 112
25 Herringston Farmhouse – near Dorchester — 113
26 Tithe Barn – Abbotsbury — 115
27 Barton Barn – West Stafford — 118

28 Long Barn – Woodsford Farm, Woodsford ... 119
29 Lower Lewell Barn – near West Knighton ... 120
30 North Barn – Affpuddle ... 120

Chapter 7
31 Thomas Hardy's Cottage – Bockhampton ... 123
32 Yalbury Cottage Restaurant – Bockhampton ... 125
33 Hangman's Cottage – Dorchester ... 126
34 Butcher's Shop – Piddletrenthide ... 128
35 Memorial Seat – Tolpuddle ... 130
36 Pixie's Cottage – Tolpuddle ... 130
37 The Ring – Briantspuddle ... 132
38 Bladen Valley Estate Cottages – Briantspuddle ... 133
39 Post Office – Milborne St Andrew ... 134
40 Butcher Shop and Post Office – Bere Regis ... 136
41 Village Street – Milton Abbas ... 136
42 The Old Malt House – Winterborne Stickland ... 139
43 Bridge Cottage – Winterborne Zelston ... 141
44 A Thatched Wall – Winterborne Zelston ... 142
45 Cottage in Abbey Street – Cerne Abbas ... 143
46 Wessex Barn Guest-House – Frampton ... 145
47 Southover House – Southover, near Frampton ... 146
48 Terrace of Cottages – Charminster ... 146

Chapter 8
49 Solicitor's Office – Sturminster Newton ... 149
50 Barton House – Newton ... 151
51 Cottage by Pond – Ashmore ... 156
52 Thatch at Gold Hill – Shaftesbury ... 159

Chapter 9
53 Museum and Avice's Cottage – Wakeham, Portland ... 162
54 Information centre (RSPB) – Radipole Lake ... 163
55 Post Office – Preston, near Weymouth ... 165
56 Cottage by Waterside – Sutton Poyntz ... 166
57 Cottage – Sutton Poyntz ... 166
58 Terrace of Cottages – Sutton Poyntz ... 167
59 Wayfaring Cottage – Corfe Castle ... 173
60 Post Office – Moreton ... 174
61 Group of Cottages – Whitcombe, near Dorchester ... 176
62 Bus Shelter – West Stafford ... 177
63 Cottage with Thatched Apron Roof Layer – West Stafford ... 178
64 A Thatched Gabled End – Little Bredy ... 179
65 'Eyebrow' Windows – Little Bredy ... 180
66 Latticed Window Cottage – Little Bredy ... 181

Chapter 10
67   Group of Cottages – Tarrant Monkton   185
68   Marigold Cottage – Spetisbury   186
69   A Long Straw Thatched Cottage – Witchampton   190
70   Ornamental Thatch and Timber Framed Cottage –
       Witchampton   191
71   A Long Stretch of Thatch – Manswood   191

Chapter 11
72   The Cottage – Charmouth   199
73   Cottages in Main Street – Chideock   200
74   An Outshut End Thatched Cottage – Chideock   201
75   Seventeenth-century Cottage Chimneys – Chideock   201
76   J. C. and R. H. Palmer's Old Brewery – Bridport   204
77   Terrace of Cottages – Abbotsbury   207
78   A Cottage Group – Melbury Osmond   208
79   Post Office – Rampisham   210
80   An Ornamental Thatched Cottage – Chantmarle, near
       Evershot   211

Line Drawings

Fig.

1 Dorset Chalk Belts — 21
2 Cottage Types — 23
3 Wall Materials — 24
4 Corn Rick on Staddle Stones — 28
5 Dorset Marsh Reed Beds — 32
6 Dorset Spar Hook — 35
7 Long Straw Finishes — 40
8 Roof Types — 42
9 Renovated Thatched Roof — 44
10 Chimney Types — 47
11 Thatched Ridge Ornamentation — 48
12 Elaborate Ridge Ornamentation — 49
13 Woodsford Castle – First Floor — 55
14 Hammoon Manor House — 58
15 The Thimble, Piddlehinton — 76
16 Eaves Types — 94
17 Cottage Orné Lodge (Demolished) – Shroton — 99
18 Farmhouse Types — 105
19 Barn Roof Designs — 117
20 Thatch Fire Hook — 135
21 Sketch Map of Dorset — 213

Introduction

Eighty million years ago, a warm shallow sea covered present-day Britain and the 1,025 square miles which now comprise modern Dorset. This ancient sea deposited a soft limestone over many southern regions of the country. It also gave Dorset its large expanses of ground which are now underlaid with this soft limestone, in the form of chalk. The passage of time and the subsequent erosion of softer materials, such as clay, left the chalk behind to create the highest hills in Dorset.

At the end of the four Ice Ages, which later followed and lasted over the period from one million to ten thousand years ago, the climate became warmer. The Dorset landscape gradually became etched by rivers, which now flow through rich clay vales and downland valleys to the sea. This sea was originally swollen by the thaw after the last Ice Age and this flooded the land bridge which had joined England to the continent and Britain became an island.

Sandy regions also evolved in Dorset, giving rise to the unique great heathlands around Wareham, towards the eastern side of the county. As well as the softer (fine particle) chalk, much smaller deposits of a harder (coarser particle) limestone known as oolite also formed. These were eventually to provide excellent materials for building, such as Portland and Purbeck stones. These early beginnings, giving rise to a lush fertile varied land, together with the slowly ensuing temperate climate, guaranteed that Dorset was to become and remain an agricultural county. This meant that corn could be grown on the chalk uplands and a by-product of this, the straw, could be used through many centuries, to the present day, as a thatching material.

The first true inhabitants of Dorset were Neolithic or late Stone Age, about 4,500 years ago. They were nomadic herdsmen, with flocks of sheep and cattle which they had bred from the wild species. They kept mainly to the grassy hills. A race of farmers followed the tribal herdsmen. These cultivated edible grasses until they were able to sow regular corn crops. They cleared the trees around the edges of the valleys, reaped with sickles and ground the corn into flour with portable millstones. They lived in permanent houses, mostly roofed with thatch, waiting for their crops to grow. The thatch at this time was probably brushwood, bracken, or turf. The technique of using straw had not yet developed. The late Stone Age people therefore laid the foundations of our present civilization, by the domestication of livestock and the early practice of agriculture. They buried their dead in long barrows and many of these still exist in Dorset. Very good examples remain at Longbredy and Pimperne, although some have been ploughed over.

Later invaders into Dorset (2000 BC) brought knowledge of how to smelt metals. These were the men of the Bronze Age. The round barrows or mounds raised over the burials of their dead may also still be seen. For example, on the surrounding hills of Dorchester, particularly along the ancient highway known as The Ridgeway, between Dorchester and Weymouth, are about 200 round barrows. These form one of the most marked concentrations in the British Isles and many exist near Winterbourne Abbas. During the Bronze Age, farming had reached a relatively higher degree of efficiency. Each family group lived in its own farmstead which consisted of a primitive thatched farmhouse and often thatched outbuildings and granaries, enclosed by a ditch or fence. The thatch used was the nearest available suitable material. The art of thatching was already progressing in Dorset.

About 500 BC another race, the warlike Celts, introduced a new hard metal called iron to Britain. The superiority of the metal for weapon and tool manufacture enabled them to overcome the bronze users. They eventually ruled all England and Wales. As regards agriculture, the Celts introduced the first significant crude plough. They lived in circular-shaped structures, covered with thatch but with a hole cut in the roof to allow the escape of smoke from a fire lit within. They were also great builders of fortified camps and perhaps Maiden Castle remains the most famous. The Celts had brought the Iron Age to Dorset with them – the age which also created the Roman Empire.

The Romans were possibly the first to introduce common wheat into England but despite this they were not great users of thatch, because of the fire risk, particularly in times of war. They preferred stone slabs and tiles, especially in towns. However, the Romans occasionally approved thatched roofs for their dwellings in country areas. They established a few villas in Dorset, for example, along the Frome Valley and Blackmore Vale and it is possible that some of these were thatched. This is despite the fact that Roman roof tiles have been excavated in these areas giving tangible proof of their more definite use.

The Romano-British population of Dorset kept the Saxon invaders at bay for a considerable time. It was not until well after AD 650 that they became established in the Dorchester area. These early Saxon settlers were great exponents of the use of thatch, laying rushes on a support of wattle and daub. Later Saxon settlers built more elaborate houses of a barn-like nature and shared them with their animals, who were housed in separate bays. These larger houses were thatched with straw, probably rye straw as the Saxons were the first to introduce rye into England. They also thatched with water reeds. The laying and securing of the reeds by this time must have developed to a relatively high standard. The foundations for the present-day laying of reeds in Dorset therefore dates back to at least the tenth century. The Saxons built up sizeable estates in Dorset and village sites were nearly always built near streams and on fertile soil. Most buildings were constructed of timber, including the churches which were also often thatched.

The Norman and feudal period which followed meant in effect that all land became the property of the king. He granted estates to his servants, or vassals, on certain conditions, taken under the oath of allegiance. The chief stipulation was the rendering of military service to the king. The powerful tenant of the land, or lord of the manor, then granted portions of his land to his own supporters but again only under strict binding contracts. These often included service (military and domestic) or the pursuit of agriculture. Many of the owners did not live in the county and only made fleeting visits. By the end of the twelfth century, Dorset belonged to large landowners, the families of whom were to dominate the agriculture in the county for the many centuries which were to follow. The Crown also retained vast estates.

Most people under the feudal system, which lasted into the fifteenth century, lived in humble dwellings made from wattle and daub and roofed with thatch. Even much later, thatch continued to be used widely in Dorset. This was due not only to its wide availability but also because it was inexpensive and thought ideal to roof the many labourers' cottages. Cheap walls (such as cob) and rafters could easily support the relatively light thatching material. However, the use of thatch in Dorset was not always confined to humble dwellings. Large expanses of thatch were laid to cover a number of very substantial houses, including several manor houses and farms which still stand today. However, in general the better types of houses were usually roofed with stone-slates or tiles.

The fire hazard with thatched buildings was particularly great in feudal times, mainly because of the lack of proper chimneys and the practice of burning open fires below a smoke hole. In country areas, such as Dorset, fires were not such a great problem as in the large towns, because the cottages and farm buildings were more sparsely dispersed. However, in the year 1212, thatch as a roof construction material for all new buildings was banned in London. In due course, other towns followed suit but at Wareham in Dorset, for example, thatch was prohibited for new buildings only after the great fire which nearly destroyed it in 1762.

During the medieval period, most of the people who worked on the land in Dorset lived in primitive thatched cottages. Traces of the strip

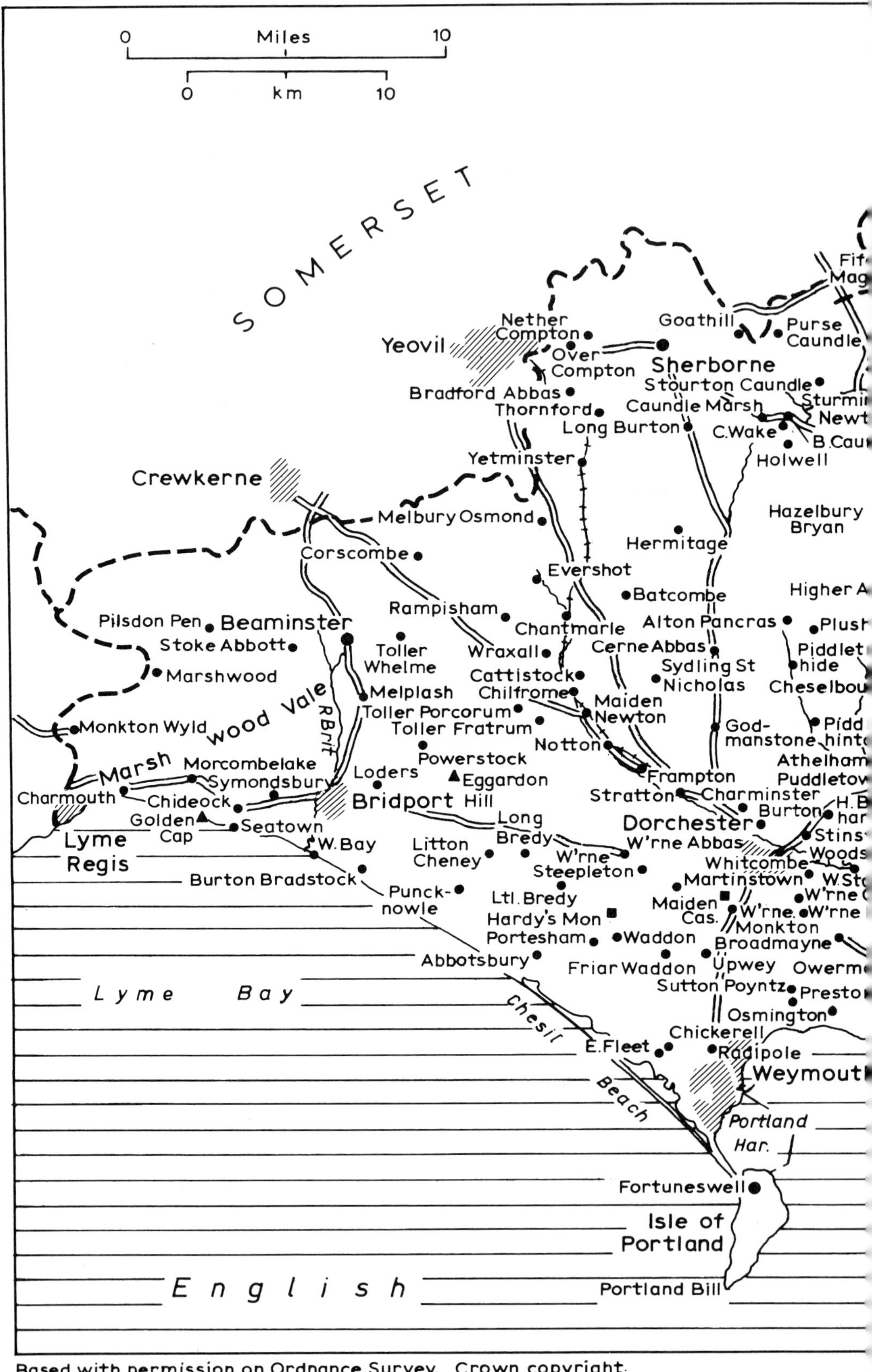

Based with permission on Ordnance Survey. Crown copyright.

WILTSHIRE
Gillingham
Motcombe
E. Stour
Shaftesbury
Stour Provost
rnhull
Margaret Marsh
Ashmore
Tollard Royal
Cranborne Chase
Fontmell Magna
ford
Hammoon
Iwerne Minster
Sixpenny Handley
Farnham
HAMPSHIRE
Childe Okeford
rd aine
Tarrant Gunville
Chettle
Cranborne
Wimborne St. Giles
Shroton
Tarrant Hinton
Stour-paine
Iwerne Stepleton
Tarrant Launceston
illing-tone
Hod Hill
Pimperne
Durweston
Tarrant Monkton
More Crichel
oberton arrow
T. Rushton
Tarrant Rawston
Manswood
Hinton Martell
Blandford Forum
T. Keyneston
Witchampton
on
Winterbornes
T. Crawford
Holt
ickland & Houghton
Badbury Rings
enston
Spetisbury
Shapwick
Milton Abbas
Sturminster Marshall
Winterborne Whitechurch
Almer
Pamphill
Wimborne Minster
W. Kingston
W. Zelston
Corfe Mullin
R. Stour
Milborne t. Andrew
W. Muston
W. Tomson
ddle
Bere Regis
Morden
Affpuddle
Bloxworth
Lytchett Minster
nts-ddle
Turnerspuddle
Poole
Christchurch
Bournemouth
Clouds Hill
Puddle R.
eton
Bovington
Poole Har.
Wareham
Brownsea Is.
ghton
Wool
Stoborough
Sandbanks
Shell Bay
Winfrith Newburgh
Blue Pool
Isle of
aldon
Coombe Keynes
E. Lulworth
Studland
Old Harry
W. Lulworth
Corfe Cas
Ch. Knowle
Kimmeridge
Purbeck
Swanage
Worbarrow Bay
Lulworth Cove
Peveril Pt.
Durlston Hd.
St. Aldhelms Hd.
Channel

lynchets they worked on the hillsides can still be seen today in many areas. Their cottages were thatched with rye straw or water reeds depending upon the most readily available material. Most landowners and farmers probably preferred to use straw as it was cheaper. However, water-reeds grew readily in certain areas such as Abbotsbury and Radipole. The financial lot of the small farmer, to build better accommodation, was not eased by the monastic system which imposed the system of the payment of tithes. As thatch was a cheap material in Dorset, landlords and farmers usually favoured its use not only for the thatching of their farmhouses but also for their barns, cart-sheds and later their granaries and ricks.

The Black Death came to Dorset during the period 1348 and 1349, with a catastrophic effect on the population. It was unfortunately introduced by the crew of a ship which berthed at Weymouth. The depletion of the population created a labour shortage and about thirty years later, there came the Peasants' Revolt against the feudal conditions under which they still toiled. The concessions they gained changed life in the village communities. The disintegration of the feudal system became the beginning of the rise of the yeoman farmer.

During Tudor times, the yeomen farmers who were the first middle-class, independent, small landowners, desired to live in better and larger types of houses. They also strove to extend their land holdings in modest ways but not on the scale of the great Dorset landowners who built up vast estates. After the 'Dissolution' by King Henry VIII's commissioners, many monastic estates passed into the hands of powerful families who still own and administer the lands today. As well as the yeomen farmers, many skilled village craftsmen also wanted better housing than that which the poor peasants had to endure. During the first half of the sixteenth century these improved yeomen houses were built within the village. In Dorset, they were frequently still thatched.

It was only later, when the enclosing of land became more customary, that the better class thatched farmhouse could be built on the farm itself. The enclosing of open fields took place at various times in different regions of the country. The majority of enclosed fields, with surrounding hedges or stone walls, appeared in most parts of the country during the Parliamentary Enclosures between 1760 and 1820. In Dorset, the enclosure of land was sometimes resisted and in certain areas many fields remained unenclosed until after these dates.

During the Elizabethan period, there was a demand for an increase in food production to feed England's expanding population. For the first time, produce was moved from county to county. Many more labourers took to the land and they were again usually sheltered in simple primitive thatched cottages. The extra corn produced yielded the straw for the thatching of the roofs. These types of cottages remained utilitarian and austere for many generations. Even in the late seventeenth century most still consisted of only one, or occasionally, two rooms.

Inside the cottages, a bake oven was usually built into the wall beside a very large fireplace. Many of these cottages had hipped rather than gable ends to their thatched roofs. This was because the thatch under an exposed gable end was, at that time, thought more prone to be lifted by the wind. The simple cottages were mainly of single-storey construction and the thatch was laid to flow around the small window spaces.

The enclosure or the fencing off of land, formerly subject to common rights on the open field system, gathered momentum in the Elizabethan period. This was later greatly accelerated in the new wave of enclosures during the second half of the eighteenth century. This forced many workers who were deprived of land to move to large towns, where they were to supply the labour for the Industrial Revolution. This was a most difficult change for agricultural labourers who had been allowed to grow up without the advantages of education. Destitution became widespread. Farm labourers who managed to find work in Dorset toiled for low wages, under bad conditions and for extremely long hours. In desperation, some rioting and rick-burning occurred and newly introduced threshing machines broken. This later led to the activities of the now famous Tolpuddle Martyrs of Dorset.

However, all the hardship was not confined exclusively to the labourers. Many small independent Dorset farmers did not survive the post-Napoleonic years of crisis and recession in agriculture. Unfavourable grain and land prices overwhelmed them. They did not have the security of the inherited landowner's wealth and so the large estates expanded at the expense of the smaller farmer.

The power of the large estate owner was still nearly absolute in the eighteenth century. A good example of this was the complete demolition of the original village of Milton Abbas by Joseph Damer, the first Earl of Dorchester, who wanted to build his mansion close by but without the village spoiling his view. Fortunately, he recreated Milton Abbas as an integrally planned thatched village, which today draws many visitors to view its beautiful thatched roofs. The thatched village of Witchampton in East Dorset is another example. This village was moved from its original site in 1765, when Crichel House was enlarged by the owner to create a Palladian palace within its own park. Although the power of the large estate owners ensured that most of their decisions remained unchallenged, the end result in several cases was a better class of thatched cottage for the farm workers.

In the eighteenth century, Dorset's wealthy landlords built several picturesque thatched cottage groups to house their tenants. It was the start of the tied cottage system. However, a more common occurrence in the late eighteenth century was the building of rows, or terraces, of thatched cottages for the estate workers. Many were built only one and half storeys high with dormer windows in the thatch. A few had two storeys. They were usually designed one room wide but a second service room was often provided in the form of a small outshut.

Sanitation in the cottages was primitive. Cottage life remained much the same for at least another century. Oil lamps lit the cottages but made the low ceilings very black, which did little to add to their cheerfulness. Cottagers relied on wells, or the village pump, for their water and most grew their own vegetables. Later the more fortunate, who worked on the large estates, kept a couple of pigs and also bees to provide honey. Villages still had to be self-supporting and each trade, such as the thatcher, served the requirements of the whole community. People walked everywhere. The shortest routes between village and farmstead were well-trod and happily many of these paths still survive in Dorset today.

In the first half of the nineteenth century, slates became available in cheap commercial quantities from Wales. However, they could not be easily brought to Dorset to threaten thatch until the railways grew in size. Distribution problems were then eased and slates could be imported and used in the county. They then competed as a cheap roofing material with the traditional thatch. By coincidence, at this time wheat straw in particular, was becoming more expensive because of the reduced supply caused by the earlier Napoleonic Wars. The wealthy then began to favour thatch again for their own houses and it became fashionable to include some thatched buildings on country estates. Thatched cottages even appeared on fashionable sea fronts, such as Lyme Regis, and rich Victorians spent their holidays in them.

In the present century, the mechanization of farms has meant that machines have replaced men working on the land to a very great extent. The agricultural industry is no longer labour intensive. A small dairy farm of about 300 acres can now be comfortably managed by one farmer working with his son. Similarly, the numbers working on the huge farming estates have also dwindled. A few of the large private land-owners of the nineteenth century have now been replaced by institutional and city investors. Although this trend has had the effect of improving land prices, it has not increased employment opportunities due to the economic advantages of using machine technology.

This is illustrated vividly when one considers that the total population of Dorset is now over half a million people, yet only about 6,000 of these are actively engaged in agricultural work. This means that the majority of people living in the villages and hamlets are no longer connected with farms, despite the fact that they are surrounded by vast acreages of farm land.

Nevertheless, agriculture still remains Dorset's chief, highly productive industry. Strangely, the different types of people living in the thatched cottages of the new rural community probably offer the best guarantee that traditional Dorset thatched cottages, many dating back to the seventeenth and eighteenth centuries, will be preserved. Many of the new wealthier owners have not only maintained them but also renovated and modernized them without ruining their original exterior appearances. The fresh class of residents has prevented many villages from becoming sparsely populated and left to decay. Thatch is now a very expensive material but fortunately the people who now live in such homes are mostly prepared to pay for its rustic and delightful appearance.

However, many farmers have inherited numerous large farm buildings covered with thatch by their forefathers. They were originally thatched not for their appearances' sake but because it was economical to do so. The cost of re-thatching such buildings, as outmoded barns, is now prohibitive unless the owner is extremely wealthy and is much influenced by the preservation of his heritage. One way of saving some of the many old large thatched farm buildings, such as barns, is their possible conversion to other non-agricultural uses, such as residential units, craft centres or even restaurants. This is only possible if the thatched barns are in or near village locations rather than situated within enclosed farmsteads.

Thatching straw has become very expensive because special varieties of wheat now have to be grown for the purpose and then harvested using a labour intensive method to ensure the straw stalks remain long and unbroken. Before the advent of the combine harvester, all wheat was harvested by this old method but labour costs were low. It seems amazing that at the outbreak of the First World War in 1914, the wage of a Dorset agricultural labourer was sixteen shillings a week. Furthermore, it had only risen to this modest level from the eleven shillings a week paid in 1880. Nearly all farm labourers still had to work extremely long hours for this wage, often under hazardous working conditions and on a diet that frequently consisted largely of bacon fat and cheese.

The high cost of producing modern thatching straw may lead to an increased use of marsh reeds for thatching although traditionally, these have always been more expensive than straw. However, in the future the price differential may eventually disappear, especially if existing water-reed beds are carefully conserved, gradually expanded by cultivation and then harvested by reed cutting machines.

The combined effects of changed farming methods, social customs and the present high price of thatching material has already led to the disappearance of many familiar things from the countryside that were formerly thatched. For example, it is now an extremely rare sight to see a thatched corn rick but happily, the occasional thatched farm boundary wall may still be glimpsed. Milk stands by the roadside were once a common feature when milk was placed in churns awaiting collection, before the advent of the modern milk lorry which now collects directly from the dairy farm. The milk stands were often sheltered with a thatched roof, to keep the milk cool and to prevent the adventitious entry of rain-water. Little thatched canopies were also sometimes used to protect notices posted outside of the village church or hall. They prevented the ink running in the rain. Country privies were also frequently protected with a thatched roof as were thatched garden sheds. In heathland areas of Dorset, heather was sometimes used as a roof covering for sheds.

At one time, several Dorset schools and almshouses were furnished with thatched roofs but none are still retained for their original purposes, although several have been adapted for other uses. A few thatched bus shelters also still remain in different Dorset villages. After Saxon times, it was not the custom to thatch churches in Dorset but the practice continued throughout the medieval period in several other counties of England and many are still preserved, especially in East Anglia. Fortunately, a host of thatched pubs may still be found in Dorset and although the cost of maintaining their roofs is high, their quaint appearances and charm probably attract many customers who might have passed by.

An additional expense of maintaining a thatched building is the fire and storm damage insurance premium payable for the roof. This is always appreciably higher than the equivalent premium for a tiled or slated roof. Although straw and reeds are combustible materials, whilst modern roofing materials are not, a well maintained thatched building with safe electrical wiring and sound chimneys often allows insurance companies, specializing in thatch, to offer more acceptable insurance rates, although these are still higher than for a conventionally roofed property. The fact that many thatched buildings have survived through several centuries suggests that the fire risk may not be as great as one might first contemplate.

1

Building Materials

The materials used for the construction of the walls of the older thatched buildings of Dorset were taken from the rocks and soil. Nature had ensured a rich variety was available and also that they could be fairly easily extracted from the earth. Chalk, clay and sand covered about seventy-five per cent of the total surface area of Dorset.

The main chalk belt stretched across the county from Cranborne Chase in the east to above Beaminster in the west (Fig. 1). This whale-back chalk spine formed the North Dorset Downs or Dorset Heights and it overlooked the rich clay areas of the Blackmore Vale to the north. A small chalk spur also branched off, just west of Beaminster, in a south-westerly direction to rise above the Marshwood Vale, another rich clay region. The South Dorset Downs were shaped by a further and more significant chalk ridge which extended from the Beaminster region to the Isle of Purbeck, where it then formed the Purbeck Hills, overlooking Swanage. The area trapped between the

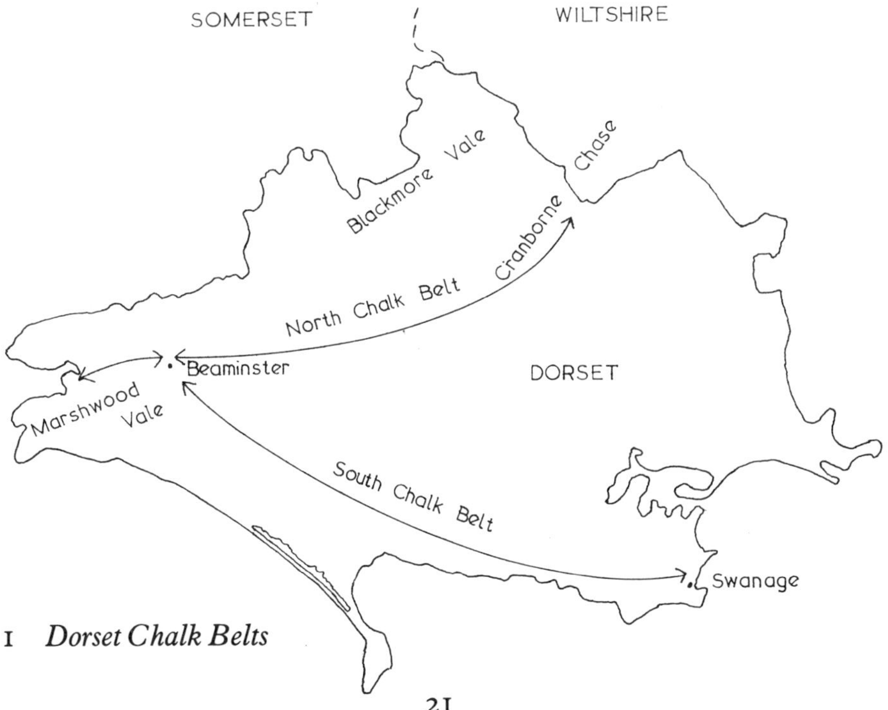

1 *Dorset Chalk Belts*

North and South Dorset Downs constituted the Frome river basin. The eastern section of this consisted of the sandy regions around Wareham and Poole Harbour. This more barren flat terrain created the heathland.

In view of the large quantities of chalk and clay available, it was not unexpected that many of the humbler dwellings in Dorset were originally constructed with cob walls. This was very common in the chalk belt areas but the structural limitations imposed by cob restricted its use mainly to cottages, barns and small farmhouses. Slightly better class houses were sometimes finished with a flint facing on the cob. This protected the cob against the weather better than the traditional coat of limewash employed on the labourers' cottages.

The cob consisted of a mixture of powdered chalk and clay but with the addition of straw to bind the mix together. On occasions the straw was introduced in the form of soiled straw, contaminated with horse dung. In the sandy heathland regions heather was often substituted for the straw.

The proportions of the various ingredients varied considerably but usually at least three parts of chalk were incorporated for each part of clay. Higher proportions of chalk produced a stronger wall. Early cob walls of the sixteenth and seventeenth centuries were built without the aid of shuttering. This gave them their delightful uneven appearance. The cob was thrown onto the wall and then trampled down. Each layer of cob had to be allowed to dry before the next could be placed on top. The base of the wall was always made thicker than the upper section and the average wall thickness was often in excess of two feet.

Later the technique was slightly changed so that a cob wall could be built with more accuracy and in less time. This resulted in a straighter and also a slightly thinner wall. In this revised method the cob mixture was moistened and then rammed between wooden planks that acted as a mould, and left to harden. The process was again fairly laborious, as each layer of cob (approximately two feet high) had to set and dry before another layer could be poured on top. The wall was built on a stone, or sometimes later on a brick foundation, to protect the base of the cob from the damp rising from the earth. The finished wall height was usually that required for a one-storey or one-and-a-half-storey cottage and two storey heights were rarely exceeded (Fig. 2). Headroom in the latter types was always very restricted. Barns tended to be some of the higher buildings constructed with cob because from a practical point of view, they had to be tall enough to accommodate a laden wagon.

In Dorset cob buildings were nearly always roofed with thatch. This tradition was maintained primarily for cheapness but a very important secondary factor was the essential need to protect the cob from damp. Water broke down the cob structure under prolonged wet conditions, especially if the water gained access to the top of the wall. Thatch, with

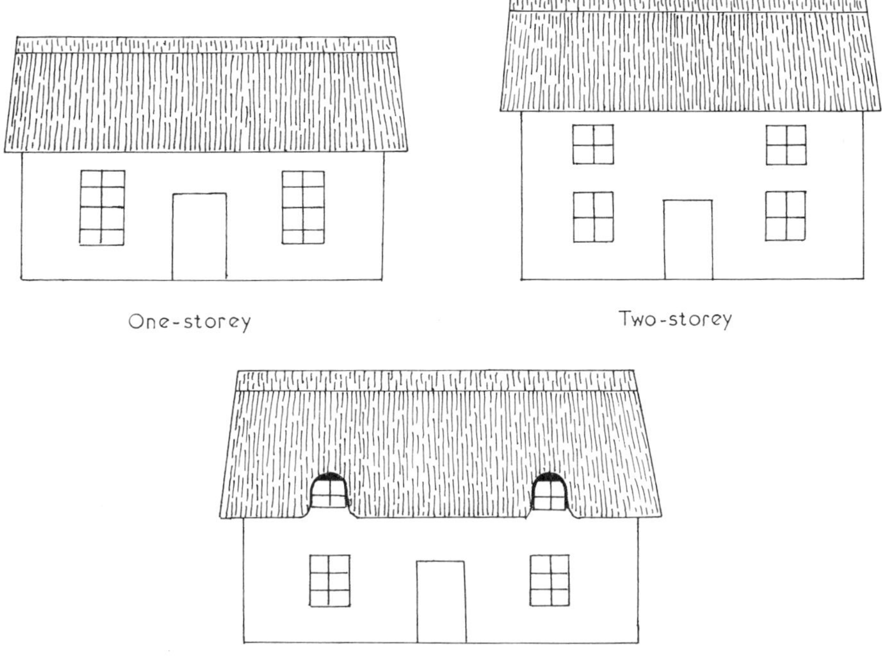

2 *Cottage Types*

its wide low overhanging eaves, threw water completely clear of the walls and so formed a much better roof cover than alternative materials.

Protected cob walls lasted for centuries with their stone bases and thatched roofs. This led to the expression which concisely sums it up – 'All cob wants is a good hat and a good pair of shoes.' The countryman always selected a sheltered site, often by the side of a bank, to gain an additional shield against driving rain which came mainly from a south-westerly direction. The cottager also frequently painted an exterior base band of black pitch around the walls to waterproof them against the rain drips and splashes bouncing up from the ground. Drips cascaded from the whole perimeter of the thatch as modern guttering and downpipes were of course not used. The host of cob buildings surviving in Dorset today offers tangible proof of the durability of cob when adequately protected from the weather.

As well as cob, blocks of chalk or chalk ashlar were sometimes used to build cottages in Dorset. These were fashioned when a suitable local chalk supply was available. Chalk was easy to quarry and cut because it was softer than other building stones. Chalk rubble which had not been squared, or dressed, was also often used for the building of walls for the more humble dwellings. The walls were made with a considerable thickness and were often in-filled with smaller pieces of chalk rubble. As with cob, it was again essential to protect such walls from water by the use of a wide overhang of thatch and to treat them annually with limewash (hydrated lime). A coat of limewash adhered well to the chalk because it was of a similar softness and composition. Over the years a considerable thickness of lime was built up on the walls by the repeated application of annual coats. There was no great tendency for it to peel away after the first few coats had stabilized the wall surface and therefore the lime admirably protected the chalk underneath. At the same time, the limewash was porous and so allowed any rising damp in the wall to dry out. For these reasons, limewash is still preferred to modern masonry paints for the treatment of cob and chalk walls.

Flint, a hard variety of quartz used by early man for shaping tools and weapons, is often found in chalk and limestone regions. It was therefore not surprising that an abundance of flints were readily available in such a chalky county as Dorset. The flints were mainly used for wall construction from the beginning of the seventeenth century onwards and were often incorporated with alternating bands, or courses, of stones. Decorative banding became a common feature in the chalk belts of Dorset, particularly after the middle of the seventeenth century, for

3   *Wall Materials*

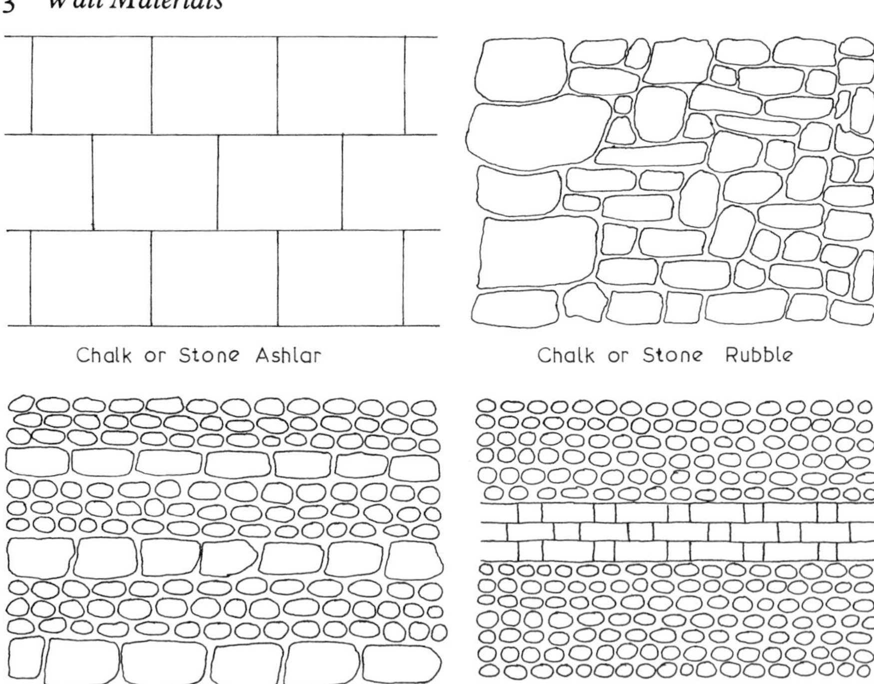

the slightly better class homes (Fig. 3). Most of these cottages were thatched but others were roofed with stone slates.

Many less elaborate cottages were also built entirely from rough stones picked up at random from the ground. These stones were locally called 'pudding' stones because their appearance resembled that of a plum pudding. In effect, they were composed of a conglomerate mass of rock containing dark rounded pebbles which nature had once embedded in the rock. In view of their unappealing colour such walls were inevitably whitewashed. The cottages were usually thatched and more commonly built in north Dorset. Sometimes the 'pudding' stone was mixed with flints, or bricks, to produce a mixed wall effect. Stone rubble was also used in both north and central Dorset for wall construction, the rubble being unsquared and undressed. Many of these cottages were also thatched, although this was not so essential with flint and stone as with cob or chalk-constructed walls.

For the wealthier owners, it was not essential to rely on materials available in the immediate locality. Stone was often transported a few miles from other areas of the county which offered good building stone. Dorset was fortunate in possessing several outcrops of hard limestone which yielded stones that were excellent for building. They occurred at Portland, Purbeck, Marnhull, Sturminster Newton, with small deposits also found between Bridport and Weymouth. A further small stretch of hard limestone existed between Portisham and Poxwell. All these deposits were quarried at various times. The stones produced were relatively easy to work when first quarried and this made it possible to dress and carve them. Many of the quarries are today still yielding excellent stone employed widely for building, not only in this country but also across the Atlantic. Portland stone stands as the prime example.

Oddly enough, the grey-coloured Portland stone was not favoured for house building in Dorset until the eighteenth century. This was well after its virtues were highlighted and proved in many London buildings designed by Inigo Jones and later by Sir Christopher Wren. More houses in south Dorset were built with the grey limestone quarried from Purbeck and Portisham. In the central and northern districts of the county the golden-brown coloured Ham Hill limestone was favoured. This was obtained from just across the border in Somerset and the stone often became even more attractive after it had weathered and become covered with lichens. Although the majority of the larger houses constructed of limestone in Dorset were not thatched, many substantial farmhouses made from stone were roofed with straw or water reed. Manor houses, such as Hammoon and the massive Woodsford Castle, were both constructed from Purbeck limestone and thatched.

Despite the presence of London clay type deposits in parts of Dorset brickmaking made little progress until the seventeenth century. Houses constructed with brick then appeared first in the more sandy regions in the east of the county. The practice of using bricks only spread slowly to the other districts of Dorset. However, several substantial farmhouses were constructed with brick and roofed with thatch in the eighteenth century. Throughout the county, the use of brick for house building accelerated with the coming of the railways in the nineteenth century. Even a substitute brick was tried during the early half of this present century. The brick was made from concrete and a few cottages built with it were roofed with thatch in the Briantspuddle region of Dorset. This was a most unusual combination – modern concrete and traditional thatch. The concrete bricks were experimental and were designed to reduce the condensation which occurred on cottage walls. Concrete bricks were made with three air cavity spaces in each brick in order to increase the inner wall surface temperature, compared to that obtained when solid building blocks were used. The concrete brick slightly improved the condensation problem but never became widely adopted.

Oak trees grew well in the London clay regions of the county and so oak-framed brick cottages were constructed in these areas, for example, at Holt in eastern Dorset. However, in general little timber framed or cruck house construction took place in the county, except for these few specialized regions and also in the more wooded areas of the north, near Sherborne. Many of these homes which incorporated timber in their walls were thatched.

With regard to thatched roof construction, the main thatching material favoured in Dorset for many centuries was straw because of its ready availability from corn production. Nowadays, it is always wheat straw that is used. Rye tolerated poorer soils than wheat and when it was once commonly grown its straw was utilized for thatching. However, farmers do not grow rye now to any significant extent due to its rather limited demand for only making specialized products, such as ryebread. Rye was also once occasionally sown as cattle fodder. Nevertheless, the rye straw that used to be produced was an ideal material for thatching as the straw stalks were not only long and strong but also less brittle than those of wheat straw.

Wheat requires more fertile soils than rye. Conditions in Dorset favour its growth and much wheat is sown on the higher chalk areas. This helps to reserve the richer valleys for the traditional dairying. The modern varieties of wheat grown are normally the heavy-headed types and their yields are now much increased by the use of nitrogenous fertilizers. Modern wheats grow rather short in height (about eighteen inches). They are also stiffer and are not so easily damaged and flattened by winds and rain. They are harvested at high speed by the combine-harvester, which threshes the wheat as it reaps it and pours the resultant grain into storage containers. The straw suffers much mechanical stress in the process with the result that the stalks become damaged and broken as they pass through the machine. The straw is then pressed into bales which are tied with baler twine and stacked in barns. Storage is no longer carried out in corn-ricks. Modern produced straw is unfortunately not suitable as a thatching material, because good thatching straw must be long and in an unbroken condition. Nowadays it is therefore in short supply due to the combine-harvester's wide usage on modern farms.

Before the advent of the combine-harvester the wheat varieties grown were much taller. They were harvested by the reaper and binder machine which tied the corn into convenient bundles (sheaves) so that they could be arranged in self-supporting stooks to dry and ripen in the sun. The bundles of wheat were always collected from the fields in wagons and then stored in ricks built from the sheaves by the farmer. The wheat was kept in the rick to allow it to dry before threshing. The building of a rick was a most skilful operation but the combine-harvester has now made rick-building nearly an obsolete art.

Corn-ricks were usually made in rectangular or more occasionally circular shapes, either in groups in the open fields or in rickyards adjacent to the farm. Rickyards became really dominant features of arable farmsteads during the eighteenth and nineteenth centuries due to the increasing demand for cereal crops. The ricks were often built on staddle stones, or timber bases, to impede mice gaining entry to the bottom of the rick and damaging the corn (Fig. 4). The bound sheaves of corn were stacked one upon another with their butt end outwards. The circular rick was started in the centre and stacking progressed towards the perimeter. Sometimes the ricks were built around a hollow cone to prevent them from overheating from self-generated spontaneous combustion. The construction process was highly skilled in order to prevent the rick from collapsing. At the top of the rick the middle was always built up substantially so that the outermost layer of sheaves could be laid slanting down at an oblique angle to shed rain water.

Well-made ricks had to resist the ingress of rainwater until the thatcher was able to give them their waterproof roofs; some farmers thatched their own ricks. Rick thatching resembled house thatching to a great extent, except that longer spars were used to secure the thatch to the top of the rick. The making of ricks in Dorset continued well into the twentieth century. During the Second World War, the thatching of ricks became the chief occupation of many Dorset thatchers, as very little house thatching was allowed.

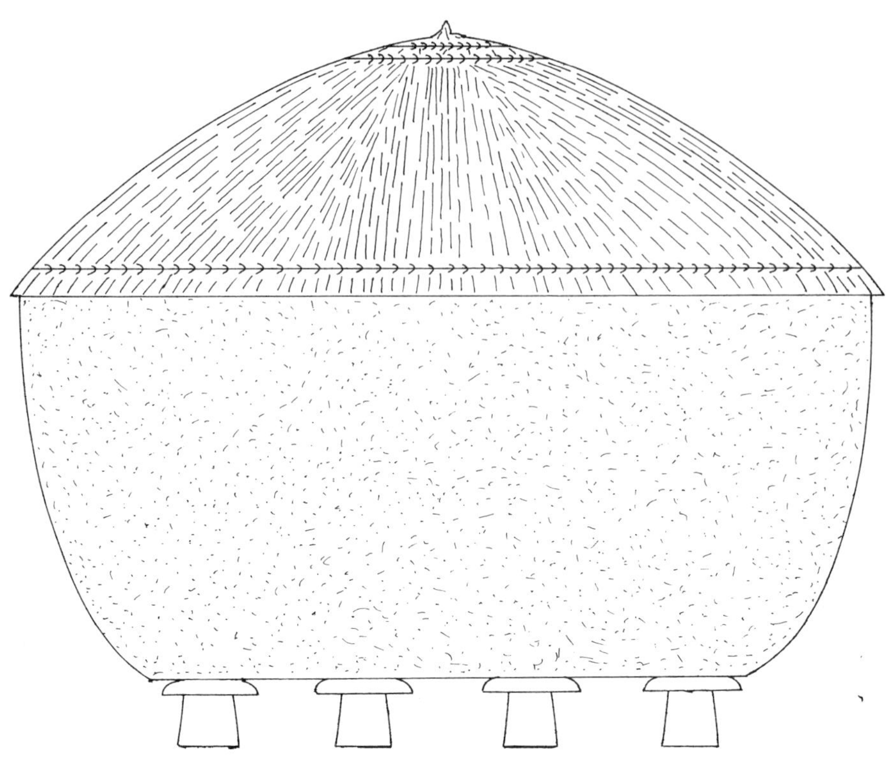

4   *Corn Rick on Staddle Stones*

The ricks presented a delightful sight when their tops were ornamented by the thatcher. Common rick finials were cockbirds and animals made by the thatcher from bundles of straw, often tied together with binder twine to form the desired shape. The birds or animals were not made from woven or plaited straw like the corn dolly. The tradition of rick decoration no doubt originated in the distant past, to prevent mishaps occurring to the rick. Superstitions were rife. An imitation straw-bird on the top may have been placed there to prevent witches from landing on the rick and it was also thought to protect the rick from fire, lightning and storm damage. On rectangular ricks two ornaments were sometimes displayed. One marked the end at which the rick was started and the other showed the end where it was finished. From the two distinguishing ornaments the men knew later at which end of the rick to park the threshing machine. It was the practice to thresh the corn first which had been in the rick the longest.

The custom of fixing ornaments to the ricks appears to be closely related to the making of corn dollies. This ritual is also steeped in antiquity and mystery. It was thought that the earliest farmers were in fact women and not men and that they worshipped a corn goddess who protected the crop. Many believed that the spirit of the goddess resided in the crop and so she would die if the last stalks of corn were not saved, as these formed the last refuge for the corn spirit to hide in. This 'neck' of corn, as it was sometimes called, was always carried home with rejoicing after the harvest. The traditional custom followed that an image of the goddess should be made in straw from the last sheaf of corn of the final wagon-load of the gathered summer harvest. This corn dolly, as it became known, was kept throughout the winter and the grain preserved was sown the following spring. The tradition became a good-luck charm to ensure a bountiful harvest, after the grain had been sown and the corn spirit reborn.

In many other regions of the world, various goddesses associated with harvests were worshipped both in the fields and on the threshing floors. Ceres, the Roman fertility goddess of the earth and the growing corn, may be naturally identified with the equivalent Greek goddess, Demeter, who was the mythical goddess of corn, harvest and fruitfulness. Isis was worshipped as the ancient Egyptian nature goddess and all three goddesses developed into mystery cults representing seasonal cycles. Each of these goddesses also became symbolized by a sheaf of corn and a straw dolly to represent her image. Harvest ceremonies became strongly linked with religious practice over the ensuing years and during the last century the Church, in this country, officially accepted the Blessing of the Harvest.

It seemed a logical step that rick ornaments would ensure the stacked wheat would also be protected during its stay in the rick. The corn remained in the rick for about three months, when it was ready for threshing. If the straw was to be used for thatching purposes the threshing operation to obtain the grain was carried out carefully. This originally was done by hand on the threshing floor but the threshing machine took over in the nineteenth century. The sheaves were gently handled and opened, then fed singly to the threshing machine drum which separated the grain from the straw. The straw, deprived of its grain, was then tied in bundles for the thatcher. The straw, often bent after being through the thresher, was not subjected to any further processing, so it could be termed to be in its natural state. Later, the thatcher, after slightly wetting the straw, straightening it and gathering it together in handfuls from a heaped pile, would employ such straw to thatch a roof in the style known as long-straw thatching.

To produce a different type of thatching straw the wheat was once combed by hand to remove the grain and leaves so that the stalks would not be bent or damaged. The stalks were then gathered with all their thicker butt ends together in a bundle and therefore not in random array as for the natural straw used for long-straw thatching. This type of straw became known as wheat reed and was, and still is, much used in Dorset to thatch in the style known as reed thatching. The old-fashioned, tedious, hand-combing method using an iron comb, was once a familiar sight carried out in Dorset barns when the weather was wet. Thomas Hardy in *Tess of the d'Urbervilles* describes such a scene very vividly.

A later development was the attachment of a special device known as a reed-comber to the conventional threshing machine. The sheaves were fed into the thresher and comber with all the straw stalks facing in the same direction. The machine removed the grain from the ears and the leaves from the wheat but prevented the straw from entering the threshing drum beaters. The unbroken stalks came out from the machine in a parallel form, lying in one direction. They were then tied into bundles with thicker butt ends together. The bundles were then ready for the wheat reed thatcher, after their bases had been tidily levelled by tapping them on a wooden spot-board.

Nowadays, few threshing and combing machines survive but one or two farmers in Dorset still retain them to process the wheat they grow specially for thatchers. The limited number of acres which still grow this longer variety of wheat have to be harvested in the old-fashioned way, using the reaper and binder. This is very labour intensive and therefore expensive compared to using a modern combine harvester. The gathered sheaves are stooked in the fields before being stacked into ricks, as they were in bygone ages. Therefore, the very occasional ricks still to be glimpsed on a few farms, mainly in west Dorset, will be thatching wheat waiting to be processed in one of the remaining old style threshing and combing machines.

Farmers growing thatching wheats on chalk regions lose on yield because only a little nitrogen fertilizer can be utilized. Fertilizers, because of the enforced growth rate, tend to make the straw brittle which could render it unsuitable for thatching. However, to compensate for the yield loss, farmers can obtain an extra few hundred pounds an acre for the long wheat and at the same time they can sell the corn in addition to the straw.

From the thatcher's point of view, the wheat should be harvested when slightly green as this ensures a stronger more durable straw. However, the farmer will always want to produce ripe corn in order to sell the grain. The wheat is winter sown to allow a longer season for it to reach naturally, the height and strength required for thatching. The seeding must not be heavy because overcrowding weakens the base of the wheat stems. The optimum straw length for thatching lies in the range of two and a half to just over three feet. Special machines are available to trim the wheat bundles before they are used by the thatcher which ensures that they do not extend too much over three feet in length. Longer wheat reeds tend to wear more quickly when in the thatched roof as the ends are more exposed. The wheat must be thoroughly dried after harvesting, as straw with pith in the centre is not suitable for the thatcher. It tends to darken in colour and break much more readily than hollow straws. The latter type therefore lasts much better in the roof.

Farmers growing the old-fashioned varieties of long wheat prefer those which offer reasonable grain yields. Some Dorset thatchers used to like the variety known as Red Standard but this is now uneconomic for the farmer to grow because of its poor yield. A compromise crop may be a variety such as Maris Huntsman, which gives strong long straw as well as an improved yield. However, the popular strains of wheat are changed constantly over the years in order to achieve disease resistant varieties.

Another different more durable and much tougher thatching material used by Dorset thatchers originates from the marsh reed beds of the county. The water reeds (*Phragmites communis*) are more expensive and also less readily available than the more commonly utilized wheat reed and long straw. However, over many centuries, marsh reed beds at the Abbotsbury Swannery have been regularly grown, irrigated and cut for thatching. The management of the reed beds involves the burning of old reed growth to get rid of debris and unwanted weeds. It also helps to create potash and provide the best conditions for the new reed shoots to grow. Within three months the new reed stands out from the old.

The swannery itself is situated on the western brackish water of the Fleet, the seven-mile-long lagoon sheltering behind the Chesil Beach. The lagoon opens to the sea at its eastern end towards Portland. The Fleet was commandeered for a time during World War Two by the RAF to practise their dam-busting experimental runs. The swannery now provides a breeding and nesting ground for about five hundred mute swans in summer and a region of shelter for about nine hundred in winter. The colony is protected and has been managed at Abbotsbury since the fourteenth century. The swans originally formed a source of food for the monastery which was once established here. Nowadays, special plant food, the eel grass (*Zostera marina*) is grown locally to ensure the preservation of the swans. In addition to the swans, a decoy lures visiting ducks so that they can be ringed and released later for research purposes. A decoy duck was first established at Abbotsbury in the seventeenth century and a thatched house, which was one lived in by the man responsible for the decoy, still stands at the swannery.

The extensive reed beds provide an ideal habitat for many other marsh birds. The reeds grow to very tall heights, in the region of ten feet or so and they therefore provide excellent thatching reed. The cut reeds, or 'spears' as they are sometimes called, are stored in the magnificent Abbotsbury thatched tithe barn which stands nearby. The supply is rather limited and mainly reserved for use at the swannery for thatching and fencing. It is also used on the roofs of the attractive thatched cottages at Abbotsbury village. Many of the thatched roofs made from Abbotsbury reed last for the best part of a century, compared to the approximate forty years for combed wheat reed and the twenty-five years for a long-straw roof. This of course, assumes that occasional repairs are carried out, especially to the ridges when they are needed.

Another good source of water reeds in the past has been Radipole Lake at Weymouth. The marsh reeds from here were once quite widely used for thatching in Dorset, but in recent years the supply has gradually decreased making the reed difficult to obtain. The Radipole Lake area has now been made into a bird sanctuary by the Royal Society for the Protection of Birds. Although reed cutters' rights are still observed, the area allowed for cutting has been drastically reduced and the right is not now often exercised. Unfortunately, if the reeds are not cut regularly, the beds will deteriorate from the thatcher's point of view.

Marsh reed beds also exist at Lodmoor at Weymouth (Fig. 5) and reed cutters now work these to supply a limited quantity of reed to Dorset thatchers. Water reeds grow at an extraordinary rate and may even show perceptible growth in the space of a few days. The men cut the reeds only during the winter, from the final days of November to about the end of March. By this time the frost has killed off most of the leaves but as mentioned, the reed beds must be semi-cultivated to produce the high quality long and straight reeds suitable for thatching.

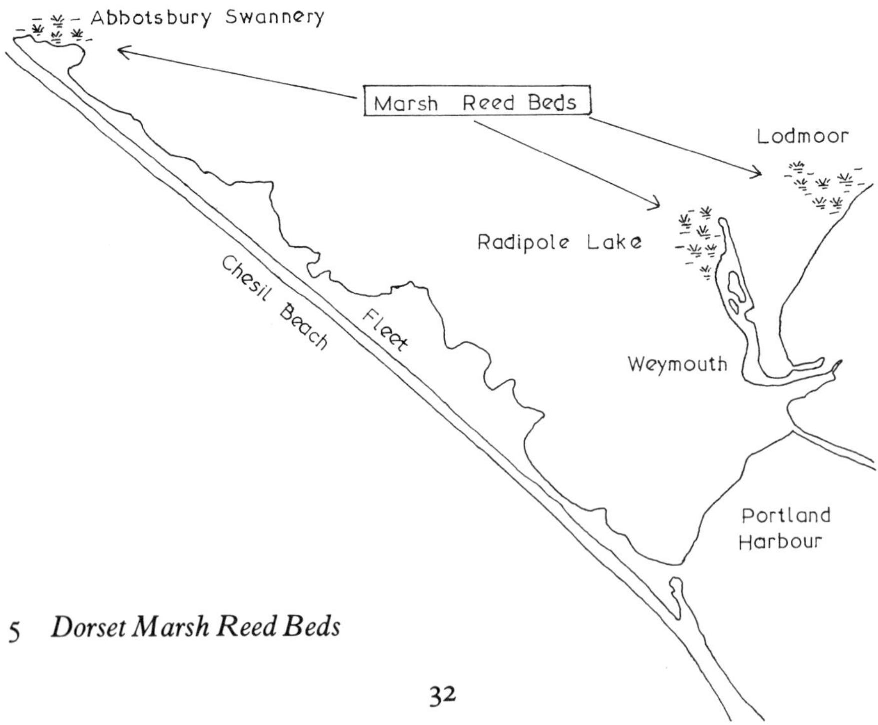

5 *Dorset Marsh Reed Beds*

The cutters trim the old growth and burn it, retaining only those reeds which lie between about four feet and nine feet. During suitable weather conditions, a special hand-operated machine cuts the reeds. The reeds are then tied into bundles and loaded by hand into a suitable conveyance for delivery to the thatcher. At one time all water reeds were harvested by hand cutting, with a special scythe or sickle, but the advent of the mechanical cutter has considerably speeded up the operation. A machine can cut several hundred bundles of reeds per day. Nevertheless, hand-cut reeds were once thought to be superior to machine-harvested ones.

The Lodmoor reed beds provide a natural watercourse for the streams which flow through them. They also provide a haven for wild bird life, such as the reed warblers and bearded tits, especially during the winter period. The delightful bearded tits are more commonly found at Radipole Lake, where they are normally resident during the breeding season and where they have now established a strong colony. They first arrived in Dorset during the 1960s. Fairly large reed beds composed of the phragmites reeds form the only suitable habitat for the birds.

The unusual bearded tit spends much of its time at the bottom of the reeds, particularly when the weather is windy. It is therefore difficult to see. Its body is a beautiful tawny-brown with black under its long tail. The name 'bearded' arises from the black 'moustache' present on the white cheeks of the male bird. The reed warbler displays brown on top and a paler colour underneath and it is also rather a shy bird. It lurks in the reed beds and during the breeding season it builds a suspended nest around the reed stems. Unfortunately, the reed warbler is victimized by the cuckoo. The reed warbler gains its name from the distinctive warbling nature of its song. The cutting of the reeds appears not to upset the birds, as they return to Lodmoor each year and in any event the reeds are only cut during the winter months.

In 1983 a new sea life centre was opened at Lodmoor as a tourist attraction. This displays native marine life in Britain in a series of walk over and through tanks, filled with octopus, sharks, monk fish, conger eels, giant rays, lobster and salmon. However, it is likely that the reed beds at Lodmoor will remain safe from further urbanization schemes. The reeds will survive not only to provide a habitat for the reed birds but also to supply marsh reeds to Dorset thatchers for years to come. Without the reed beds, many more water reeds would have to be imported into the county. For many years, supplies of both the famous Norfolk reeds and also phragmites reeds from Scotland and Hampshire have been used by local thatchers, mainly because Dorset-grown water reeds have been in limited supply. In more recent years marsh reeds have also been imported from Austria, Holland and even Poland and

Romania, in order to supplement the thatchers' needs for high quality marsh water reeds.

In addition to the actual thatch material of wheat straw and marsh reed, a very important additional item required by the thatcher is a constant supply of thatching spars made from hazel. These are used to fix the thatch to the roof and traditionally spars in Dorset have always been obtained from hurdle-makers. These rural craftsmen did not only make hurdles and spars; once they also bound together the feathery tips of the hazel to make faggots for heating the bread ovens in cottages. At the moment there are still about half a dozen hurdle-makers left in Dorset but thirty years ago there were over forty.

The decline in this rural craft has been caused by the drop in demand for hurdles. They are not needed any more by modern sheep farmers who no longer fold sheep on the downs with hurdles. Only a relative few are now made, for such purposes as garden fences or screens. However, there is still a demand for thatching spars and this forms an important sideline trade for the few remaining hurdle-makers. The hurdle-maker leads a lonely life working alone in the woods for many hours each day, with nature's wildlife as his sole companions. His working day is even more solitary than that of the thatcher who also spends most of his day alone on a roof-top but the thatcher, if he feels inclined, can watch the modern world pass by below him.

Spars made by the hurdle-maker in Dorset are frequently called spar-gads but in other parts of the country they are known by many other strange sounding names, such as withynecks, brotches, rouvers, sparrods, spics, spikes, splints and tangs. The best spars are made from hazel wood, although willow is also very occasionally utilized. Both woods are relatively soft and fairly easy to split, although they remain tough and flexible enough for use by the thatcher. The number of hazel copses tended in Dorset has dwindled in line with the fall in demand for sheep hurdles. Nevertheless, the remaining hurdle-makers still maintain a few copses, usually paying a farmer a percentage of their turnover for the privilege of cutting the wood on his land.

By nature, hazel spreads and unless the shrub is satisfactorily coppiced (lopped near ground level), it will not produce the straight pliant branches needed by the hurdle and spar-maker. The hazel copses must therefore be cut down every seven or eight years in rotation. This ensures a continuous crop, as hazel possesses a natural capacity to regenerate from a stump, or stool, as it is more commonly called. However, the art of making a coppice demands skill because the tops of the severed stems must be left with oblique angles on them so that rain-water will run off and not rot the stump. Deer create great havoc to the coppices because they eat the young shoots and cause the hazel to sprout into a much more bushy form. This type of damage is on the increase as the deer population of Dorset has considerably expanded over the last few decades. They roam at will in the more remote areas of Dorset and jump even the most formidable fences.

A few farmers restrict the number of hazel copses they allow to be regularly stripped by the hurdle-maker, mainly because they have been persuaded to leave some areas for wildlife by the conservationists. On economic grounds, it makes sense for the farmer to leave the less fertile patches for wildlife preservation, rather than land which is easy to farm. Therefore the coppice is often left to nature and becomes a scrub woodland for any wildlife which is able to survive in this type of habitat. The regular cutting down of the hazel to near ground level by the hurdle-maker would not give a good permanent cover for such wildlife. Although, in nature's unique method of compensation it would allow many wild flowers such as bluebells and violets to thrive.

The hurdle-maker cuts and selects hazel twigs especially for the thatcher. The slender rods, or wands, as they are occasionally called, are all chopped to the same length of about three feet. They then have to be clefted and pointed by the spar-maker. This is often done by the hurdle-maker but some thatchers prefer to do the job themselves. They work at the task when they are unable to carry out thatching, such as when snow, frosty or windy conditions prevail. The rods for the spars have to be cut at the beginning of the winter when the sap is retreating in the hazel. If the wood is severed when green, it becomes brittle and proves useless for the manufacture of thatching spars.

The hurdle-maker and thatcher both develop extremely tough hands as nearly all of them work without gloves when making spars. The three feet lengths of hazel rods are split down the centre with the use of a Dorset spar hook (Fig. 6). This requires considerable skill, practice and a steady strength of hand. The skill, acquired only by experience,

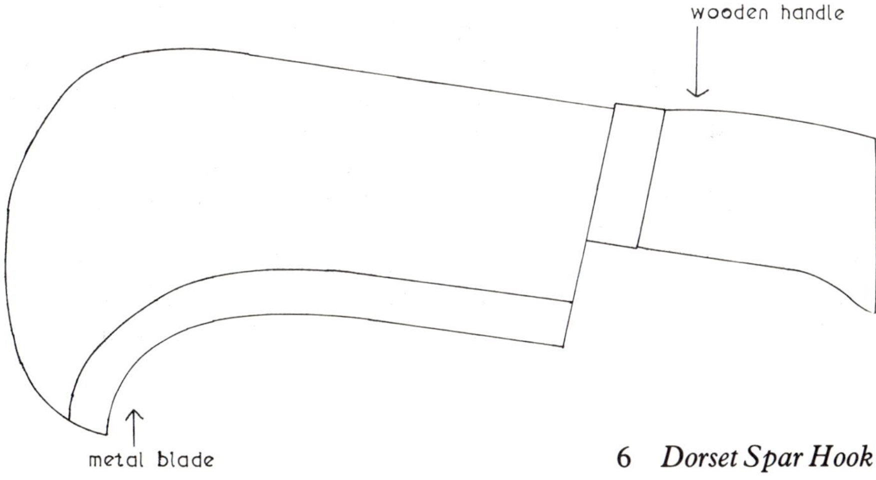

6   *Dorset Spar Hook*

entails the knack of turning the wrist in a special twist action as the wood is split and forced apart. Many spar makers manage to strip eight spars from each hazel twig, although some prefer to make only four. This means a true central cut must be made each time the hazel is split down its full length. The operation is therefore extremely dextrous, especially as it is often carried out at great speed by the spar-maker and hardness variations in the wood constantly try to divert the blade from travelling its selected course.

The finished lengths of spar wood possess two flat white sides and a slightly rounded side with the bark still on it. They are normally tied up in bundles to ease the task of transportation. The spars are pointed at each end by the thatcher (if the task has not already been done) and then twisted into a hairpin shape. This is done by first holding the rod near the centre. The thatcher then twists his hands in opposite directions and the spars are doubled over into the required hairpin shape. The twisting operation must be carried out within a period of two or three months after the wood has been cut by the hurdle-maker. The twisting action then does not break the fibres in the wood and the springy nature is retained. One leg of the spar is usually made shorter than the other.

Many hundreds of spars are employed by the thatcher in the construction of a roof. Their configuration enables the spars to grip and remain firm when pushed into the thatch during roof construction. Many spars are used to hold the adjacent bundles of thatch tightly together on the roof. As well as spars, longer lengths of unsplit hazel are also needed to secure the thatch. Nine foot long lengths, called sways, are utilized to hold down securely the underlying layers of thatch; the long hazel rods themselves being pinned over the thatch bundles to the roof rafters with iron hooks. This method of fixing is very commonly employed when the thatch material consists of the tougher water reeds. The sways are never visible on the roof surface as they are eventually covered by an overlapping top surface layer of thatch.

In addition to the sways, shorter five foot lengths of hazel which have been split along their full lengths are used to peg down some of the top layers of thatch. These five foot lengths are known as liggers and the spars are driven over them into the thatch to press the liggers down onto the thatch and hold it down firmly. Liggers are always visible on the surface of the thatch in the ridge and in the case of long straw roofs, also at the eaves and along the gable ends. Two parallel liggers are normally pegged to the ridge and decorative patterns are created in the space between them with small crossed hazel rods, called slats, which are also held in position with spars.

2

Thatching Styles

It is perhaps interesting to note that threshing machines in the south and east of England were introduced much later than in the north and west. This may have played some role in the persistence of thatch in Dorset because it meant that good thatching straw was available for a longer period of time.

Thatching has remained a family business in Dorset and the skills have therefore been handed on from father to son. For example, one Dorset thatching family still operating in north Dorset has carried out its trade in unbroken succession for well over two hundred years. Very unusually, a daughter of this family also became a highly skilled thatcher, despite the harsh uninviting nature of the outdoor work. In general, before the days of motor transport, thatchers concentrated on their own localities and built up a tradition of thatching most of the buildings and cottages there. Although most still prefer to obtain jobs in the near vicinity of their homes, many more now travel and are prepared to thatch in any district. They are always kept very busy and most have work booked many months ahead.

Practical experience and tuition from a master thatcher constitute the only way to learn to thatch. As mentioned, this means that individual styles have been transferred from generation to generation. Thatchers usually take on apprentices when they have no son in the trade but here again the recruit learns the art and style as dictated by his master tutor. The apprenticeship normally runs for five years. Many thatchers are proud of the certificates they possess for their teaching ability as well as for their thatching achievements. Most skilled thatchers are members of the Master Thatchers Association. In more recent years, the Council for Small Industries in Rural Areas (CoSIRA) have introduced training schemes for new entrants to thatching. They organize instructional courses but the student must also be sponsored by a Masterman in the thatching trade in order to gain his practical experience.

Thatching still thrives in Dorset today because there remain approximately four thousand thatched homes in the county, as well as many thatched pubs, barns and other buildings. Recently, the West Dorset Council decided to give grants to owner-occupiers towards re-thatching their homes. Previously, grants were only made when substantial structural repairs to the roof timbers were also required, which necessitated the removal of the thatch and its eventual replacement. Grants were not previously available for the mere renewal of thatch. This new policy of assisting owners to meet their expensive thatching repair bills must generate even more business for the thatcher and hopefully allows him to employ additional apprentices. An average size cottage will cost about £5,500 to re-thatch at present day prices.

Thatchers spend a great deal of their time on the roof and so require a special ladder to make them comfortable when working aloft. The design eliminates sharp corners on the inside uprights of the ladder because the thatcher often presses and rubs his knees against them when working. The inside lengths are thus rounded in contrast to the straight edges of a normal builder's ladder. The thatcher's ladder is made of wood so that he is less likely to slip than if he used a modern light-weight aluminium one. The special wooden ladders often possess as many as forty-eight rungs and they are long and heavy. Thatchers also need smaller lighter ladders for use on the roof. These are called hang-ladders and they are fitted with spikes which enable the ladder to grip when laid on the thatch to reach the ridge. Thatchers also frequently wear knee pads to protect themselves further against abrasions when working on the roof.

Thatchers employ two main methods to lay thatch; the first involves sewing the thatch to the rafters and the second consists of pinning it down with a system of wooden rods. As mentioned earlier, these rods are called sways when they are securing the underneath layers of the thatch and liggers when they hold down the outer coat of thatch. Some thatchers use a combination of the sewing and pinning down techniques. Many wooden spars are utilized in both methods.

The most commonly used thatching material in Dorset is combed wheat reed. Most thatchers sew the bundles of reed securely to the roof with a tarred twine, threaded through a two-foot-long flat needle. The bundles are made slightly wet by the thatcher before use to assist the packing of the reeds close together. Two overlapping coats of thatch are laid to ensure a perfect waterproof cover, about eighteen inches thick on the finished roof. As the roof is thatched, many spars in conjunction with the twine, are utilized to pack the bundles tightly. The reeds are also 'shut' snuggly together by beating the exposed straw butt ends constantly upwards with a tool called a leggett. This implement is perhaps most commonly known as a 'biddle' in Dorset or sometimes as a 'beater' or 'pomiard'. It consists of a flat piece of wood with ridges cut along its face to assist the driving of the reed ends firmly upwards to tension them and ensure they are evenly compacted. The thatcher always works in 'lanes' which extend from the eaves to the ridge and moves across the roof from right to left in 'courses'. In this way the whole roof surface is eventually thatched. A thatcher and his apprentice will lay about a hundred bundles a day, removing the old thatch as they proceed. The ridge of the roof demands extra attention and additional thatch material to ensure the straw bent over the apex forms a completely water-tight seal. The gable ends of the ridge are sometimes finished with pinnacles which give a more rustic appearance to the roof.

The thatcher normally trims the butt ends of the reeds on the roof surface with a hook to tidy the finished appearance. The completed reed roof then displays a smooth bristle or quill-like look, as only very small lengths of the reed butts are left exposed on the roof surface and these are tensioned outwards.

Finally, the thatcher cuts the eaves of the wheat reed with an eaves-hook. In Dorset, it is common practice to taper the eaves when they are cut to give them a distinctive appearance. This also applies to the thatch swept over any 'eyebrow' dormer windows at the eaves level and also the thatched hoods above any full dormer windows in the roof. This tapering of the thatch gives rise to a dainty look but the style also helps the admission of more light through the windows. The practice of sweeping thatch in a scallop shape around the upper windows at eaves level is very common in Dorset. It is a pleasant sight on many long thatched buildings and it is quite usual to find a whole series of such windows. These 'eyebrows' are much more numerous in Dorset than the full dormer, with its window projecting vertically from the sloping roof and having its own thatched hood.

Although combed wheat reed dominates as the chief thatching material in Dorset, many roofs thatched in the long-straw style may also be found. The density of these is more pronounced towards the eastern side of Dorset. In contrast to combed wheat reed, the long straw used for thatching is placed in a more random array and the butt ends are not all arranged together. The long straw is also applied to the roof using a different technique and this gives rise to a much looser aspect than the more bristly appearance of a combed wheat reed roof.

The long straw bundles, or yealms as they are called, may be sewn to the roof or pinned down. They are wetted to make them pliant and then applied lengthwise to give eventually a gentle, more moulded finish. The straws are not tensioned outwards, with only the ends exposed, as in the case of reed. During roof construction, the long straw is combed downwards to remove small pieces of loose and bent straw. This contrasts to the upwards dressing, or beating, employed in reed laying. The combing action results in longer lengths of the straw being visible on the completed roof surface. This is the reason the end-product is much more hair-like and loose than the regimented structure of the combed wheat reed. Although the long straw thatcher does not pack the straw as tightly, he makes very sure the surface is level so no area is prone to sag. If sagging occurs, then rain-water soon exposes it and channels down along its route to the eaves. This seriously shortens the life of the roof.

When the long-straw roof is completely thatched and the ridges finished, the thatcher rakes and then shears the thatch to tidy it up. The amount of shearing depends upon the individual thatcher's preference. The eaves and barges are always finished with liggers and spars (Fig. 7). The liggers secure the thatch before the eaves and barges are neatly cut. These liggers, which are also decorative, make it very easy to distinguish a long-straw thatched roof from a combed wheat reed one.

Water reeds taken from the marshes are without doubt the toughest thatching materials. They are extremely durable and Norfolk reed is the most famous. Although the *Phragmites communis* reed grows in other counties, it is only correctly called 'Norfolk reed' if it originates from the semi-cultivated reed beds of Norfolk. Abbotsbury and Radipole reeds from Dorset are as durable as the Norfolk reed but because of their limited quantities their fame is confined mainly to Dorset.

Norfolk reed finds a market demand in most counties of England,

7   *Long Straw Finishes*

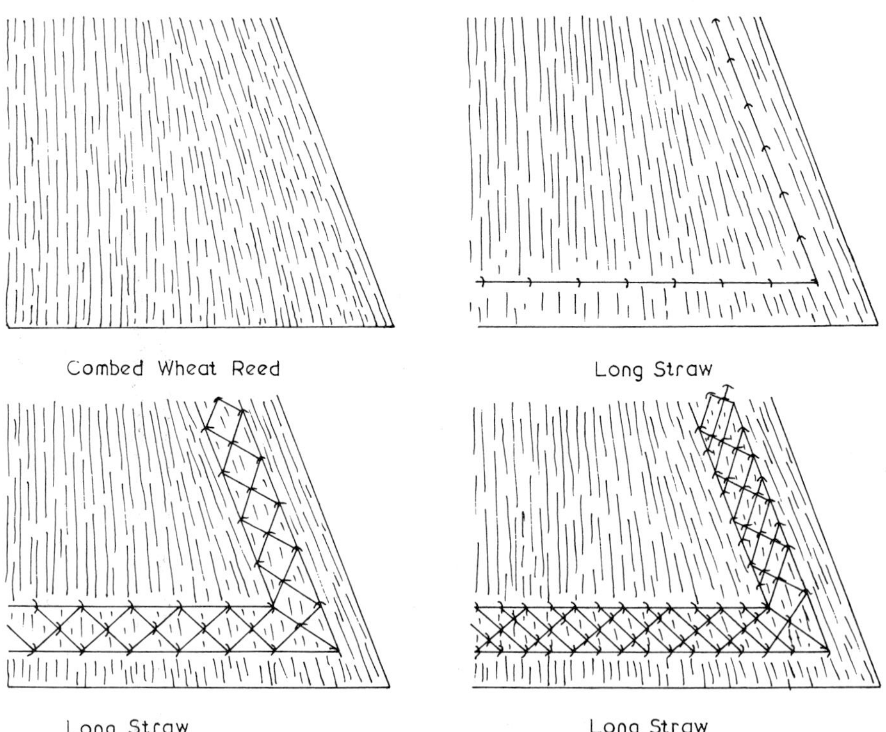

and Dorset is no exception. Norfolk reed thatch may be found on a number of houses scattered throughout the county but Radipole reed roofs are also discovered on quite a number of buildings. For example, Radipole reed may be seen covering the Thatched House pub at East Howe, Bournemouth whilst Norfolk reed shelters the beautiful thatched manor house at Toller Whelme. Abbotsbury reed roofs are not so widely dispersed but many examples may be viewed in the village from where the reed takes its name.

The thatcher lays a marsh reed roof in a similar manner to combed wheat reed. However, the marsh water reeds require no preliminary wetting treatment and are simply dressed by the thatcher on a board to level the butt ends. The thatcher may also cut off any feathery tips still present on the tops of the reeds. In contrast to combed wheat reed, the marsh reeds are more frequently secured to the roof with the use of sways and iron hooks and the reeds are again beaten upwards with a leggett to pack them tightly.

Unlike wheat straw, marsh reed is not flexible enough to bend over the apex of the roof to make a waterproof ridge. In Norfolk, sedge is traditionally used for ridge construction but in Dorset it is common for the ridges of roofs thatched with Norfolk reed to be built with straw.

Norfolk and marsh reed roofs attain a beautiful golden-brown colour on ageing, whilst combed wheat reed changes to a more greyish-like hue. Another distinguishing feature shows in the finish of the eaves and gables of the thatch. The ends of the Norfolk reed are never cut to shape whilst the combed wheat reed is always trimmed by the thatcher to the line or taper required with an eaves-hook.

The great advantage of thatch over alternative roofing materials, such as tiles and slates, is that it can be swept with an elegant flow over any complex plan of building. This cannot be done with any other material. Thatch is therefore very versatile and can form hipped, half-hipped, quarter-hipped and gabled roofs with equal ease (Fig. 8). It also is ideal for making outshut and catslide roofs whilst its use on winged and cross-winged houses offers no problems. In fact, it allows roof valleys to be readily made with soft gentle curves in these types of houses. The only practical limitation on the use of thatch is that the pitch of the roof must be steep, so that rain-water and snow are quickly shed from the roof surface. This makes thatch more suitable on longer narrower buildings than on larger square double-pile houses, which are more than two rooms deep. However, this restriction made little effect on the wide traditional usage of thatch in Dorset because the double-pile house in the countryside was rare and it did not become established at all until the middle of the eighteenth century onwards.

With regard to the various types of thatch, the long-straw style looks especially pleasing on small cottages, around small dormers and also on

Hipped
Half-hipped
Quarter-hipped
Gabled
Outshut
Catslide
Winged

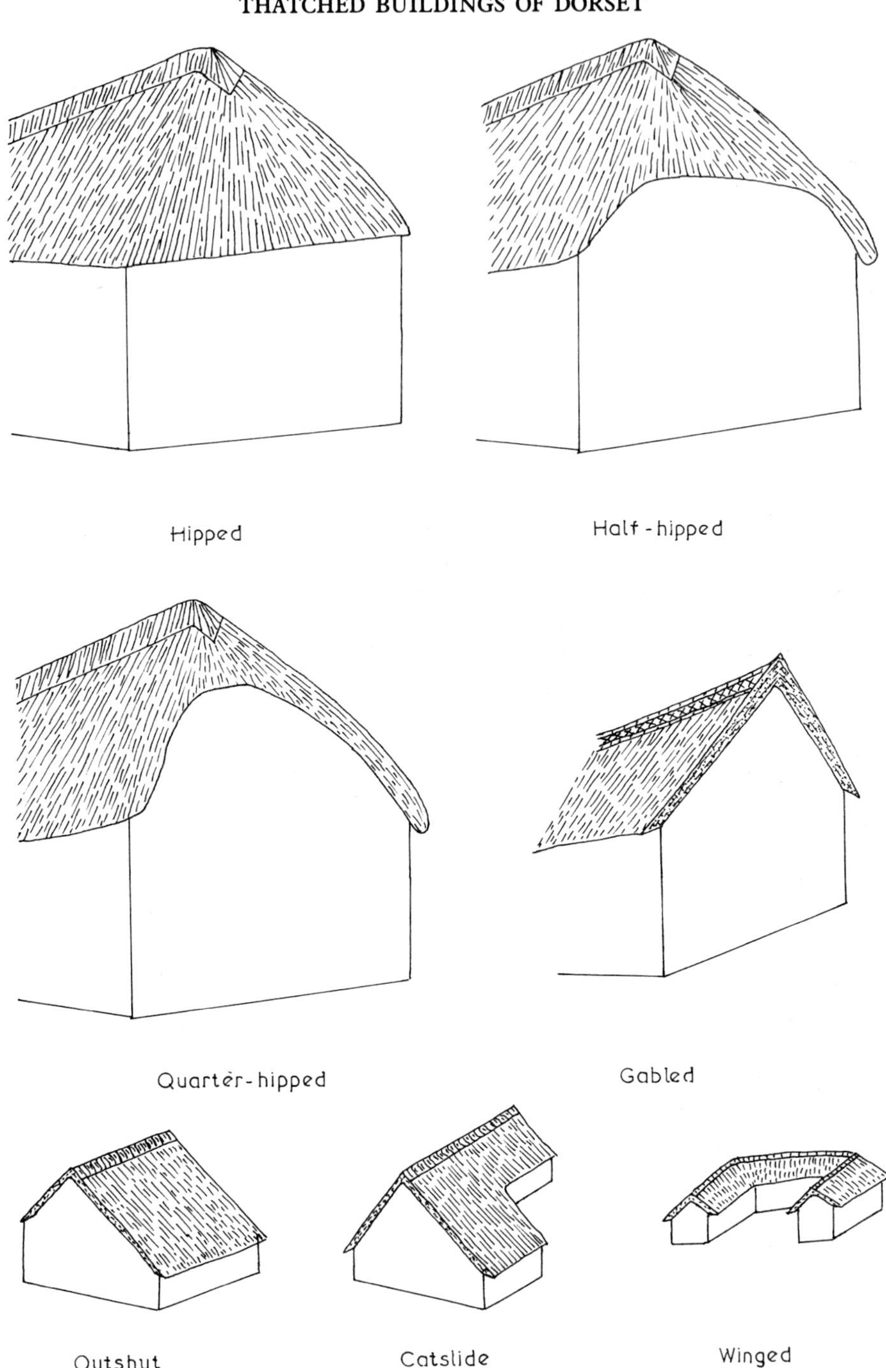

8   *Roof Types*

buildings which possess different roof levels. The natural look of a long-straw roof in these cases seems more appropriate than the smarter more regulated style of a combed wheat reed or marsh reed roof. Long straw also appears less severe on porches and these types of small roofs are made even more rustic when jaunty pinnacles are fashioned on top. Combed wheat reed is a particularly good thatch for medium-sized cottages, whilst marsh reed is perhaps ideally suited to larger buildings. However, much of this depends upon personal opinion and the three main types of thatching material may be found on all sizes and shapes of buildings, depending upon the different owners' preferences. The thatcher will also be keen to give advice on the best material to use in individual cases. Cost will also play a role.

Roofs thatched in the long-straw style do not last as long as those constructed using the reed technique. A long-straw roof needs a new top coat after about twenty years. However, the roof remains perfectly watertight during this period. This is illustrated by the fact that the undercoat hardly ever requires replacement and may remain for a century. Thatchers sometimes find pieces of old debris, such as scraps of paper, left behind by the previous thatcher. These are still usually bone-dry, thus paying tribute to the excellent waterproof qualities of the long-straw roof.

The finding of other more interesting items in the lower coat of thatch, or often on the top of an attic wall at the eaves level, is also quite common. In fact, small things were often deliberately left, rather than lost in the thatch by accident. The older the building, the more likely is the discovery of a concealed object. The superstition that hiding something in a house will bring good luck to the building, probably dates back to the fifteenth century. The custom has survived over many centuries and a favourite thing to hide seems to be an old worn shoe. The practice of concealment may also be connected with the human desire to leave a mysterious link of personal identity for a stranger to find later.

It was rare to secrete a pair of shoes but an interesting case was reported in a local newspaper a few years ago. A tiny pair of roughly made but hand-sewn shoes, were discovered in the loft area of a house which was being re-thatched at the village of Winterborne Stickland in Dorset. One of the shoes had nearly disintegrated but surprisingly, the other one was in a better condition. Nevertheless, the heel had been badly flattened and the shoe was also shapeless, which suggested it had been worn by a lady whose foot was too large. The age of the shoe remains unknown, as well as the identity of the mysterious stranger who had walked many miles in it.

Instead of the more usual repair of a top coat of thatch, fixed in the traditional manner, some thatched roofs are occasionally renovated by

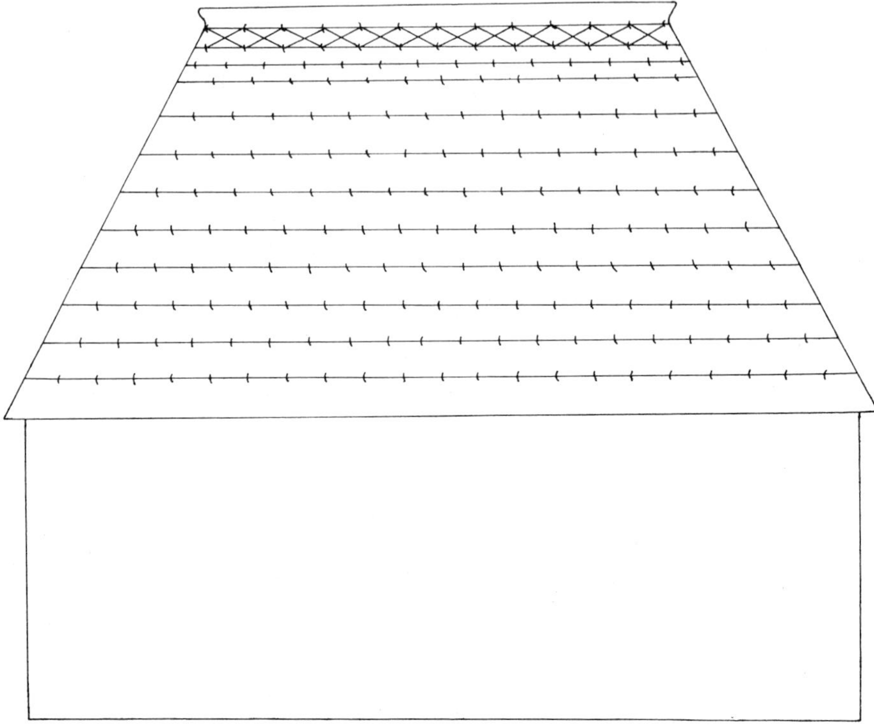

9   *Renovated Thatched Roof*

binding the entire surface over with a whole series of horizontal liggers, held down by spars (Fig. 9). This Dorset style of repair may sometimes be seen on older roofs and especially those made from Abbotsbury reed. This method of renovation proves to be effective but the expected look of the thatched roof is entirely changed. The liggers form ladder-like steps which extend from the eaves to the ridge of the roof.

On the subject of prolonging the life of a roof, a difference of opinion often arises between thatchers on the relative merits of wire-netting to protect the thatch from bird damage. Some think wire-netting on a straw roof is an unnecessary expense because bird damage is minimal if the straw is initially clean and the ears devoid of grain. They also hold the opinion that any increase in roof life obtained by reducing the number of straws pulled out by birds, is offset by the damage caused to the thatch by the wire-netting itself. Strong winds rub the exposed straw ends against the wire and this causes abrasion and the breaking of some of the straws. The wire-netting also slightly impedes the shedding of rain-water from the roof, as it slows up its flow over the surface. In addition, any broken straws trapped under the wire and turned into the thatch offer potential routes for the ingress of water.

However, all thatchers will agree that long straw is more likely to be damaged by birds than roofs made from combed wheat reed or marsh reed. This is because the long straw is more loosely packed than a reed constructed roof and longer ends of straw are exposed for the birds to grip with their beaks. The main culprits are sparrows and starlings. Most thatchers will not recommend the use of wire-netting when the thatched roof is close to trees. The netting tends to trap fallen twigs and leaves. This impedes the water shedding properties of the roof and hastens the onset of thatch rot. It also encourages the growth of moss on the roof which becomes very unsightly and also retains moisture. In any event, many people think that the presence of wire-netting itself on a thatched roof greatly detracts from its appearance and charm.

Some countrymen suggest that birds damage thatched cottage roofs more frequently now that ricks are no longer a predominant feature of the countryside. The pulling of straws by birds from thatched roofs, especially at the places most prone to attack, such as under eaves, gables, ridges and chimney junctions, does not appear to be connected purely with the nesting season. Birds seem to derive pleasure from pecking at thatched roofs during all the seasons of the year and then dropping the straw to the ground. They have initially been attracted to the straw when searching for insects as food.

Wire-netting was also once considered to be a method of preventing mice or other vermin gaining entry into the roof. However, most people who have lived in a thatched house will agree that this has never been a problem of any significance. It is extremely rare to find mice in the space below a thatched roof. Insurance companies do not favour the use of wire-netting on thatched roofs because of the increased fire damage risk. It takes time to remove the netting before the burning thatch can be reached by the fire brigade. This is despite the fact that the netting strips are joined in such a way that they can be easily released in the event of a fire.

With regard to fires, some thatchers believe a few of these are inadvertently caused by the new type of owner who now lives in the older thatched cottages. The present-day owner sometimes prefers to install a modern enclosed fire in his hearth, rather than enjoy the traditional open fire. Unfortunately, many old cottage chimneys have a tendency to smoke which is a further incentive for the owner to install rather quickly a modern fuel burning appliance with a forced draught. However, many old cottage chimneys have a roof timber intruding into them and the forced draught causes any sparks which may alight on the timber to be constantly fanned to a higher temperature. This causes the beam to smoulder and eventually a fire to start. Yet the chimney may have given no problem over the last century or two with an ordinary open fire.

A habit which irritates the thatcher is when owners push TV aerials through the thatch. This not only destroys the waterproof nature of the roof but also grossly interferes with the charm of the thatching style and the overall appearance. In addition, some residents allow creepers to grow over the thatch which helps to ruin the thatch and also encourages rot. This is because the creeper hinders the shedding of rain-water from the roof and traps falling leaves.

A considerable difference exists in the thatching styles adopted by thatchers in the various regions of England; Dorset is no exception. Some thatchers prefer to work with water reed, others with combed wheat reed and some with long straw. This preference is not always strictly related to local availability, as all three types of thatching material are obtainable to varying extents in Dorset.

The individuality of the thatcher relates not only to the material he selects and prefers to work with but also to the artistic touches he creates on his finished thatched roof. These are most noticeable in his treatment of the ridge of the roof which is normally decorated with attractive patterns fashioned from hazel wood liggers and spars. Often the underside of a raised ridge will also be cut into various neat shapes, as if they were a trademark of the particular thatcher. The individuality of the thatcher shows not only in the surface decoration of the thatch but also in many other ways, such as his preferred method of shaping the thatch around dormer windows, or the way he may cut the thatch at the eaves or gable ends of the roof.

Some thatchers proudly display a more obvious trademark such as a pheasant, shaped in straw, on the top of the roof. Other thatchers may prefer to use a different straw bird, or an animal, on the ridge but pheasants are especially popular in Dorset. They may be displayed singly or, quite commonly in twos, thus making a brace of pheasants perching on the ridge. The birds may be made within wire-netting and moulded to the required shape, or they may be sculptured from straw bound to wooden sticks or alternatively, on the outside of a wire-frame. However, some thatchers will not agree to this type of ornamentation. They hold the view that when rain runs off the straw bird, it encourages a 'guttering' effect on the roof below which slowly spoils the thatch.

It seems that fashion also plays a role in the decorative work carried out by thatchers on the ridges of thatched roofs. A sense of competitiveness comes through even at the vernacular level to highlight the pride and work of the individual thatcher. The selected ornamental pattern adopted by the thatcher will be somewhat affected by the architectural style of the building and also the chimney location. Many thatchers favour a large apron along the underside of the thatch ridge below the chimney position, but this can only be done when the chimney passes through the actual ridge of the roof. Some thatchers will even create a

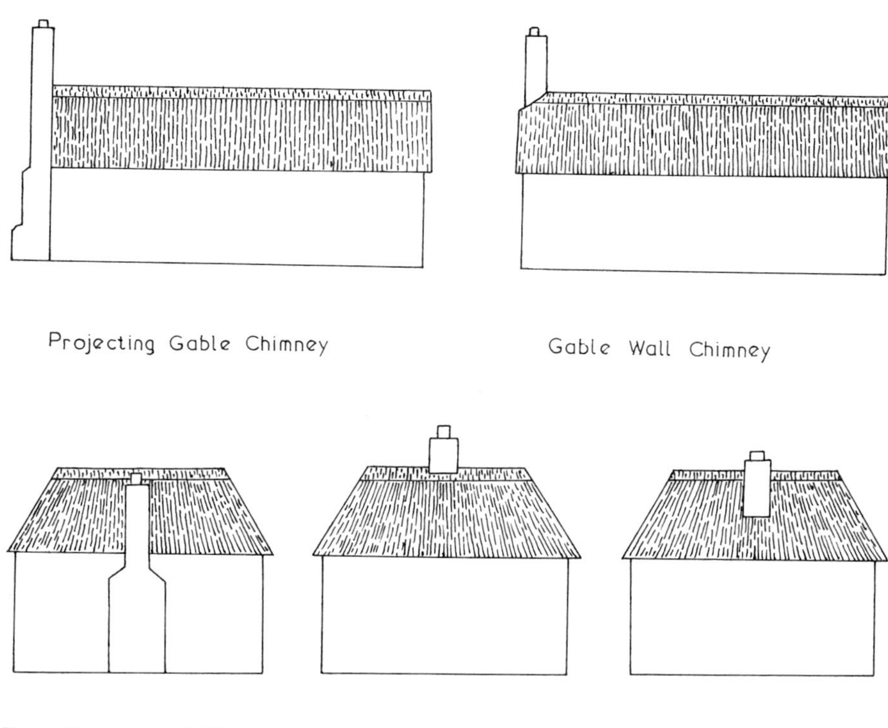

10   *Chimney Types*

huge thatched apron which may well extend half-way down the main roof and also run the full length of the roof. This adds a considerable cost to the work but the effect is delightful. A good example of this type of thatching may be viewed on cottages at West Stafford in Dorset.

Many early cottages were constructed with chimneys projecting from the gables to keep them well clear of the thatch (Fig. 10). This was done to reduce the fire risk but later the chimneys became incorporated into the gable walls of the cottages. With early hipped roofs, it was again often the practice to position chimneys so that they projected from the side wall to avoid the thatch at the eaves. However, this design badly affected the ability of the thatch to shed water at the chimney junction and later it became customary to build chimneys which passed through the ridge. The siting of chimneys in the middle region of the main thatch slope to avoid passing through the ridge, are rarely found in thatched cottages. Again this type of design grossly interfered with the shedding of water from the roof and presented problems with water-proofing. Water tended to gather at the thatch interface with the chimney.

In general, the ridges of thatched roofs may be divided into two main

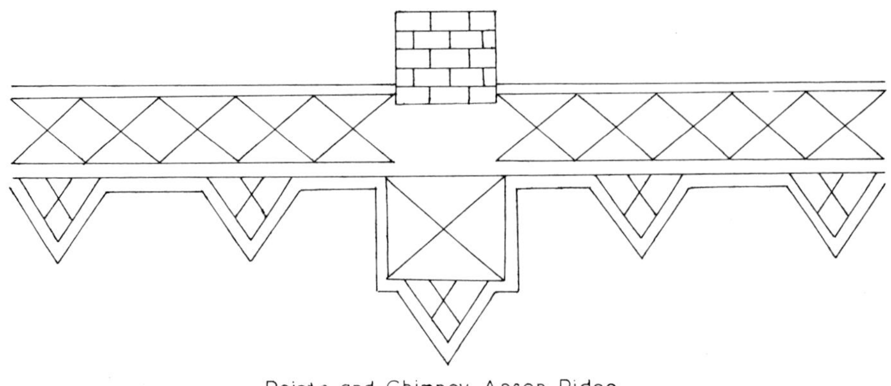

Points and Chimney Apron Ridge

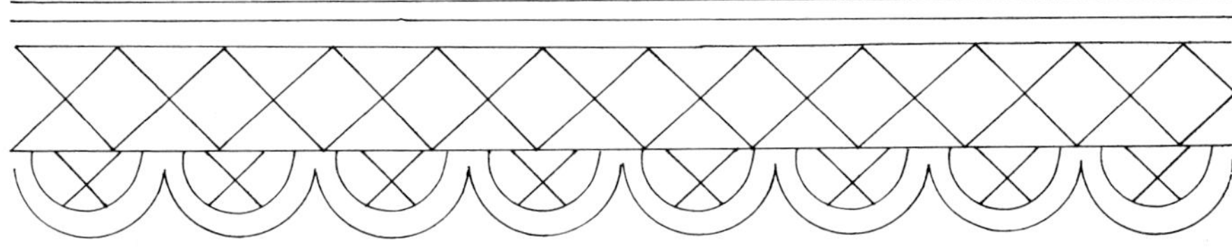

Scallops Ridge

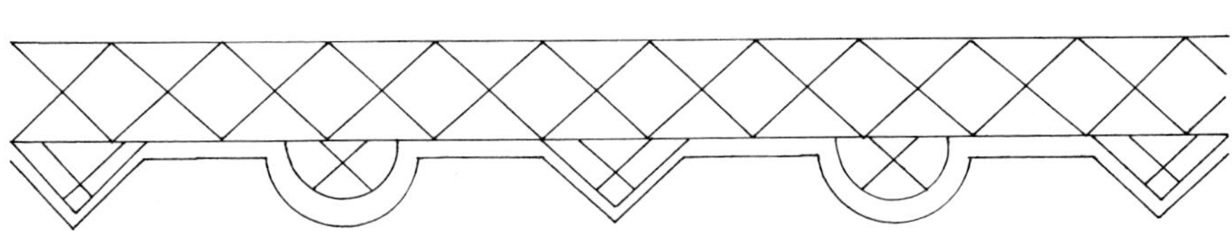

Scallops and Points Ridge

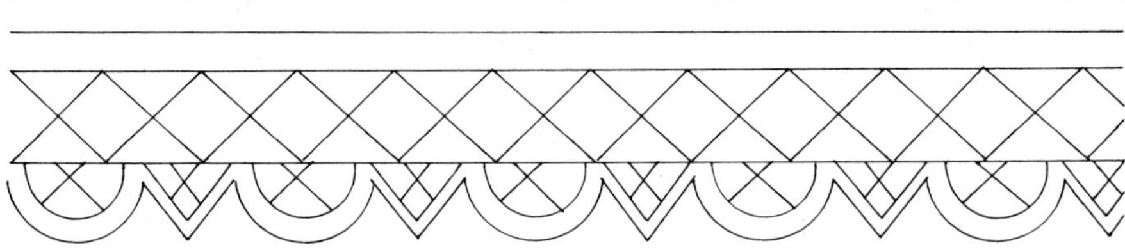

Scallops and Points Variation

11 *Thatched Ridge Ornamentation*

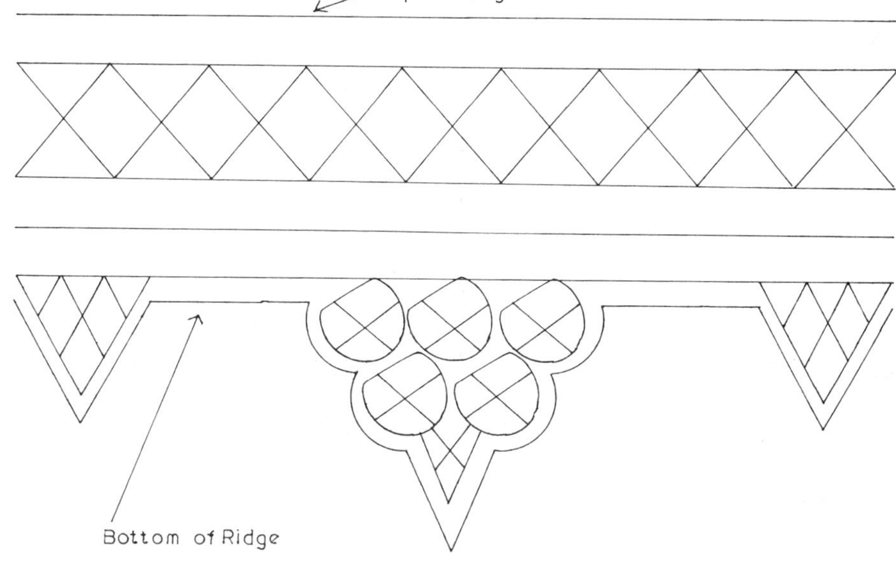

12 *Elaborate Ridge Ornamentation*

types, depending upon whether they are flat or raised. In the former case, the ridge follows the same surface plane as the main roof, whilst in the latter the ridge may be raised up to approximately four inches above it. This gives a richer look to the roof but uses considerably more thatch material. A raised ridge allows the thatcher an opportunity to indulge in a great variety of artistic shapes, fashioned along the bottom of the ridge. With a flat ridge, the only distinctive embellishment which can be made are patterns created from liggers and spars. It is also common to decorate raised ridges with similar such patterns, thus making these even more elaborate. The decorative design may be constructed from a series of liggers and crossed slats to form a diamond type image or, perhaps less commonly in Dorset, a complex herring-bone picture.

Many Dorset thatchers prefer to cut a series of points along the bottom edge of a raised ridge, with a rectangular-shaped apron also carved below any ridge chimney which may be present (Fig. 11). Points are more common than scallop shapes, although these are also seen on roofs. Ridges with just points, or more occasionally only scallops, are much more popular in Dorset than using a combination of both shapes, as frequently favoured by thatchers in East Anglia. However, many elaborate shapes derived from the basic scallop form are found on many roofs (Fig. 12). The individual rounded enlarged portions of the scallops are frequently decorated on their surfaces with D-shaped designs made from hazel wood rods and spars. A scallop of a similar type may even be furnished with a large point at the bottom to make a large distinctive emblem. Good examples of these types of decorative ridge finishes may be viewed, for example, on Preston Post Office (near Weymouth) and larger versions of the ornamentation may be found on the thatched roof of East Farm at Osmington.

Long-straw thatched roofs offer the thatcher an even more extensive opportunity to grace the roof with hazel wood patterns. As mentioned earlier, combinations of liggers and cross-rods are used not only on the ridges of such roofs but also along the eaves and gable or barge ends of the thatch. The liggers may be fixed in a single row with spars, which gives rise to a stitch-like image, or in parallel pairs. In the latter case, a series of slats made into the shape of crosses adorns the space between the two parallel liggers. The crosses themselves are secured with spars in a neat row.

<h1 style="text-align:center">3</h1>

Thatched Manor House Buildings

The lavishness of the architectural design, the splendour of the interior furnishings of the house, the extent of the grounds, the formal gardens, the retinue of servants and the number of acres of land owned, all reflected the prestige and power of the great lord of the manor. Without doubt, the most important of these assets was the land, as this allowed the owner and his descendants to be accepted through many centuries as members of the ruling class of England. The lord of the large manor owned vast estates of land but he did not usually farm them himself. He may have managed a small home farm to supply the fresh food needs of his household but the rest of the land was rented to tenant farmers, to generate a source of income for the estate.

As the owner was not tied to his land by the need to farm it, he could be away for long periods. The lord therefore often lived in a town or city house and participated in affairs of state, or served as one of the judiciary. He also often travelled widely and by this experience was able to introduce new concepts and ideas to his local manor. He frequently formed the only link between the outside world and the villagers working on his estates. The lord recognized the great value of education and learning so he always provided the best possible for his heirs.

In addition to the nobility who had acquired vast acreages of land, there were many lesser squires who possessed land and lived in the smaller manor houses. They played a much more active role in the farming of their lands and normally the manor house was their sole home. They also enjoyed a good education and gave service to the community by acting, for example, as local magistrates, contributing to the upkeep of the church and supporting other parochial activities. As with the great lords of the manor, most squires gave distinguished military service when called upon by their country in times of need.

Manor houses built before the end of the sixteenth century inevitably included a defensive element in them. The households were also predominantly male, in order to maintain a fighting force which was immediately available for action. Strength at arms ensured power. The custom of 'Beating the Bounds' was also practised to claim for each manor its lands and limits. The emphasis on a fighting force in the manor house waned in the seventeenth century and the domestic side became important. However, the change took place slowly and it was not until the nineteenth century that the number of female servants in the household generally became greater than the number of male servants. Manor houses through the ages were frequently used as places of entertainment for visiting nobles. Wandering minstrels and jesters often performed in them on festive occasions and many manor houses brewed their own ale and beer.

The power of the country landowners in the ruling of England decreased slowly in the nineteenth century with the coming of the Industrial Revolution. This shifted some of the power base and wealth to the expanding industrial towns. The establishment of county and rural district councils in 1888 also gradually reduced the power of the lords and country squires.

Nevertheless, at the beginning of the eighteenth century, the landed nobility anticipated the need for agrarian change and some took steps to make agriculture a more profitable industry. New improved methods of cultivation were introduced and the great landowners sought out novel developments to experiment with on their estates. The eighteenth century saw the emergence of a new social class, termed the gentleman farmer. The nobility recognized land as a profitable source of income, as well as a symbol of power and social prestige. Farming thus became a fashionable occupation with the upper classes and this continued through the nineteenth century. During this present century, many more large landowners have become farmers on a very extensive scale. This is due to changes in the law which have made a tenanted farm a less attractive proposition for the landowner.

Many of the manor houses in Dorset have now become in effect large farmhouses, as they are so inextricably associated with the working of the land. On the other hand, some manor houses have undergone complete changes in use. Several have been converted into hotels, others into educational institutions and some into homes for wealthy but previous city and town dwellers.

Despite these alterations to their original functions, a very large number of manor houses still survive in Dorset. Most were originally built with locally quarried stone-ashlar, with mullioned windows and they were roofed with substantial stone slates. Perhaps surprisingly, a few were also roofed with thatch but despite their rather large and grand appearances, they mingled in complete harmony with the smaller thatched cottages and farm buildings of the villages. Many other manor houses, although not thatched themselves, possessed outbuildings which were thatched, such as barns, stables and gate-houses. Many of these types of ancillary buildings illustrate the close relationship which developed between the lord of the manor and the agriculture carried out on his land.

Woodsford Castle

The largest thatched manor house in Dorset lies beside the River Frome, about four and a quarter miles to the east of Dorchester, just along the road outside Woodsford village. It is a most unusual building as it is a fortified manor house and yet it is furnished with a huge thatched roof. The manor house bears the name Woodsford Castle. It boasts two main claims to fame, it is the only thatched castle in England and it is also the oldest one which has been lived in throughout its entire history, including the present day.

This history dates back to 1337 when the licence to crenellate a manor house at Woodsford was first granted to William de Whitefield by King Edward III. The exact dates the building work was started and eventually completed appear to be lost in the past, but there is no doubt the house was standing in 1368 when Sir Guy de Bryan lived in the manor. As the Hundred Years War with France began in 1337, it appears likely that the permission obtained to build a manor house with battlements and loopholes at this particular time may not have been purely coincidental. The crenellation licence made Woodsford offici-ally a castle. When first constructed, it was most unlikely that the castle would have been thatched, as this would have made it too vulnerable under siege. Its position near a ford over the River Frome was probably the chief reason for its original fortification.

After the decease of Sir Guy de Bryan in 1391, his heiresses lived in the castle until it passed to John Butler, who was the Earl of Wiltshire and a few years later to Sir Humphrey Stafford, who was to become the Earl of Devon for a short while before his death. Both earls met similar fates at the hands of the executioner. The Earl of Wiltshire was executed after the Battle of Towton, which was fought along the River Aire in Yorkshire in 1461. The Earl of Devon was beheaded a few years later at Bridgwater in 1469 for forsaking the Yorkist cause. Woodsford then passed to his heiresses, one of whom married into the Strangeways family and it remained part of their estates for the following centuries, under the various Earls of Ilchester. The castle was extensively restored in about 1850 and it then became used as a farmhouse. It is now a private residence with a modern stepped entrance made in the east wall.

The most striking feature of Woodsford Castle is its vast expanse of thatch which covers a roof area in excess of three thousand square feet. The exact date the castle received its first thatched roof is not clear but the walls were probably raised at the same time, although this was only done at the northern end of the house. There are therefore two different roof levels today. Over a period of time, the top coat of thatch must have been renewed many times and the roof has again recently been re-thatched. The present ridge is straight and therefore is not cut with any ornamented shapes. The plain nature of the ridge conforms well to the overall character expected of a slightly austere fortified building.

Woodsford Castle still stands with most of its fourteenth-century stonework, as it was originally built with squared Purbeck masonry which has lasted through the many centuries. The manor house was constructed in the form of a very long narrow building but there have been a few alterations, including a small seventeenth-century block added at one corner in the place of the original north-west tower of the castle. There are also several seventeenth-century stone mullioned windows. The original castle possessed a square tower at each corner and possibly also a fifth; one near the centre of the long east wall (Fig. 13) but only the north-east tower now survives. This remaining square tower still displays its defensive arrow-slit windows.

The projecting turret visible along the exterior of the west wall has a small rounded stone roof. This turret hides the original circular newel staircase still situated within the building. Corbels are also visible on the exterior walls of the castle and some of these may have supported a projecting gallery with holes in its floor to drop stones through on assailants below. This gallery would have been reached from a parapet walk. The position of the corbels on the wall indicates the northern section of the house which had its walls heightened, as the corbels were no doubt at the original parapet level.

A further indication of the defensive nature of the house was that it

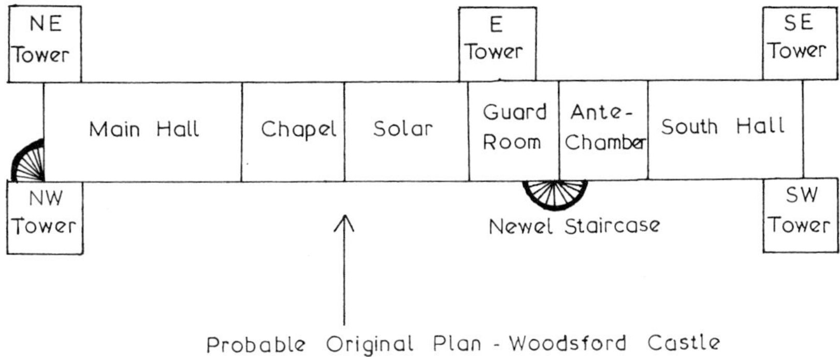

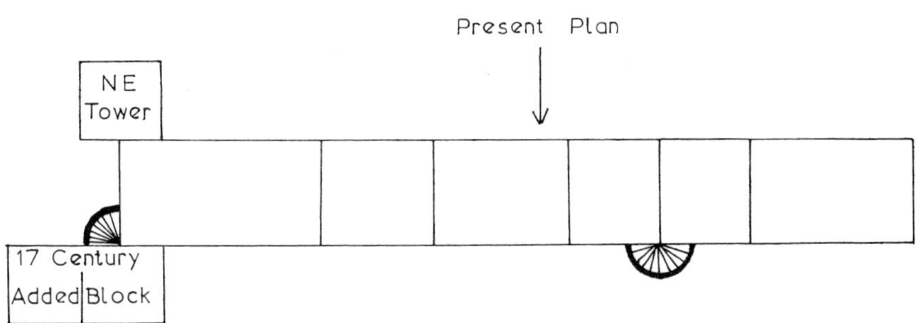

13 *Woodsford Castle – First Floor*

was built with two storeys but only the first floor was used for living accommodation. The ground floor consisted of a series of vaulted rooms, all intercommunicating but employed only as service and storage rooms. The central room of these probably served as the kitchen. The use of spiral staircases in turrets or towers was a common feature of many houses constructed in Britain for first-floor living, combined with defensive purposes. They were easier to defend than open staircases and this was the reason such stairs were installed at Woodsford Castle. A water well was also always an essential require-ment within the confines of a castle and one was present at Woodsford, near the north-west corner of the house.

As with the ground floor, all the first floor living-rooms were built in a long interconnecting box-like chain. There were a total of six rooms in the original block. The main living-room on the first floor was the large hall at the extreme north end of the building. One doorway from this led into the surviving north-east square tower, which originally enclosed a privy and laver for hand washing. A second doorway from the main hall gave access to a spiral staircase in a round turret projecting from the north wall. It would have originally been built to allow the parapet to be easily reached. The room to the south of the main hall, reached by a third door, was a small private chapel and this led into another principal chamber with a guard room attached. The next room in the chain was an antechamber at the entrance to the south hall. This hall was also intended for living accommodation but it was smaller and not so elaborate as the main north hall situated at the extreme opposite end of the long building. The projecting, round turret on the west wall, containing the circular newel staircase, gave access to both the guard-room and the antechamber. Entry was therefore gained via these two rooms, to all the interconnected rooms on the first floor.

Another thatched manor house with a somewhat more tranquil appearance may be seen in the village of Hammoon. This peaceful tiny village lies beside the River Stour, approximately two miles to the east of Sturminster Newton. Hammoon Manor House, which has now become a farmhouse, rests between Manor Farm and the Church of St Paul. The church (parts of which probably date back to the twelfth century) exhibits on its roof an unusual wooden Victorian bell-turret of 1885, fitted with a weathercock which enables the church to be easily recognized as a landmark. The strange sounding name Hammoon means the 'river-land of the Mohuns'. The de Mohuns were a Norman baron family who once owned several manors, including the one at Hammoon. They had originally come over with William the Conqueror, accompanied by a retinue of forty-seven knights. The Trenchard family succeeded the de Mohuns as lords of the manor towards the end of the fifteenth century.

Hammoon Manor House is nearly adjacent to the church and it possesses an appreciable expanse of thatch. The manor house is in a simple L-shape, constructed of stone-ashlar and rubble, which contrasts quite charmingly with the darker colour of the thatched roof. A huge old sycamore tree towers beside the house and casts a shadow on the roof. This shade has now encouraged moss to grow on an area of the thatch. The roof material consists of combed wheat reed with a straight ridge construction and the thatch is snuggly wired-in. A small dormer type window peeps through the thatch. An attractive walled garden lies next door to the house and the walls of the garden are now fitted with tiles on their tops but feasibly the walls were also once thatched. A few years ago the village green of Hammoon lay immediately opposite the manor house but it has since been enclosed.

The history of the construction of the manor house makes an interesting study. Various parts of the house appear to have been added, altered and rebuilt over a period of several centuries, despite the building's relatively elementary layout (Fig. 14). Nevertheless, there is nothing simple about the grand porch at the front of the house. This is made of Purbeck limestone and it is of classical proportions, displaying

Hammoon Manor House

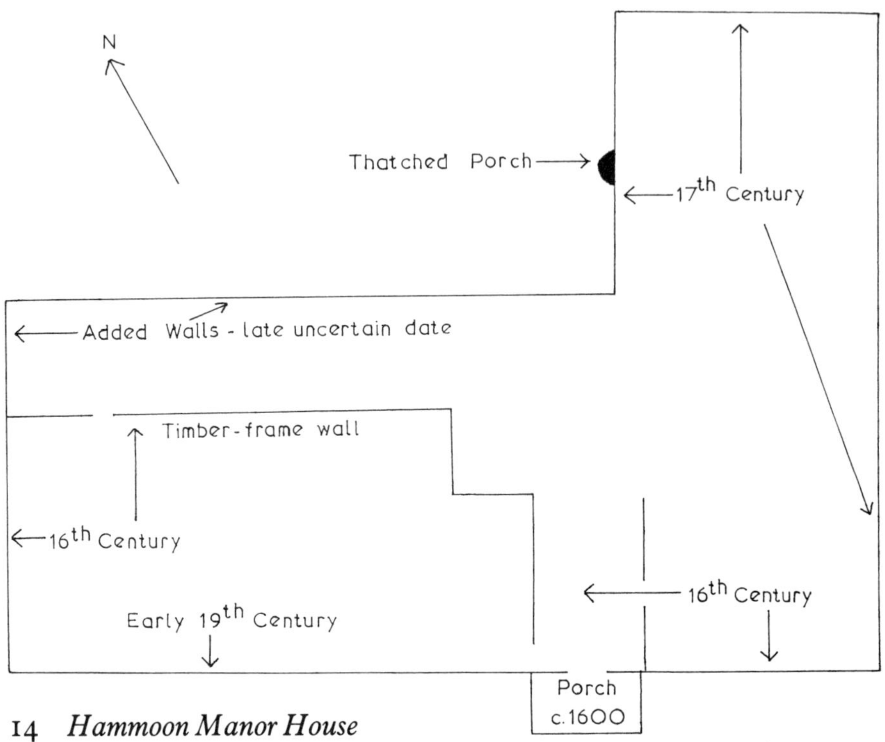

14 *Hammoon Manor House*

a shaped gable with strapwork. As shaped gables with multi-curved sides became fashionable in the first half of the seventeenth century and strapwork decoration with interlaced bands in the sixteenth century, then it is fair to assume the porch is probably of the Elizabethan or Jacobean period. A date of about 1600 is probably right. Strangely, the banded Tuscan columns of the doorway fail to harmonize in scale with the porch itself, so it seems likely they were introduced separately. Incidentally, it is understood that the inside of the house still contains some Jacobean panelling.

The main part of the house behind the classical porch is thought to be approximately a century older than the porch and it dates therefore to the beginning of the sixteenth century. The south-east section, to the right of the porch, is a very attractive part of the house built with a beautiful two-storeyed bay with mullioned windows. These are high-lighted by their arched heads over them. This side of the front of the house also displays a narrow polygonal angle-shaft in the corner and there is a matching one by the porch. The long north-east wing which stretches back to form the L-shape from this front section was probably a rebuilding carried out during the seventeenth century, as the type of mullioned windows on the ground floor suggest. An attractive, newly thatched, small porch shelters the door at the rear of the wing.

The portion of the house, to the left of the main porch by the sycamore tree, is another area where rebuilding has been carried out, most likely at the beginning of the nineteenth century. It was done in cottage style to match the rest of the house. However, the rubble stone wall at the extreme west end seems to be the original early sixteenth century one, so the house was not extended during this rebuilding programme. The walls at the back of this particular section of the house are weather-boarded and there is evidence of the original timber framing.

Another thatched manor house which hides in the heart of the Dorset countryside and is extremely difficult to find, stands at the small village of Toller Whelme. It may be reached by following the narrow bumpy road branching off from the minor road to the south which leads towards Hooke village from Beaminster. Alternatively, it may be reached from the north on an exit from the B3163. The south approach road to the manor passes by a lake and the house itself rests beside a small stream and overlooks beautiful wooded hilly countryside. The church lies just above the house. Many years ago, monks kept carp in the nearby water, as the manor house was once a grange belonging to Forde Abbey. The so-called English carp was first imported into England by monks in the fourteenth century as a source of food. The fish eat mainly plants and survive well in ponds, lakes, slow-moving rivers and even withstand stagnant water. It was thus an ideal fish to sustain the monks living in isolated communities as long as there was some form of water available in the near locality. Plenty of water still

Toller Whelme Manor House

gushes forth at Toller Whelme, as it forms the source of the River Hooke.

The manor house as it stands today is a mixture of the monastic and the seventeenth century. The porch doorway at the front of the house is dated 1470 and must have originated from a demolished range. The rest of the house is mainly seventeenth century, built of stone and covered with a thatched roof. The building is long and has stone mullioned windows. A small wing at the back of the manor house was also thatched at one time but only the main roof now remains thatched. At the beginning of the 1960s, the house was in a rather dilapidated condition and many windows were missing. The building has since been beautifully restored by its present owners and the main roof has just been re-thatched.

The new thatch consists of Norfolk reed but the deepness of the thatch is hidden, as the roof is trapped between the raised parapet walls at the gable ends of the house. The parapets rise to the level of the surface of the thatch. The ridge of the thatched roof is constructed from wheat straw because Norfolk reed is unsuitable for ridge making. The thick raised ridge has a series of points cut along its bottom edge and a rectangular-shaped apron lies below the centre ridge chimney.

A few miles away, another Toller village called Toller Fratrum also offers an old grey-stone manor house with reputed monastic connections but only one section of the building on the east side is thatched.

Thatched Range of Toller Fratrum Manor House

Toller Fratrum lies in delightful secluded countryside about three-quarters of a mile off the A356 road, a little outside of Maiden Newton. The twisting road, leading to the manor house, passes by one or two old thatched cottages in the tiny village, one of which is heavily buttressed at one end. The manor house, now known as Little Toller Farm, stands just to the west of the small medieval church.

The name Toller Fratrum means 'Toller of the Brothers' and they were Brethren of St John of Jerusalem, or the Knights Hospitallers. This religious military order arose out of the crusades to the Holy Land and included knights, clergy and brothers of the order. The long thatched range of the manor house was reputed to have once been the site of the refectory of the knights, who were established here from 1300 until the Dissolution of the Monasteries.

In 1540 Toller Fratrum was purchased by John Samways, who lived at Winterborne Martin (Martinstown) but worked in Dorchester as a merchant. He built the manor house and was responsible for the Tudor windows in the thatched section which was later to become the stable range of the main house. There is a carving of John Samways' initials and crest on a shield set in the stone of the thatched building. The crest consists of a hammer held in a claw. John Samways died in 1586 and then the house passed to various members of the Samways family. By marriage, the property was then inherited in 1645 by Francis Fulford of Great Fulford in Devon and it remained in this family for many generations. In 1867, Lord Wynford bought the property.

The long thatched one-storeyed stable block possesses a continuous string course (a horizontal moulding set in the surface of the wall) and this passes above the Tudor windows. These are decorated at their heads by small fanciful carvings of Renaissance character. In addition to the Samways's shield, there is a carving set in the wall which appears to be a young man playing the bagpipes. There is now an open-fronted cart-shed attached to the end of the thatched stable. Vertical stout timbers support the tiled roof of this extension. The thatch of the main roof consists of combed wheat reed and it is covered with wire-netting. An inspection of the rear of the building (viewed from the churchyard) reveals a series of round ventilation ports inserted just below the thatched eaves level.

The main manor house also deserves attention and commands much interest, although it is not thatched. It displays two spectacular tall twisted chimneys on a central-gabled chimney breast, which projects from the main roof. Rather curiously, a carved gable finial of a chained monkey holding a mirror rises between the two chimneys. This is intriguing because a similar effigy is associated with another famous manor house of Dorset. The chained monkey constitutes the crest of the Martyns of Athelhampton who lived in the manor house in the fifteenth and sixteenth centuries. Folklore relates that a ghost in the form of a monkey still haunts Athelhampton, as the animal was once accidentally bricked up and entombed in the manor.

Athelhampton House lies one mile east of Puddletown on the legendary site of King Athelstan's palace. King Athelstan was the grandson of Alfred the Great. The present house was built for Sir William Martyn who was Lord Mayor of London in 1493 and ever since it has remained a family home. Successive owners have enlarged and improved the house and its surrounding gardens, both of which are open to the public on several days of the week during the summer months.

The earlier parts of the magnificent house were built with Portesham stone-ashlar and the later parts included the contrasting colour of Ham Hill stone. The present house was first started in 1485 and it was well battlemented. The main roof consists of stone slates. A unique timbered roof shelters the great fifteenth-century hall and there is an oriel window, heraldic glass and linenfold panelling. Spiral and secret staircases are hidden in the house and other interesting features include the Tudor great chamber and the wine cellar. The heraldic monkey of the Martyns may also be discovered on the octagonal buttresses outside the house.

The impressive interior of this fine house reflects the elegance and splendour of the age in which Athelhampton was built but the surrounding grounds and formal gardens are equally impressive. They are laid out as separate enclosed stone-walled gardens and include a topiary, yew hedges, rare trees and plants. There are also water gardens with fountain pools, waterfalls and the River Piddle runs through the grounds which extend over about ten acres. A sixteenth-century circular dovecote dominates the scene to the south-west of the house and this is topped with a conical tiled roof and louvre.

A long thatched stable range stands by the wall of the main gate to the south-west of the house. The stables may be seen from the road immediately outside the entrance drive. The stables were built in the first half of the seventeenth century, with ashlar walls but also with some brickwork and cob. The building was constructed with one and a half storeys and provided with a ridge chimney. It possesses several diamond pattern leaded windows in the main long section as viewed from the drive. There are also 'eyebrow' windows at the thatch eaves level.

The thatched roof consists of combed wheat reed with a raised ridge. Ivy has now intruded and crept over one area of the thatch. The roof is hipped at one end but the other end links with a shorter stable section, thus forming an L-shaped block with a continuous thatched roof. The shorter section on the east side also has two seventeenth-century

Thatched Stable Range of Athelhampton House

windows and a wide doorway. These two right-angle sections surround the stable yard at the back. The smaller stable section is open-fronted on its inside to the yard and its thatched roof is supported by timber posts in the style of a cartshed. A further rectangular-shaped thatched building completes the third side of the stable yard.

The disadvantage of a thatched roof on a stable block would have been the fire risk but smoking, for example, would have been strictly banned in its vicinity, when horses were housed there. A similar smoking ban was similarly always applied to personnel working in rickyards. An advantage of a thatched roof over a stable in the winter was that its insulating qualities helped to retain the body heat emitted from the line of horses in the building. In summer, the coolness of the stable made it more comfortable for them. The design of stables has always remained a major interest to man, due to his high regard for the horse over many centuries.

In large country manor houses, the horses kept in the stables would have been carriage and riding horses. Each horse would have been housed in a separate stall with a substantial partition on each side of the animal. This was to prevent the horses kicking each other and the partitions were always high enough to stop them biting one another. It was also normal practice to have a large loose box available in the stable to treat a sick horse or assist a foaling mare. The stables were always placed so that they could be conveniently reached from the house.

However, the direction they faced was dictated by the need to give the horses maximum protection from the weather. Horses enjoyed looking out of their stalls onto the yard and the building of stables around a rectangular yard also offered some shield against direct cold winter winds.

Lofts containing hay were often built over stables and the 'eyebrow' windows of the Athelhampton thatched stable range probably suggest the level. The lofts were normally reached by a ladder and trap door from within the stable. It was sometimes possible to feed the horses from the loft by dropping the hay directly into each manger. Many years ago the loft also sometimes served as a form of temporary accommodation for staff connected with the horses, the horses below acting as a source of heat for the men above. A thatched roof above the loft would also have been beneficial in retaining the heat. Grooming equipment and tackle were usually stored in a separate 'tack' room but always adjacent to the stable.

A far less elaborate manor house than Athelhampton but built with a main thatched roof in a rural style, stands in the hamlet of Winterborne Muston, about two and a half miles from Bere Regis. The hamlet may be reached by turning left at the Red Post on the main A31 road when travelling towards Wimborne. The minor road passes by Anderson

Winterborne Muston Manor House

Manor on the way to Winterborne Kingston. The Winterborne Muston manor house is a little difficult to find but it can be viewed by looking northwards, about half-way along the Winterborne Kingston to Anderson Manor road. Incidentally, the Red Post is a scarlet signpost reputed to commemorate the bloody reign of Judge Jeffreys in 1685 in Dorset's courts.

The thatched manor house at Winterborne Muston was mainly built in the late seventeenth century but was extended at both ends during the eighteenth century to make a longer, more spacious home. It then looked much more like a miniature manor house than its previous cottage appearance. The house consists of two storeys with a total of eight multi-pane cottage-style windows at the front of it, four on the ground floor and the other four arranged symmetrically above these at the first floor level, immediately below the eaves of the thatched roof. The thatch has been shaped to flow fully around the upper windows; the roof is thatched with reed and displays a straight raised ridge. Two chimney stacks pass through the ridge and the roof is half hipped.

The most striking feature of the house is the unusual polygonal (five-sided) two-storeyed porch at the centre of the front of the building. This tall porch imitates the one at the nearby but much larger Anderson Manor. The thatched manor house at Winterborne Muston, although small was built with rich decorative taste and two of the upper rooms boast unusual vaulted ceilings. Most rooms are also panelled.

A member of the powerful Turberville family once lived in the house. The Turbervilles possessed many manor houses in Dorset but perhaps their better known ones were those at Bere Regis and Woolbridge. Although Tess of the d'Urbervilles existed only in the pages of Thomas Hardy's novel, the d'Urberville family was in fact based on the actual Turbervilles who had lived in Dorset for many centuries before the male line became extinct in the eighteenth century. The Turbervilles had originally come over to England with William the Conqueror.

Woolbridge Manor House stands on the banks of the River Frome, close to the village of Wool by Hardy's Egdon Heath. The house was once much larger than it is today. It was here in Hardy's novel that Tess and Angel Clare spent their unfortunate wedding night, when Tess made her tragic confession. The wall paintings of Julia and Francis Turberville on the upstairs landing, which so frightened Tess by their sinister faces, still survive in the manor. The manor house has now become a farmhouse and an hotel, with Woolbridge Manor Farm adjoining the grounds.

When the manor was the seat of the Turbervilles, Nicholas Turberville was stabbed by his brother-in-law in 1579 when travelling in the family coach, over the old bridge near the manor house. Legend relates that after this murder, a ghostly coach with spectral passengers, driver and footmen was often seen along the Dorset roads. This apparition continued for a couple of centuries after the tragedy but the only people who were able to view it were those with Turberville blood in their veins. The ghostly coach thus disappeared when the last of the Turbervilles died. As Tess in Hardy's novel was remotely connected with the family it was feasible for her to have imagined she saw the coach passing over the bridge.

Woolbridge Manor has its origin in medieval times and before the Dissolution of the Monasteries it belonged to Bindon Abbey. Thomas Turberville acquired the mansion towards the middle of the sixteenth century and it stayed in the family until the eighteenth century. It was restored in the middle of the seventeenth century. The house consists of a mixture of brick with stone and the front has a two-storeyed porch. The attractive imposing chimney stacks are made of brick and the roof is stone tiled.

There are some attractive thatched outbuildings in the grounds of Woolbridge Manor. Two separate thatched cottages, built close together at right angles to one another, are roofed with combed wheat reed. They display raised ridges with points cut along their underside edges. A thatched wooden building also stands near the cottages. The thatched buildings, although dwarfed by the large manor house, provide a soft rustic touch. They offer a pleasing contrast to the grey stone of the main house and the Elizabethan stone bridge which carries the road over the River Frome just outside the manor house. The bridge contains five arches and provides refuges, or retreats, cut into the side for the use and safety of pedestrians crossing the bridge.

Another Dorset manor house which offers an interesting thatched outbuilding is Waddon Manor. This is located about one mile east of Portesham, on the road linking Portesham with Upwey. With regard to the main manor house, only a late seventeenth-century wing and a little office court remain of the vanished Tudor mansion which was burnt down in 1704. The walls of the remaining wing are constructed of grey ashlar-stone and the roof is stone slated. Massive stone gate-piers guard the entrance to the house and these hint at the previous splendour of the original manor house. The mansion became a farmhouse in the first half of the eighteenth century but became the manor house again in 1928. The original owners of the manor were a family named the Gerards and one of these married a Colonel Reymes in the seventeenth century. He later became the MP for Melcombe Regis. The colonel was a frequent and keen London play-goer and was a friend of Samuel Pepys, the diarist.

Just outside of the main gates of the manor house a magnificent thatched barn, known as Waddon Barn, remains as a reminder of the previous links of the manor house with agriculture. The barn has now

Thatched Barn of Waddon Manor House

been converted into a shop selling high quality dress materials. Car parking facilities are available just opposite the thatched barn and the manor house. Splendid views over open countryside and a superb long view to the sea may be enjoyed from the road due to its high commanding position alongside the house.

The main large wide door of the thatched barn faces the manor house and there are three smaller doors in the side wall of the barn. A stone lintel over one of these doors displays the date 1702 and there are chamfered jambs to the doorway. The barn was built with grey ashlar-stone; there are two small upper windows and three lower ones with stone mullioned windows and hood-moulds. The large thatched reed roof over the barn has both ends hipped and the roof is furnished with a straight ridge. A small neat pinnacle decorates one end and there is a weather-vane in the shape of a fox.

4

Thatched Pubs

Dorset serves its locals and tempts its visitors with a variety of well-run pubs, generously sprinkled around all parts of the county. Many of the most attractive lie in the country, rather than in the towns and some offer the rustic flavour of a thatched roof. These especially lure holidaymakers from the city and also the local residents of the towns of Dorset, who enjoy many a warm summer's evening under their cool roofs. The motor car brings many customers to the country pub, not only to drink but also to eat. The serving of good value pub food forms a very pleasant social habit. It is difficult to visualize that many busy country pubs once catered only for the local village trade. Before the motor car, the few visitors either walked or came by horse.

The art of ale making in Dorset dates back to at least early Saxon times. A form of ale was no doubt brewed earlier than this but the Danish invaders can claim the name ale, as it is derived from the Danish word 'ol'. It was not until the fifteenth century that an improved beverage, called beer, was perfected by the introduction of hops. Sherborne brewed ale for sale in 1228 and Weymouth has also brewed since the thirteenth century. Church-wardens at Wimborne made church ales from 1403 onwards. These ales were brewed for everyday drinking and their sale raised much revenue for the church.

Through many centuries, beer has been used as a medium for raising money for charitable causes, as well as taxes for governments. For example, a civic brew-house existed at Dorchester in 1628 'for the maintenance of the hospital' and at a later stage it made contributions towards the poor of the parish. Dorchester has since become one of the leading brewing centres of the county.

Milton Ales were at one time brewed at Milton Abbas, using local hops grown at Milborne St Andrew and the beer was considered excellent enough for supply to London. Unfortunately, the brewery was pulled down when the old town of Milton Abbas was demolished in 1786 on the order of Joseph Damer, the first Earl of Dorchester. A smaller Milton brewery arose in 1848 in the new village and this survived into the middle of this century. Cerne Abbas brewed quality ales which were supplied to the London market in the eighteenth century. Large quantities of malt for the brewing industry were also made at Cerne Abbas and the malt-house continued to thrive there until approximately the end of the nineteenth century. Up to about the same time, many small brewers and publicans in the villages and towns of Dorset also made their own home-brew ales, which were, no doubt, much appreciated by the locals. Nowadays, Dorset boasts one thatched brewery and several other breweries which supply a range of excellent local beers to their respective pubs. These breweries, independent of the major national companies, are now all located in the larger towns of Dorset.

In the twelfth and thirteenth centuries, the monasteries provided simple hospices for travelling pilgrims and the monks managed their own brew-houses. The hospices were generally built at strategic distances apart, mainly in isolated areas. The monks usually offered free lodgings for two days to genuine pilgrims, but other travellers normally had to pay for their accommodation. One of these original hospices still survives in Dorset today, in the form of the thirteenth-century Shave Cross Inn. It stands at a remote crossroads, about two and a half miles north of Bridport off the B3162 road, in the Marshwood Vale. The unusual name of the inn derives from the travelling monks who stopped there and had their heads shaved, as an outward sign of humility, before their visit to the shrine of St Wita at Whitchurch Canonicorum.

A delightful thatched roof, with a raised ridge, now protects the inn; the original walls of which were constructed of a mixture of cob, rubble and flint. The inn has been much altered over the centuries, including the incorporation of an old barn formerly attached to the house. This explains the existence of the hipped end of the thatched roof which formerly covered the barn. The kitchen floor of the inn hides the original well, the water from which the monks used to brew their ale. In view of the age of the house, it comes as no surprise that the inn claims the oldest skittle alley in Dorset and this was formerly furnished with a clay surface. The skittle alley is thatched but has now been converted into a children's room. The inn has two storeys and it offers one main bar. This is beamed with a slate slab floor and a huge ancient open fireplace. There is ample overflow space in the garden which enjoys excellent views over the surrounding countryside and there is also a thatched wishing well. It is reputed that the ghost of Atte the Shaver, who shaved the monks' hair, may sometimes be seen in the garden.

Dorset also possesses another thirteenth-century thatched inn but with an entirely different history. The house, now called the Smugglers Inn, overlooks the sea from a valley in the Dorset hills at Osmington Mills. The old part of the inn was originally called The Crown and at a later date the house became known as The Picnic Inn. Its present name is probably the most apt as it was formerly a smugglers' haunt. It has

Smugglers Inn – Osmington Mills

also served fishermen and farmers during the seven hundred years of its history. Today it attracts many tourists. Beautiful views across the sea towards Portland and Weymouth may be gained from its large car park.

A narrow path leads to rocky coves along the seashore below the inn. There are also coastal path walks which form part of the five-hundred mile south-west Peninsula Coast Path. A stream runs through the gardens of the inn and a series of tiny foot-bridges span it. The grounds also offer garden seats with thatched beehive-shaped shelters over them. The thatched roofs of the shelters are adorned with raised pointed ridges.

The white-coloured inn has been much altered over the centuries but the original thatched building still remains. This was formerly a fisherman's cottage built of cob and stone. Brick and stone constructed extensions to the inn have since been added, the centre block with a slate roof and the end part with a red-tiled roof. Two thatched porches guard the doors to the inn. The extensions allowed the inclusion of a restaurant and residential accommodation, in addition to the bars. The thatched roof section of the inn displays a raised decorated ridge, with a brick chimney protruding through it. The ridge is furnished with a series of points and a thatched apron ornaments the area immediately below the chimney.

The most interesting part of the interior of the inn is the main bar, in the oldest section of the building. This contains the original huge inglenook fireplace with a bread oven; the exposed walls of the bar are rough-hewn stone. It must still appear similar to the time when it formed the smuggling headquarters of the notorious Pierre Latour, known as French Peter. Much of the success of his smuggling activities was due to his very fast boat, the *L'Hirondelle*, which always managed to outpace the cutters of the revenue officers. French Peter later married the daughter of the landlord of the inn and retired as a rich man with her to his native France.

Dorset's spectacular coastline, containing many coves and quiet little bays etched into the cliffs, offered many opportunities for smugglers to land their booty undetected. They were often in league with the local farmers and in certain instances the squire and parson. French brandy was the most favoured contraband and when landed, it was hidden in a variety of safe places. Many of the old cottages kept secret cupboards for the purpose, various caves such as Tilly Whim, near Swanage, were also used and caches on church property were not uncommon. However, the formation of the coastguards and the invention of the telegraph in 1837 brought considerable success for the authorities and hastened the end of large scale smuggling.

Another thatched pub with a history of use by smugglers is located just a few miles away from Osmington Mills. This house, called The Sailor's Return, lies inland from the coast at the rural hamlet of East Chaldon (Chaldon Herring), about one and a half miles south, off the A352 Dorchester to Wareham Road. The picturesque thatched house has been a pub for about a hundred years but the building is older. It was built early in the eighteenth century as two cottages, each two storeys high, with walls of cob under their thatched roofs. A porch protected the entrance to the cottages.

The thatch which covers the present pub has one gabled end and one hipped end to the roof. A chimney stack arises from the gable end wall and a further chimney protrudes through the ridge of the thatch. Another separate thatched house stands behind the pub and it is alleged that a tunnel was built to connect the two, when the smugglers were active in the eighteenth and nineteenth centuries. Stone flags cover the ground floors of the pub. The rooms have low ceilings and many old beams.

As well as smuggling connections, the pub also boasts a literary heritage. In view of its rural nature, it was perhaps unusual that it became a fashionable venue for both writers and artists. At one time, several travelled from neighbouring counties and London to visit it. Later Edward Garnett in 1926 selected the name of the pub as the title for his novel.

The inn sign shows a woman greeting a sailor but another mysterious figure hides in the background. Two theories relate to the meaning of the pub sign and the name, The Sailor's Return. The first suggests that it depicts an unfaithful wife greeting her husband on his return from the sea but at the same time she has surreptitiously hidden her lodger in a cupboard. The second theory offers the more moral explanation that the wife had thought her husband lost at sea but much later he unexpectedly returned to discover, tragically, that she had remarried.

The digging of secret tunnels between houses by smugglers appears to have been fairly common. This is despite the fact that the building of a tunnel of any length demands considerable skill. It is also hazardous and a difficult operation to keep secret when the work is being carried out. However, a tunnel existed at the site of another pub, The Thatched House, which stands at East Howe Lane, Kinson, Bournemouth. It is believed that the gentleman smuggler, Isaac Gulliver, constructed the tunnel to link his manor house to it. At the time he was thought to be a respectable merchant trading in wines, spirits and tea. He died in 1822 at the age of 77, having made a fortune from his smuggling operations, before retiring to Wimborne. King George III protected Gulliver from the authorities, in gratitude for saving the King's life by exposing a French assassination plot. Nevertheless, Gulliver had proved on many occasions that he could well look after himself. Once he evaded a search by Customs officials by pretending he was a corpse, by whitening his face and laying out in a coffin.

The Thatched House was opened as a pub in 1953, when it was roofed with quality Radipole reed. It was previously a private house which in Gulliver's day had been constructed of cob and stone. The ghost of an old gardener haunts the pub, and there are two bars for him to visit.

Gulliver expanded his smuggling activities over a wide area and distributed his booty further afield from a thatched pub called The Stocks Inn, situated at Furzehill, near Wimborne. Large cellars existed under the inn and these concealed the smuggled goods but the entrance to them has now been sealed. A false floor in the bar has also been filled in and there was once an escape tunnel from the cellars for use when the Customs men approached. The inn stands at the foot of Smugglers' Lane, an apt reminder of its former days as a centre of the contraband trade. The lane leads to the village green where vagabonds were formerly punished in the stocks. Upon release, many begged for a drink at the inn. A gibbet also stood on the crossroads to deal with the more persistent rogues, such as smugglers and highwaymen.

Stocks are now displayed outside the inn but the original ones are kept on a wall inside the house. The inn sign portrays a man in the stocks, philosophically drinking his beer. The original parts of the low long thatched building were probably constructed in the late sixteenth century but before becoming a pub and coach-house, the premises were used as the local post office. Two small extensions have been added to the property in more recent years.

The picturesque inn's brick walls are now painted white, which highlights the browns of its long thatched roof. The building, although of two storeys, is low and the thatch sweeps around the series of dormer windows at the eaves level. A raised ridge, with scallops, tops the wired-in wheat reed roof. The inn offers the choice of two bars, a restaurant and a garden. Low beamed ceilings shield the main bar and a ghost of a man called Holloway, who committed suicide, sometimes roams through the premises.

Cranborne Chase in the east of Dorset was once a huge royal hunting forest and many battles of wits took place between the poachers and the keepers. The Chase also formed a distribution centre for the smuggling trade and the men who carried their ill-gotten gains to it from the coast, often rested at a site near Ferndown. This was located at Tricketts Cross, about five miles from Wimborne. The original building on the site was burnt down in 1938 but a new thatched pub was opened in 1957, called The Smugglers' Haunt. This incorporated many ships' timbers which had been brought to Dorset from Yorkshire. The inn sign shows three smugglers walking by in a line, the first carrying silk, the second a keg of brandy and the third a tea-chest.

The new building consists of two main sections, partly built in brick with a little timber framing and there are attractive leaded light windows, with wooden lintels. The main thatched building has two storeys, with towering square chimneys but a second single-storeyed bar adjoins with a good height of thatch. Both roofs are immaculately fashioned with reed and possess raised ridges. A separate thatched porch covers the entrance to the main building. A large open fireplace warms the main bar and attractive brass and copper ware, including many horse brasses adorn the interior. Unfortunately, a thatch fire occurred during 1983 but the pub has remained open.

A fishermen's pub, with further smuggling history, stands on the edge of the village of Burton Bradstock on the west coast of Dorset. This thatched pub, named The Dove, was used as a smuggling distribution house up to the nineteenth century. Holidaymakers now drink there around a table made from the hatch cover of the schooner *Flirt*, wrecked under Burton Cliffs in 1897. The building was originally constructed as a cottage in the seventeenth century, from stone and cob under a thatched roof. The thatch moulds neatly around the upper-storey windows of the building which has a gable end with an old projecting chimney stack.

There are two bars and thatched brick-built porches shield the entrances. An unusual pub game has been revived at The Dove. Once a year, on the last Sunday of October, a conker competition takes place. Strangely, the inn sign, supported on a post outside, shows a picture of a fantail pigeon, rather than a dove. However, the original inn sign (now removed) did depict a dovecot and doves, the dove representing the religious emblem of peace.

Burton Bradstock also has another thatched pub, The Three Horseshoes, situated in the centre of the village with a car park opposite. The inn is built of mellowed stone and displays a very attractive thatched roof, with a gable end, facing the main village street. The ancient inn has now been much modernized. The thick ridge of the thatch has a smart set of points cut along its bottom edge. Thatched canopies shelter the doorways to the inn. In addition to the bars, there is a spacious garden, ideal for visitors with children. The corner of the inn by the main street was once a grocer's shop and the bow window, still present to the left of the entrance, was the original shop window. The inn sign shows three horseshoes and this signifies the Blacksmiths' coat of arms. Any inn seen with this type of name would most likely have housed a forge sometime in its past.

Dorset was once rich with blacksmiths and forges were found in nearly every village. The agricultural nature of the county demanded it. Many horseshoes had to be made in the hot forge, with the hammer and anvil, to shod a wide variety of horses. These included massive horses, often a ton in weight, such as the beautiful Shires, the Clydesdales and the Suffolk punches which were much used in Dorset on the farms. In addition there were the gentry's carriage horses, riding horses and ponies. Bullocks also laboured on the farms and as their hooves were cleft, they had to be shod with half shoes – a most tricky and delicate operation.

The craft of the blacksmith was not confined purely to shoeing animals, he made and repaired many tools including those of the thatcher and he also produced a large selection of much larger farm implements. He also toiled hard alongside the village wheelwright, fashioning the large metal tyre rings for fitting to heavy wagon wheels and carriage wheels. The intense heat of the forge, created by the apprentice pumping the huge bellows to maintain the fire temperature at a very high level, as well as the physical work, produced much sweat. Many a smithy kept a supply of beer to quench the thirst and also refresh a weary traveller on horseback. Horse traffic increased markedly in the seventeenth century but officially the blacksmiths required a licence to supply refreshment.

The thatched pub, The Smiths Arms, at Godmanstone on the Dorchester to Sherborne Road provides the best known illustration of this fact. King Charles II personally licensed it in 1665 when he stopped there, to have his horse shod whilst out hunting. He asked for a drink and the blacksmith replied 'I have no licence', so there and then the King granted him one.

Due to the Royal Charter, the former blacksmith's shop became one

Smiths Arms – Godmanstone

of the few fully licensed inns in England which could serve beer, wines and spirits from just one tiny bar; in general, houses only selling beer were allowed one bar. The Smiths Arms can safely claim to be the smallest public house in England with a thatched roof. It is thought the building may date back to the late fifteenth century. The one-storeyed inn measures just about twelve feet in width and about forty-five feet in depth. The eaves of the thatch are only four feet from the ground and the ceiling height in the bar is about six feet nine inches. The walls are constructed of cob, faced with local flint stones. The roof has recently been re-thatched and it is now furnished with a beautiful raised ridge with large scallops and points. The large garden attracts visitors from the bar during the summer months. The river which runs along the side of the garden, was used many years ago by the landlord to keep his bottled beer cool. This he did by immersing the bottles in a net in the flowing water for a few hours.

Whilst on the subject of small pubs, Dorset also possesses a thatched pub called The Thimble at Piddlehinton. It consists of just one L-shaped beamed bar but it is considerably larger than the one at The Smiths Arms. The Thimble was built in the seventeenth century, although it was known as The New Inn until a few years ago, when it was renamed. This was initiated by the landlord's family who thought the pub's size and appearance resembled that of a thimble. The many multi-pane windows, when viewed from the outside, also give a vague impression of the surface undulations of a thimble (Fig. 15). The front

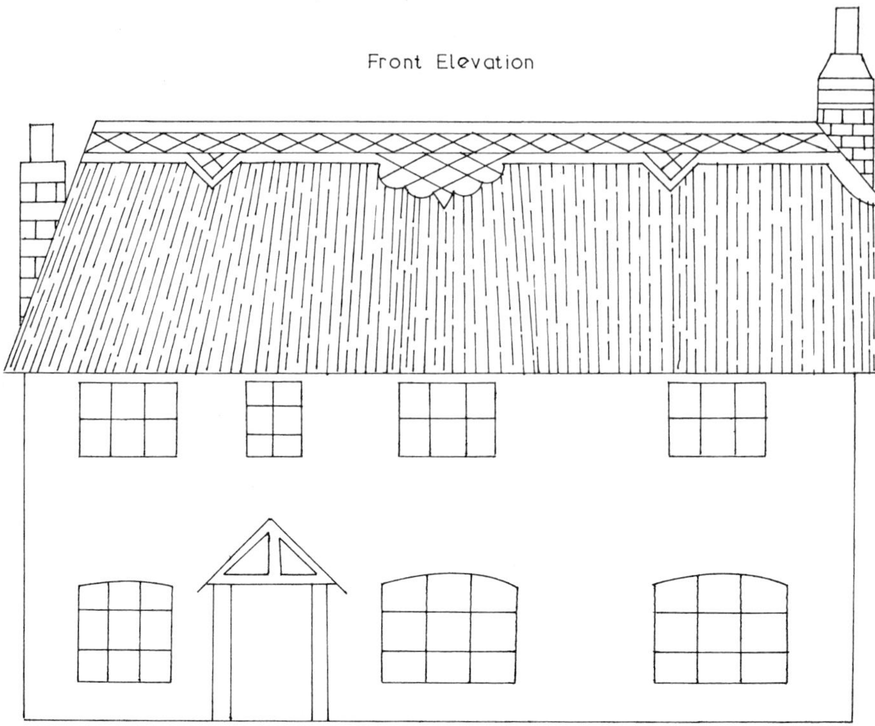

15　*The Thimble, Piddlehinton*

roof of the house is combed wheat reed thatched, with a raised ornamented ridge but the back is now fitted with a corrugated roof. The pub is rather dwarfed by its large car park at the rear, reached by crossing a pedestrian bridge over the stream known as the Piddle.

Another ancient thatched inn which once possessed a forge in its yard may be found at Cerne Abbas. The two-storeyed building, now known as The Royal Oak, was probably built in about 1540, using some of the Ham Hill stone salvaged from the nearby abbey which was destroyed at the time of the Reformation. Axed and moulded beams are still visible in the centre section of the bar. These together with the quality of the exterior roof corbels, in the form of shaped brackets supporting the eaves, suggest that items other than stone were taken from the ruined abbey. A fine stone-arched doorway stands on the north side of the inn in the alley yard below the shaped eaves brackets – this door once gave access to the upstairs of the house. The thatched inn has a dormer window positioned in the main expanse of thatch on its south side. Modernization of the interior has created one very long bar and in keeping with the age of the building, the through passages are still covered with stone slabs. An old stone fireplace which has now been renovated occupies the central position of the long bar room. The walls of the bar are tastefully decorated with a wide selection of horse-brasses and other country items.

In the seventeenth century, the inn expanded from the earlier inclusion of a blacksmith's forge into a coaching and posting house. The yard, stables and coaching gateway were all added at this time. Parts of the original stone gateway have been retained in the modernized entrance leading into the back garden. A legal document preserved in the inn and dated 1771, shows the premises changed hands for a mere five shillings and an annual rent of one peppercorn. The impressive document hangs in a frame over the mantelpiece in the bar. How the owner at that time, Robert Summers, was persuaded to sell it to Richard Cain for such a small sum remains a mystery. As in many other counties, Royal Oak is probably the most popular name used in Dorset. It, of course, commemorates Charles II's escape, following the Battle of Worcester in 1651, which he accomplished by hiding from his pursuers in an oak tree at Boscobel, in Shropshire. The inn sign depicts this scene and it is located by the clematis-clad gable wall entrance.

The other common inn name, Kings Arms, also arose from loyalty to the Crown and it became popular after the Reformation, to show that the King now owned the former church hospices and lands. The number of pubs called by this name nearly equals the number of Royal Oaks in Dorset. A Kings Arms with a thatched roof, which also once contained a blacksmith's forge, stands at Stoborough, just outside Wareham on the road to Swanage. In 1826, the premises were used both as a pub and as a blacksmith's forge but at that time it was appropriately called The Horseshoe. Earlier in 1770 the pub was known as The Hoop, a sign which signifies its association with the vintner's trade. At the beginning of this century, the inn served as a butcher's shop and the hooks where the meat was hung may still be seen on the ceiling. There is rather restricted head room inside the pub and there are beams and stone floors.

The two-storeyed inn has therefore seen many different trades since it was constructed with stone and brick on a three-foot high rubble plinth with a thatched roof in the eighteenth century. On the site of the present inn, it is reputed that some of Cromwell's troops rested here for a long spell, when Corfe Castle was under siege during the Civil War. Sir John Bankes, Charles I's Chief Justice, owned the castle at that time and it proved quite impregnable to the Roundhead forces. It eventually fell in 1646, long after most other Royalist strongholds had fallen, when a traitor inside the castle let in the enemy.

Another more trendy thatched pub, the Brace of Pheasants, hides in the remote village of Plush, in the Piddle Valley. The original pub was converted from the village forge and a pair of cottages, built in the sixteenth century of flint and brick. Unfortunately, the pub was badly gutted by fire in March 1979 but it has since been rebuilt in its original form, with a long thatched roof flowing attractively around the many

Brace of Pheasants – Plush

upper-storey windows. The white-painted pub displays a wrought-iron cock-pheasant on the exterior wall by the main entrance. Two straw birds perch on the ridge of the thatched roof and the unique inn sign consists of a brace of stuffed pheasants in a glass case over the door. Earlier this century, the pub was called The Hankey Arms, the name of the local land- and racehorse-owner. The long bar has a low ceiling and is beamed. A staircase leads to the restaurant on the first floor and there is also a small alcove for eating downstairs. A delightful large garden lies to the rear of the premises. An orchid-nursery is situated behind the pub and this breeds rare orchids, many hybrids of which are exported to a number of different countries.

In 1646, some of Cromwell's troops were stationed at Broomhill tithe barn, near the thatched Barley Mow pub at Colehill, just outside of Wimborne off the A31. A lane near the pub still bears the name, God's Blessing Lane, ever since it was called this after Cromwell's troops were given 'God's Blessing' in the lane upon their departure. The pub lies in isolated countryside but a few beautiful thatched houses are situated on the road leading to Broomhill. Nearby, there is a God's Blessing Farm which is a thatched cottage built in the seventeenth century and also a God's Blessing Green, with yet another thatched farmhouse.

The Barley Mow has thatch on the centre portion of the building only. A raised ridge with points ornaments the thatch which is wired-in with a straw bird perched on the top. The pub possesses a square-shaped thatched porch and there is a tiny thatched hut in the rear garden. The front of the inn is now faced with painted brick. There are

The Fox Inn – Corscombe

shuttered windows and the upper storey is timber-clad. The thatch is cut around the upper window. The pub has two bars and retains an ancient open fireplace. This may date back to the beginning of the sixteenth century, when the building was probably constructed as an inn for drovers.

From the mid fifteenth century onwards, sheep contributed a great deal towards Dorset's trade and wealth. Some of this wealth eventually found its way into beautifying many of the parish churches, the money having been donated by the rich landowning families who ran the sheep. However, the drovers who tended the sheep could only move the flocks slowly since they travelled by foot. Therefore special pounds were built close to suitable inns along the route to rest the animals before reaching the market. Also, in the seventeenth century, the development of new roads led to a further increase in the wool trade, when pack horses were employed to carry fleeces.

Another old drovers' inn called The Fox exists at Corscombe, just under a mile off the A356 Dorchester to Crewkerne road. The present beautiful and immaculate thatched pub gives no clue as to its former usage. Built of cob and stone in about 1600, the two-storeyed building probably provided a dormitory for the drovers in an upstairs room. By coincidence, a Puritan Act of 1612 decreed that 'none were to tipple more than one hour in one house' which confirms the life of a drover was never an easy one. However, drovers were certainly wayfaring persons, or *bona fide* travellers and may have been able to obtain drinks at times forbidden to the local residents. The inn has undergone an extension since it was originally built. A delightful stretch of thatch covers the present long building and two thatched canopies shelter the entrances.

A stream meanders alongside the grass verge opposite the inn. The Fox, like The Barley Mow, is a traditional country pub name. However, in the case of The Fox there may also be an heraldic significance, linked to the emblem of the Earls of Ilchester who were local land-owners. The inn also once featured in the film, 'Rogue Male', which starred Peter O'Toole. There are two beamed bars, both neatly decorated with a range of brass and copper utensils. Hunting prints hang on the walls, together with old agricultural implements and there are large attractive open fireplaces.

Many country inns in Dorset, including many thatched ones, were first built as farmhouses or small cottages. In medieval times, each community supported an ale-house which was mainly used by the locals for drinking purposes only. An evergreen branch or bush suspended from a pole above the doorway indicated the cottage which served the ale. Through the following centuries, the ale wife (as she was known) brewed and served the beer in the cottages. Even today, the name Brewsters Sessions (feminine) is still retained when the magistrates meet to issue licences to trade in alcoholic liquors. In the early part of the present century, nearly every country publican in Dorset was still a piece worker on neighbouring farms. His wife served the occasional visitor at lunchtime and so pub keeping at that time still remained a

The Worlds End – Almer, near Morden

sideline for a skilled farmworker. The wife contributed the major share in running the public house.

The need to have some form of licence was recognized and the first real attempt to control the opening hours started in 1550, when premises were required to shut at nine during the summer months and eight in the winter. An isolated farmhouse held the first official beer licence issued in Dorset and it was dated 1589. The house was situated at Almer, a remote area where four parishes now meet. In keeping with its locality, the pub is called The Worlds End, although at the time of the granting of the licence it was known as The Red Lion. The present pub consists of an integration of the farmhouse and is built of cob and stone, while the stables form a long low two-storeyed building with a thatched roof. Thatch also covers the wing at the end of the inn. The present thatched roof has a raised ridge ornamented with scallops and points. The Worlds End has a very attractive appearance and lies beside the A31 Dorchester to Wimborne road, although it is set a little back from the road.

Field Marshal Montgomery stopped at the inn in 1942 and it is reputed he planned the Normandy invasion there. The inn has two bars and an array of old agricultural tools decorate the walls. In harmony with the age of the building, there are low beamed ceilings, stone flag floors and an inglenook fireplace incorporating a bread oven. One of the bars once formed the stables. In the seventeenth century, the inn became a minor post house where horses could be changed; stables were an essential feature of such buildings at that time.

Another ancient thatched inn, which originated from a country farm cottage built in the late sixteenth century, stands at Marshwood, near Bridport, in West Dorset. The house is called The Bottle and the name was probably selected about two hundred years ago to indicate that bottled beer could be purchased, a fairly unusual occurrence at that time. The four-hundred-year-old inn was nearly destroyed by a thatch fire during the winter of 1982–3. Fortunately, the interior of the inn was not damaged but about half the thatched roof was affected, although the roof timbers escaped nearly intact. This meant the thatch could be renewed fairly quickly and the premises re-opened for business.

As well as being a pub, The Bottle has always been a smallholding and a source of provisions, selling to the local community. This dual function of pub and village store was a common occurrence in most isolated communities before the advent of the motor car. The inn walls are of cob, mixed with stone and the building has two storeys under its thatched roof. Two small bars serve the customers and there are again stone floors, low-beamed ceilings and an open inglenook fireplace.

Stocks Farm was built at Stoke Abbott, near Beaminster, in west Dorset during the seventeenth century with walls of stone and rubble, topped with a thatched roof. It was so named because the village stocks were kept nearby on the green. Additions in brick were made to the building and a small extension, abutting at right angles, changed the farm building into an L-shape. A tiled roof shelters this added winged section but the main roof is thatched with a neat gabled end. The building is now called The New Inn, having been converted from the farmhouse in the middle of the nineteenth century. The inn still retains its bread oven, incorporated with the original open fireplace. There are two bars, a restaurant and a garden at the rear.

Some thatched stone-walled farm cottages were built in the late sixteenth century at West Stafford, situated two miles from Dorchester, off the A352 road to Wareham. They became the village shop and off-licence but were converted into a pub in 1937. The inn was then named the Wise Man. A learned judge with a wig adorns the sign board of the inn and a poem appears on the wall outside, describing the virtues of ale:

> I trust no Wise Man will condemn
> A cup of genuine now and then,
> When you are faint, your spirits low,
> Your string relaxed, twill bend your bow,
> Brace your drumhead and make you tight,
> Wind up your watch and set you right,
> But then again, the too much use,
> Of all strong liquors, is abuse,
> Tis liquid makes the solid loose,
> The texture and whole frame destroys,
> But health lies in the equipoise.

Some attribute the poem to Thomas Hardy who lived nearby but others dispute this, suggesting it was the work of a lesser known poet.

The picturesque inn's thatched roof has a raised ridge with points and a thatched canopy shields the front entrance. Straw pheasants perch on the ridge near the chimney of the inn. Agricultural implements, such as milkmaids' yokes and shepherds' crooks adorn the exterior gable wall facing the car park and garden. The public bar of the two-storeyed inn is renowned for its magnificent collection of mugs, toby jugs and antique pipes. The lounge bar also has mugs hanging from the ceiling. The two bars are low-beamed and are fitted with attractive multi-pane windows. The Frome Valley Morris Dancers sometimes practise outside the inn as Easter approaches – during the winter months they rehearse at the West Stafford village hall.

The Union, a small thatched stone and brick pub at Childe Okeford, typifies the original concept of a cottage serving beer, with a bunch of grapes displayed on the inn sign. During the two centuries of its

Wise Man Inn – West Stafford

existence, and before the pub was recently modernized, there was no bar as such in the small room where the beer was consumed. An old kitchen range served as the sole heat source for the room and a Welsh dresser stood in the hallway. The name, Union, commemorated the Union of Great Britain and Ireland in 1801 to form the United Kingdom of Great Britain and Ireland. This was slightly unusual as the Union sign was more widely adopted in England to celebrate the union of England and Scotland in 1707.

Another pub converted from a three-roomed cottage, constructed in the seventeenth century, is The Bull at Newton. It stands on the south side of Sturminster Newton bridge. The present single-storeyed pub has an impressive and beautiful thatched roof, furnished with a raised ridge cut with scallops and an apron thatch below the chimney. The interior of the pub displays beamed ceilings. It appears that many extensions have been made to the premises over the years and a former stable block has been incorporated on the end.

The Bakers Arms at the village of Lytchett Minster was built in the eighteenth century as a two-storeyed gabled roof thatched cottage. It later supplied the bread needs of the village in its large ovens and then became a pub. The Bakers Arms now has been expanded with brick to house an extremely large rambling bar area and skittle alley. The bread ovens have been retained, together with several open fireplaces. The building is thatched with combed wheat reed and the raised pointed ridge is decorated with liggers, enclosing a herring-bone slat pattern.

The Bakers Arms prides itself on its many unique and remarkable collections of different items. These include near complete sets of English stamps, coins arranged in eras, banknotes, butterflies, fishing flies, birds' eggs, stuffed birds, a glass beehive, medals, army badges, cigarette cards, watch faces and statistics relating to the twentieth century. There are also bayonets, weapons, horsebits and a Chinese water clock. Wherever practical, the exhibits are displayed on the walls in glass-fronted frames.

The Bridport Arms Hotel is a sixteenth-century thatched pub and hotel situated virtually on the popular east beach at West Bay. The regulars call it the 'BA' and they voted it the Dorset pub of the year for 1983 in a survey carried out by a local daily newspaper. The pub was formed by the amalgamation of four thatched cottages; three originally built in a straight row with a fourth on the end at right angles, forming an L-shape. Each individual cottage was constructed with a different level thatched roof and the present pub still retains these. The terrace of three cottages each has its own gabled thatched roof whilst the end cottage displays a hipped thatched roof. It is likely that the cottages were first built as fishermen's homes but in the eighteenth century they were used by the harbour controller. West Bay is Bridport's harbour.

As mentioned earlier, the seventeenth century saw an increase in horse traffic on the roads and the passing of the first Turnpike Act in 1663, gave an impetus for the roads to be improved during the following century. Many inns were extended and new ones built to cope with the increasing numbers of coaches and passengers. This was accentuated still further in the early eighteenth century with the establishment of a postal service across Great Britain. Coach and posting inns became characterized by their high carriage arches.

The coach houses were designed to stable many horses and also house the large staffs needed to care for them and also the passengers on the coaches. The post houses were much smaller and provided the relief, or change horses, for the coaches between the larger coaching inns. The change of horses normally took only a few minutes and so gave limited time for passengers to have a drink in the inn. By the middle of the eighteenth century, nearly all the main coach routes to the West Country passed through Dorset. Many inns in country districts also ran post-chaise houses to ferry passengers to the main coaching stations and the market towns.

The seventeenth-century thatched George Inn at Chideock, in the west of Dorset, was formerly a posting house and it also provided the services of a blacksmith and wheelwright. The inn was built in 1685 but at that time it was called The Crown and Sceptre. The orchard at the rear of the premises was known as Post Boys Orchard and this suggests that the inn was probably built specifically as a posting house. There is now a neat garden at the rear of the inn and over the years this has yielded several Georgian coins to various lucky finders. The house is reputed to be haunted by the ghost of a previous landlady, known as Miss Julie, who died in the passage of the inn. The passage with its slabbed-stone floor still survives. There is also a beamed bar and a restaurant.

The premises were originally built of stone with some cob and provided with a thatched roof to protect the walls. The thatched roof now has two slightly different levels and its raised ridge is ornamented with a series of points. One end of the roof is gabled but the other end of the inn is attached to a terrace of pretty thatched cottages, all with thatched porches. The thatch material is combed wheat reed. The inn sign commemorates George II, the last king of England to take the field in person with his troops. This occurred during the Battle of Dettingen in June 1743. A battle which resulted in a victory for the King against the French.

The thatched Kings Arms pub in the centre of Wareham was also once a posting house with a carriage arch. Before this it was used by carriers, when it was built of stone and rubble in the latter part of the seventeenth century. It has now had a modern brick front added. The thatched pub enjoys fame as it was one of the few thatched houses in Wareham which survived the very severe fire of 1762. The fire razed most of the principal buildings to the ground, including 133 houses. This disaster resulted in the use of thatch as a roofing material to be banned in Wareham. The inn now trades from two bars and there are beamed ceilings, together with flagstones on the floor.

The thatched White Hart at Sturminster Newton still retains its carriage arch leading to its car park in the rear. Above the arch is a first-floor chamber. In former times, the arch was constructed to allow the horses and coaches through, when the inn was a posting house and a small coaching stage. The thatched roof now consists of combed wheat reed and two dormer windows peep through the thatch. The inn was constructed mainly with brick in 1708, as suggested by the stone inscribed 'PWM 1708' set in the upper wall. It stands opposite a thatched solicitor's office in the centre of the town by the market. Many farmers have frequented the inn over the centuries. There is one long bar with beamed ceilings and an open inglenook fireplace, with an oak bressummer, stands at one end of the room. Another fireplace, situated behind the long bar, has now been adapted to take shelving. Pistols and stuffed fish in glass-cases decorate the exposed stone and brick walls of the bar.

Another thatched pub, also called the White Hart and which was once a post-chaise house is situated at the village of Yetminster, in north Dorset. The large stable area for the horses was in the yard where the water pump is still retained. Yetminster was the original home of the famous Yetties who still give an occasional folk-evening at the pub. The White Hart was built with stone walls in the seventeenth century in an L-shape, with a thatched roof. It still displays stone mullioned windows and a very large well-preserved inglenook fireplace in the bar. The pub at one time made its own beer and traces of the original brewery are still visible in the skittle alley. The pub also offers a wooden shove-ha'penny board to test customers' skill at this popular country pub game, which has been traditionally played in Dorset for many centuries. Wooden boards are predominantly used in the north of Dorset, whilst slate boards are mainly favoured in the south-east of the county.

The common name, White Hart, for a pub usually owes its origin to Richard II, King of England from 1377 to 1399. Pliny, the Roman author, related the ancient legend that Alexander the Great many years ago captured a stag and placed a gold collar around its neck. Richard II adopted the emblem and later, many inn signs also took up the theme. A variation of the story persists in Dorset, particularly in the Vale of Blackmore. This states that Henry III, King of England from 1216 to 1272, whilst hunting in Dorset pursued a white stag all day through the Forest of Blackmore without success. The King admired the stag so much that he decreed it must never again be hunted. This order was disobeyed and the white stag was killed later by a band of huntsmen. The King was so furious that he fined heavily the Blackmore estates belonging to the offending huntsmen, who were noblemen of the de la Lynde family. The taxes on the Blackmore Vale estates were paid annually until the seventeenth century and the money became known as White Hart Silver. Later the de la Lynde family adopted for their coat of arms, three white hart heads on a red shield.

The thatched Rose and Crown Inn at Long Burton on the Dorchester to Sherborne road has an interesting history, including its use at one time as a small coaching house. Some parts of the building were probably built in the sixteenth century but many additions have been made over the centuries. Before becoming a pub, the church mason lived in the original two-storeyed house which stands next door to the village church. The walls of the old section of the house consist of a cob and stone mixture under its thatched roof. The roof is gabled and once when it was being re-thatched, a cavalier's sword was found. The present roof is thatched with wheat reed and it is wired-in. A tiled half-hipped extension has been added to the building.

The interior of the house offers a sizeable open fireplace in a large beamed bar, which is decorated with horse-racing photographs and various items of horse tackle. The inn sign hangs from the exterior upper wall of the pub and exhibits a unique feature. It displays both the red rose and the white rose. The former appears on the sign side facing Dorchester and the latter on the side facing Sherborne. All other

Rose and Crown pubs display either the red or more occasionally the white rose, but rarely the two together. The Rose and Crown sign symbolized the end of the Wars of the Roses, which had divided the country for over twenty years. The opposing factions were eventually united when Elizabeth of York, daughter of Edward IV, married Henry VII.

The thatched Crown Hotel at Marnhull in the past offered stabling for horses passing through its carriage way at the side. The carriage wall contains a stone inscribed 'James Downe, April 4th, 1725'. The pub was stone-built as a cottage in the seventeenth century with a thatched roof but additional wings with tiled roofs have since been constructed. Called The Pure Drop Inn at Marlott by Thomas Hardy in his *Tess of the d'Urbervilles*, the inn has enjoyed an interesting history. Once courts were held on the premises and a priest's hole is concealed in the main bar. There are flagstone floors, exposed stone walls and beamed ceilings.

Many inns in Dorset, including several thatched ones, have origins closely connected with several of the county's large landowning families. The thatched Ilchester Arms at Symondsbury gained its name from the Earls of Ilchester, who lived at Abbotsbury and the family have possessed several large estates in Dorset for many centuries. The Ilchester Arms at Symondsbury at one time belonged to the estate. The similarly named pub at Abbotsbury has the same connections but it is not thatched.

The Ilchester Arms at Symondsbury was built of stone in the sixteenth century but the house has been much developed since that time. However, the thatch still conceals the original roof timbers, in the form of five bays with curved trusses. The present thatched roof has a ridge smartly decorated with scallops and points. There is a quarter-hipped end to the thatch. A separate thatched roof protects the stone Gothic-type porch. The inn has mullioned windows and inside there are two small bars with chamfered-beamed ceilings. There is a skittle alley and table skittles; the latter game commands a special appeal in West Dorset, although it is also seen in other parts of the county.

Lulworth Castle was purchased by Humphrey Weld in 1641 and it remained continuously in the possession of his descendants until a mysterious fire gutted the interior in 1929, making it uninhabitable. The Weld family estate has been responsible for the names of two thatched pubs, one situated in East Lulworth and the other in West Lulworth.

The thatched Weld Arms at East Lulworth was formerly a farmhouse on the estate. It also later housed the family coaches and stabled the carriage horses. The walls were built of cob and stone in the seventeenth century and the thatched roof was gabled. The pub is reputed to be haunted by the ghost of an old man who was buried many years ago under one of the porches.

The other thatched pub, called The Castle Inn, stands opposite the village green in West Lulworth. It is within walking distance of Lulworth Cove, the famous local beauty spot. The inn takes its name from the burnt down castle but since the inn was first built of stone in the eighteenth century, it has also borne the names of The Jolly Sailor, The Travellers Rest and The Green Man.

The village of Milton Abbas has the thatched Hambro Arms, named after a member of the well-known banking family who purchased the local estate from Lord Milton. The pub was first called the Milton Arms and then The Dorchester Arms, when Lord Milton became the Earl of Dorchester. It later changed its name again to the Portalington Arms. The inn has thus had four different names, all connected with local

The Old Thatch – Uddens Cross, near Wimborne

landowners. The two-storeyed inn was originally built in about 1780 but, in spite of it having endured many alterations over the years, it has always retained its thatched roof. The present building is very long because a separate stable block has been joined to the original building under the same continuous roof. The pub is situated in the main village street, with its neat rows of immaculate thatched cottages. The inn has two bars and a car park just outside.

The curiously named The Museum Hotel at Farnham, near Blandford Forum owes its name to the Pitt-Rivers family who built a museum just outside the village in 1880. The museum has been closed for several years but it once exhibited finds from the Romano-British village which General Pitt-Rivers had excavated in the Cranborne Chase region. The thatched hotel at Farnham displays on one side of its inn sign a picture of a statue, originally exhibited in the museum. The arms of the

Pitt-Rivers family adorn the other side. The pub was built in the late seventeenth century but it has been much changed and extended. It now has two bars and for many years, tools of the cooperage trade decorated their stone walls. In former times, the thatched pub was known as The Farnham Arms and earlier still as The Ash Tree.

The Old Thatch, a picturesque thatched pub and restaurant, may be found at Uddens Cross, near Wimborne. It was formerly the lodge house to the now demolished Uddens House (which dated back to 1747) but the lodge was converted in the 1950s to the present pub and restaurant. The building consists of one storey only and it is most attractively thatched with a raised ridge. There is an appreciable thatch overhang from the walls and one end of the thatch gives an umbrella-like appearance with its cusped eaves. The building has leaded-light windows.

The interior displays an L-shaped bar inlaid with copper on its top and the room has a beamed ceiling. It was discovered by the landlord that the carved wooden front door of the pub was originally made out of several doors. There were carvings of gargoyles, thieves and various types of games on it. The date 1612 appeared on the top and another strange feature was the keyhole which was positioned in the centre of the door.

5

Thatched Cottage Orné

The term cottage orné conjures up visions of an ideally designed and beautifully ornamented cottage, usually furnished with an elaborate and decorative thatched roof. Such buildings became particularly fashionable during the Regency decade of 1810 to 1820. The thatched roof was often built at several different levels for ornamental effect and the eaves overhang from the walls was always made extremely wide. There were normally thatched verandahs around the perimeter of the house and also thatched porches shielding the doors. Most of the low overhanging thatch was supported by a number of roughly cut timber pillars. The ridges of the steeply inclined thatched roofs were frequently topped with large rustic thatched peaks or tufts. Leaded-light windows were also often included in such buildings and tall chimney stacks were sometimes employed to emphasize the cottage style. All the buildings were always individually designed and so were relatively rare when compared with the large number of ordinary thatched cottages which existed.

John Nash, the architect mainly responsible for the establishment of the cottage orné in England, designed several of these buildings at the beginning of the nineteenth century. He also planned the well-known Blaise Castle Estate, near Bristol, with its eccentric rustic designs for a thatched dairy and thatched cottages, grouped around a contrived village green. This was commissioned by a Bristol banker for his estate. However, the trend towards rustic designs in England had really begun a little earlier than this, with the building of Queen Charlotte's thatched cottage, in the Royal Botanic Gardens at Kew. The cottage dates from 1772 and was built as a summer-house and a place for the royal family to take tea. The two-storeyed cottage was constructed of brick, with timber facing boards under its thatched roof. To enhance the concept of summer leisure, the interior decor was designed to give the impression of a large tent. Similar such edifices gained favour with the gentry and the tone was set to create the purposely primitive rural building.

Nevertheless, it was a later royal connection which helped to popularize the true cottage orné style of building in England, after the thatched Royal Lodge was constructed by Nash in Windsor Great Park during 1814. This picturesque villa was built in an extravagant cottage design to create an idealized image of a traditional country cottage. It possessed thatch and much fancy work, including a multitude of tall chimneys. There were stucco gables under the main thatched roof and large mullioned bay windows with leaded-lights. Separate little thatched bonnet roofs sheltered the tops of the bay windows. There was also a huge thatched and timbered rustic entrance porch. Around the house there were thatched verandahs. The thatch of the verandahs served a practical purpose, as well as a decorative one. It kept the rooms inside the house cool by keeping the sun's rays from the windows, providing shade and protecting furnishings.

Although the thatched Royal Lodge was later demolished (due to dry rot), it had been meticulously designed by Nash and his architects in collaboration with landscape gardeners. However, the architectural style lacked the inherent simplicity of the true countryman's cottage. This was perhaps inevitable with an elegant cottage orné built for royalty but it was also true for the smaller less elaborate versions. This was because they were designed on the drawing board by the architect but the real vernacular thatched cottage was built purely by the experience of the countryman. He used locally available materials, on a carefully selected and proven site, to build a home which would withstand the worst winter weather. His approach was essentially a practical rather than an artistic one.

The cult of the romantic and the picturesque in the form of the cottage orné gained popularity in localized regions of England. Many in the cottage orné style were first built in fashionable areas near to the centre of London, such as Richmond and Roehampton. The seaside towns of Brighton and Sidmouth then became popular locations. Such buildings were usually small but there were exceptions. For example, fairly large country houses in the ornamented rustic style gained acceptance in the Isle of Wight. The architects also designed their cottage orné buildings in Dorset but most were of the smaller variety. However, they made their picturesque thatched creations look elaborate and bizarre, so that they stood out from the host of vernacular thatched cottages which already abounded in the county. The roofs were usually thatched to match the local village style but long-straw thatch was frequently favoured by the designers of the early nineteenth century. Long straw gave a more moulded gentle line to the thatched roof surface and helped to create the planned romanticized image.

Many richer landlords throughout the early nineteenth century followed the fashion of building cottage orné styles for the lodges and keepers' cottages on their estates. The buildings were pseudo-Gothic in design but they were always made to look cheerful and attractive, despite their exaggerated decorative construction. Lodges were mainly single-storeyed but they usually contained spacious attics which were

Lodge (Cottage Orné) – Holt, near Hinton Martell

often later adapted to make habitable rooms. Dainty dormer windows allowed light into the attics. Many lodges have now had extensions built to increase further the available living space. The lodges were normally located inside the main gates, along the drives leading to the house. Sometimes, they were built to abut the walls alongside the main gates.

A good example of a thatched cottage orné lodge may be found at Holt, which is situated to the north of Wimborne on the B3078 road. It lies near the redundant church at Hinton St Parva. The ornamental lodge was built about 1810 at the gateway to the park of Gaunt's House, which itself is situated about one mile away at Hinton Martell. Gaunt's House was originally a Victorian mansion but it has now been converted into a school. The lodge walls form three sides of a polygon with a longer fourth side and at first sight the shape appears rather puzzling.

The walls are made of brick with some in-filling and they are now partly creeper clad. The building has just one storey but possesses an attic. In keeping with the cottage orné style, there are pointed, diamond-shaped, leaded-light windows with stone lintels. The fantastic thatched roof which covers the lodge is conical in shape with cusped eaves, giving an umbrella-like pointed appearance to the bottom edge of the thatch (Fig. 16). The thatch material is long straw, with ornamental

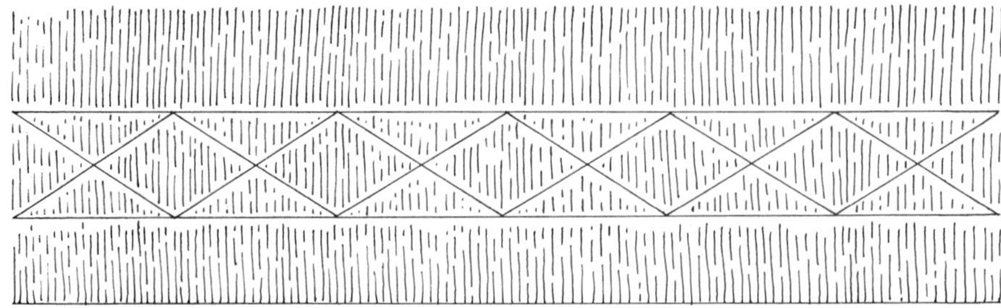

Straight Eaves

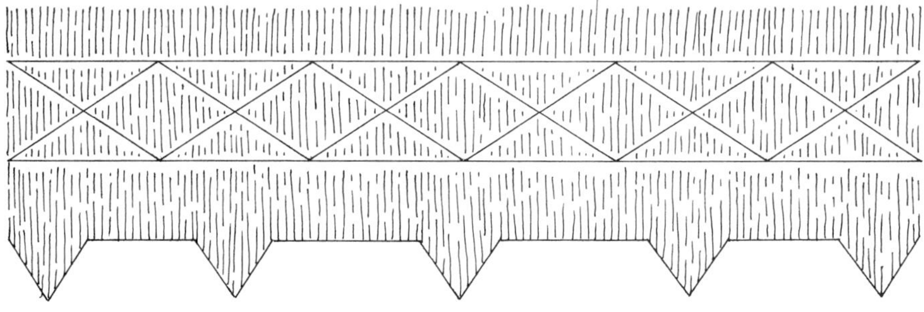

Cusped Eaves

16 *Eaves Types*

liggers and a raised ridge. In addition to the main roof there are quaint thatched doorway porches. These also have cusped eaves which are supported underneath by rough timber posts.

Another picturesque thatched lodge, in the cottage orné style, stands by the roadside about a quarter of a mile to the south of the village of Goathill, near Sherborne. In fact, the stream which rises at Goathill supplies water to the lake in the grounds of Sherborne Castle. The stream from the nearby village of Purse Caundle also feeds into Sherborne Lake. The lodge was probably built a little later than the one serving Gaunt's House but it is just as impressively thatched, with a particularly massive height to the thatch. The Goathill lodge roof is now mainly thatched with wheat reed although one portion still remains as long straw. The roof is wired-in and it has a flat ridge. The thatch has a wide overhang from the beautiful mellow yellow-tinged stone walls. There are many undulations to the front thatch of the lodge but the rear and sides are cut more squarely. Three tall chimneys arise through the centre of the towering thatch. A small thatched extension has been built to the side of the lodge.

There are several beautiful thatched houses in close proximity to the lodge and two of these may be immediately spotted across the field on the opposite side of the road. In the past, many local folk believed a ghost haunted the road just below the lodge. The ghost took the form of

94

a little old lady, clad in a shawl with a poke bonnet on her head. She always carried a basket on her arm when she was seen walking slowly along the road. Goathill also once claimed another ghost. This assumed the shape of a dog and it trotted down the hill towards Milborne Port.

Many travellers along the main A31 Wimborne to Dorchester road have admired the magnificent gateways set at intervals in the extremely long length of wall surrounding the Drax Estate. The walls enclose the very splendid landscaped deer park and grounds of Charlborough House, the seat of the Drax family for several centuries. The tallest folly in Dorset may also be found in the park and it soars well over one hundred feet high, amidst the many trees. The look-out tower was first constructed by Edward Drax in 1790 but it was badly damaged when struck by lightning in 1838. It was then rebuilt and heightened in 1839. The top of the tower gives a wide view of the surrounding country, the Isle of Wight and the English Channel. In Thomas Hardy's *Two on a Tower*, Swithen St Cleeve gazed at the stars through his telescope from the top of the tower.

Charlborough House itself was originally built in the first half of the seventeenth century but it was burnt down during the Civil War. It was later rebuilt using some of the stone and timber from Corfe Castle, which by then had also been destroyed. Three of the lodges associated with the house and park may be easily seen from the road. These are the

Lodge (Cottage Orné) – Goathill, near Sherborne

Round House (Cottage Orné) – Morden

Lion Lodge which consists of a triumphal arch surmounted by a lion, the Stag Gate with a tall brick arch carrying a stag and the East Almer Lodge which has a top pediment. There are a further two lodges which are not so familiar to the passer-by. The first of these called the Peacock Lodge is set well within the grounds of the house. The second is the thatched Morden Round House.

The latter may be found by leaving the A31 Dorchester to Wimborne road at the Lytchett Matravers turning, which is situated by the thatched Worlds End pub, about one mile west of Almer. The Lytchett Matravers road leads past The Worlds End and the Morden Round House stands a short distance up the road, by the Morden junction. The building although called round, is in fact polygonal in shape and it is pseudo-Gothic in design with its thatched roof. It was built around 1820 but the thatch is less elaborate than many of the other lodges built during the cottage orné period.

Nevertheless, the conical shaped thatch has a considerable overhang from the walls, and square timber rustic posts support the eaves, which shelter the walls in verandah style. A weather-cock sits on the apex of the thatch and porthole windows peep through the walls of the lodge. Small windows are also present in the thatch, which consists of combed wheat reed with a pointed ridge. The lodge has been much altered since first constructed and it now has a small brick extension with a slated roof.

Round Lodge (Cottage Orné) – Compton House, near Sherborne

A further thatched round house, originally built as one of the lodges to another well-known country stately home, Compton House, may be found about midway between Sherborne and Yeovil. The grounds of the house lie just off the A30 dual carriageway. Compton House and its grounds now provide the magnificent setting for the Worldwide Butter-flies and Lullingstone Silk Farm. Some of the world's most beautiful butterflies and moths may be seen here, whilst the Lullingstone Silk Farm has supplied English silk for two coronations and more recently for the wedding dress of the Princess of Wales.

The thatched Round Lodge is situated on the east drive of the main house. The conical-shaped main roof was thatched with wheat reed, when the lodge was completely and tastefully renovated in 1968. At this time, new leaded-light windows were also installed, as the old finely-designed ones had suffered deterioration over the years. The stone mullioned windows are of two lights. The lodge was probably built around 1820 and it possesses very similar carving and bossing work on its interior ceiling, as was carried out in the nearby church of Nether Compton at about this date. The circular lodge was originally built with one room downstairs and an attic room upstairs but it was later extended by the attachment of a rectangular shaped thatched block. This has one hipped end whilst the other joins the circular thatched roof at a valley junction. The thatch has a raised ridge with points.

Umbrella Cottage (Cottage Orné) – Lyme Regis

The walls are of roughly squared and coursed Ham stone and there is a delightful separate thatched pentroof over the ground floor, supported on rustic timber posts. There are therefore two roof levels of thatch; the lower pentroof follows the circular shape of the lodge and divides the upper storey from the ground floor. The windows of the upper storey look down on the surface of the lower verandah roof. Immediately over the doorway of the lodge and above the lower thatch, a round-headed niche is set into the wall. Unfortunately, the lodge roofs are often in the shade cast by the surrounding trees and this encourages moss formation on the thatch. Water flows from a spring just outside the lodge.

At Lyme Regis, in Sidmouth Road, stands an old former toll house, now known as the Umbrella Cottage because of the shape of its unusual thatched roof. It was probably built in the first quarter of the nineteenth century and it is a cottage orné. However, it was purchased by an architect who gave it many extra picturesque and extravagant additions. Details from different periods were combined in the small building to produce the desired quaint appearance sought by the owner. The plastered walls of the cottage are polygonal in shape and the cusped

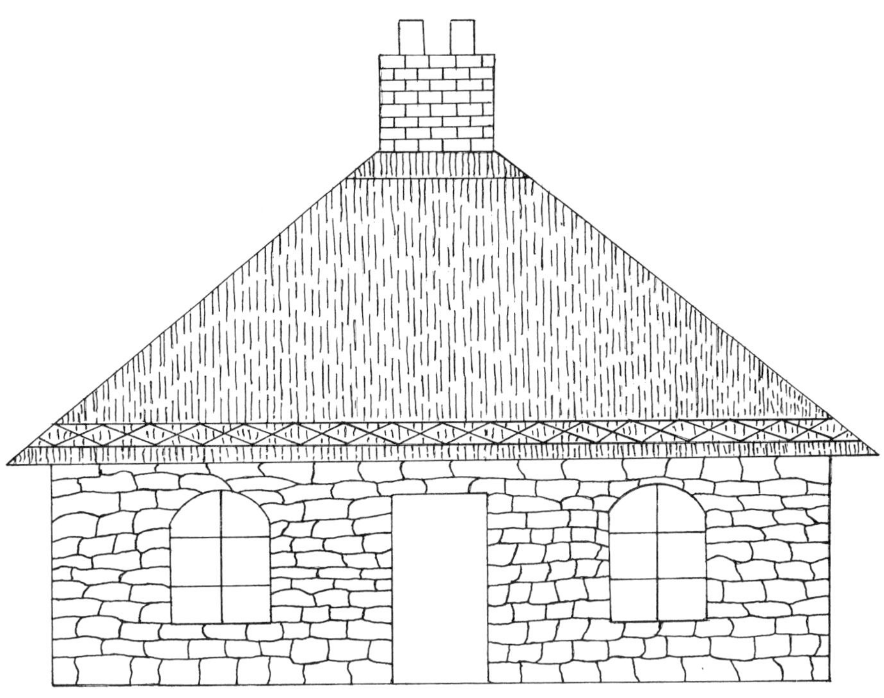

17   *Cottage Orné Lodge (Demolished) – Shroton*

eaves of the conical thatch sweep down in an umbrella-like fashion onto free-standing timber posts. The two front pillars have carved owls on the capitals. A central chimney protrudes through the thatched roof. The cottage has traceried windows and boasts a carved Flemish door, probably from the sixteenth century.

An unusual one-storeyed thatched cottage orné lodge once stood beside the main road near the entrance to the village of Iwerne Courtney (or Shroton as it is sometimes called), just a few miles to the north of Blandford. The alternative name Shroton means Sheriff's Town. The lodge was part of the large house and estate but unfortunately it was demolished in recent years after it had fallen into disrepair. A series of stones still remain where it formerly stood. However, this cottage orné was unusual as it was truly one-storeyed with no attic (Fig. 17) and it had squared walls. It therefore appeared very squat and symmetrical, with its pyramid-shaped thatch rising towards a central chimney-stack. As the lodge was low there was no separate thatched verandah level, which was often a distinctive feature of many taller cottage orné buildings.

Thatched cottage orné style buildings were not confined solely to rich landowners' estates in the shape of lodges. Some of the upper classes in the towns and cities favoured cottage orné type houses for their country retreats. Many of the middle classes also yearned to live in the rural, more primitive type of home their forefathers may once have lived in. This desire was accelerated for some by the quickening pace of the Industrial Revolution. However, with the middle classes, living in a cottage orné as the sole home was relatively economic but at the same time it offered the added advantages of prestige and fashion.

Even when the cottage orné building era dwindled, many people still gained much pleasure and contentment by living in such homes. A good example of this was the Dorset dialect poet, William Barnes, who went to live at Old Came Rectory, near Dorchester, in 1862. It was at this time, when over sixty, he became Rector of Winterborne Came, after working as a schoolmaster for forty years and a curate for two years at the tiny neighbouring parish of Whitcombe.

Without doubt William Barnes had a very wide range of interests when he came to take up his role as country parson. He was an engraver, a painter, an accomplished musician who played several instruments, an expert in the science of languages and an educationalist. In addition to his duties as rector, he also followed his other main interest of writing poetry in the Dorset dialect and reading it at many public gatherings. He also became a great friend of Thomas Hardy. They had much in common, including a deep affection for the countryside, its people and their country manners. Both were Dorset born, Barnes at Sturminster Newton and Hardy at Upper Bockhampton.

Old Came Rectory (Cottage Orné) – Dorchester

The house William Barnes lived in lies just outside of Dorchester, beside the A352 road to Broadmayne. It is situated on the left-hand side of the road, before the gates of Came Park and the hamlet of Whitcombe are reached, when travelling from Dorchester. The house was built with two storeys in the early nineteenth century in the true style of the cottage orné, but some older walls were incorporated at the rear. The rustic splendour of the building may be viewed from the roadside, by the main gate leading to the beautifully kept grounds of the rectory.

The house is attractively pink-washed over its rendered rubble walls, as is the later thatched building projecting behind. The splendid thatch of the main hipped roof has straight eaves which pass over the upper windows of the house. The main thatch is complemented by three separate thatched verandahs, visible at the front of the house. The verandahs possess similar thatch roof levels but these are much lower than the main thatch and the contrast helps to create the primitive look of the cottage orné. Neat white-painted timber posts support the verandah roofs but there are also some brick pillars. Two of these are symmetrically built each side of the white-painted main front door, beneath the overhanging verandah thatch. Two chimney stacks also rise symmetrically at each end of the short ridge of the main thatched roof.

The windows of the house are painted white and the attractive glazing-bars hold many small diamond and hexagonal glass panes. The lower windows are of similar construction but they are much longer as they are in the form of casement windows. They are fashioned in the French style and open onto the garden. The garden has well-laid smooth lawns; many old beech trees tower by the front drive and are high enough for rooks to build their nests in. The large grounds possess several old walls which possibly were once thatched to protect them against the weather. There is also an orchard and a vast variety of shrubs and flowers; all making a perfect setting for a classic cottage orné thatched home. The garden also has its own original water well.

William Barnes died at the age of eighty-six in the house on the 7th October 1886. Thomas Hardy, who lived about half a mile away at Max Gate, walked across the well-trod path through the fields to watch as Barnes's funeral cortege left the rectory. Barnes was buried in the churchyard at Came, about half a mile away from his home. He had been rector of the parish of Came for 24 years and at nearby Whitcombe he gave his first and last sermon. A few lines from one of Barnes's own poems makes a fitting epitaph:

> Zoo now I hope this kindly feace
> Is gone to find a better pleace;
> But still wi' Vo'k a-left behind
> He'll always be a-kept in mind.

A few miles away in the older part of the village of Wool, just down the bottom of the lane from the church, another charming thatched cottage orné home may be found. This is the Regency Cottage, situated by the side of the small stream which runs along its front. The stream is spanned by a series of tiny foot-bridges and there is a broad grass verge by the water's edge. The cottage was probably built during the period 1810 to 1820. Its delightful and elaborate thatched roof of combed wheat reed now displays a neat raised straight ridge. The main thatched roof undulates around the upper windows of the cottage and below there is a timber supported thatched canopy over the front door, which further enhances the rustic appearance.

The glazing metal bars of the attractive, round-headed windows on the upper floor are painted white. In similar fashion to Old Came Rectory, the long ground floor French windows open up to the front garden of the cottage, with its well-kept lawns. The front of the cottage has a symmetrical appearance, as the thatched porch is central and the windows are equally spaced in a planned fashion. Although surrounded by many other beautiful thatched cottages, the distinctive cottage orné

Regency Cottage (Cottage Orné) – Wool

style of the Regency Cottage makes it outstanding and easily identifiable to the casual visitor.

Although the cottage orné period became firmly established during the early part of the nineteenth century, the impetus towards the picturesque had started much earlier in the eighteenth century. A few wealthy landowners in Dorset built groups of model thatched cottages, landscaped into the surrounding scenery for the labourers working on their estates. Eventually, they became more ornate as the architects began to play a greater role in their design.

The eventual passing of the cottage orné period was partly due to the rich deciding that they preferred to spend their holiday leisure abroad, in warmer climes than in England. Nevertheless, even to the present time, many people still dream of living in an idyllic thatched cottage in the countryside, with visions of climbing roses, honeysuckle and clematis on the walls. The more rustic its appearance, so the greater the charm of the thatched cottage in attracting a town or city dweller. Many people retire to such cottages, to fulfil a lifetime's ambition to escape from urban surroundings and industrialization.

6

Thatched Farms and Barns

The total number of farms in Dorset today approaches three thousand and all together they occupy about half-a-million acres. Despite the size of the industry, it only employs three per cent of the county's working population. Most types of farming are carried out, including dairying, meat production, the growing of arable crops, horticultural produce and oil seed rape. Dairying and corn production are the largest individual farming aspects. Approximately one third of the farms keep dairy cows and although Dorset's arable farms are renowned for their barley production, the growing of wheat is now not far behind. Most of the cereal production takes place in the chalk belt uplands of the county. Many of the larger farms do not specialize in one particular sector of agriculture but undertake mixed farming on a closely interrelated basis.

Most of the older farmhouses and barns surviving in Dorset are vernacular buildings built with local materials and many are still roofed with thatch. Throughout the centuries, these farm buildings have undergone changes to adapt to new farming developments and to meet the domestic needs of the farmer, his family and his farmworkers. Some former farmhouses have now been converted to private residences, no longer associated with farming. There exists a large variation in the relative sizes of different farmhouses, ranging from the simple two-roomed houses originally built on smallholdings, to the larger farmhouses with many ground-floor rooms.

The few farmsteads still located in villages are likely to be survivors from the period of community open-field agriculture. More isolated farmsteads in the countryside may have been built when cultivation of wasteland was first undertaken, or more frequently, when the enclosure of common land took place with the establishment of a new central farmstead. The site for a farmstead was also often dictated by the type of farming being carried out. The lush valleys, for example, became the home for dairy cattle because of the availability of riverside pastures.

Before the middle of the eighteenth century, farmhouses were nearly always built just one room deep. This meant that multi-room houses had to be long rather than squarish in shape. The long house design suggested that the buildings could be readily thatched, as the high

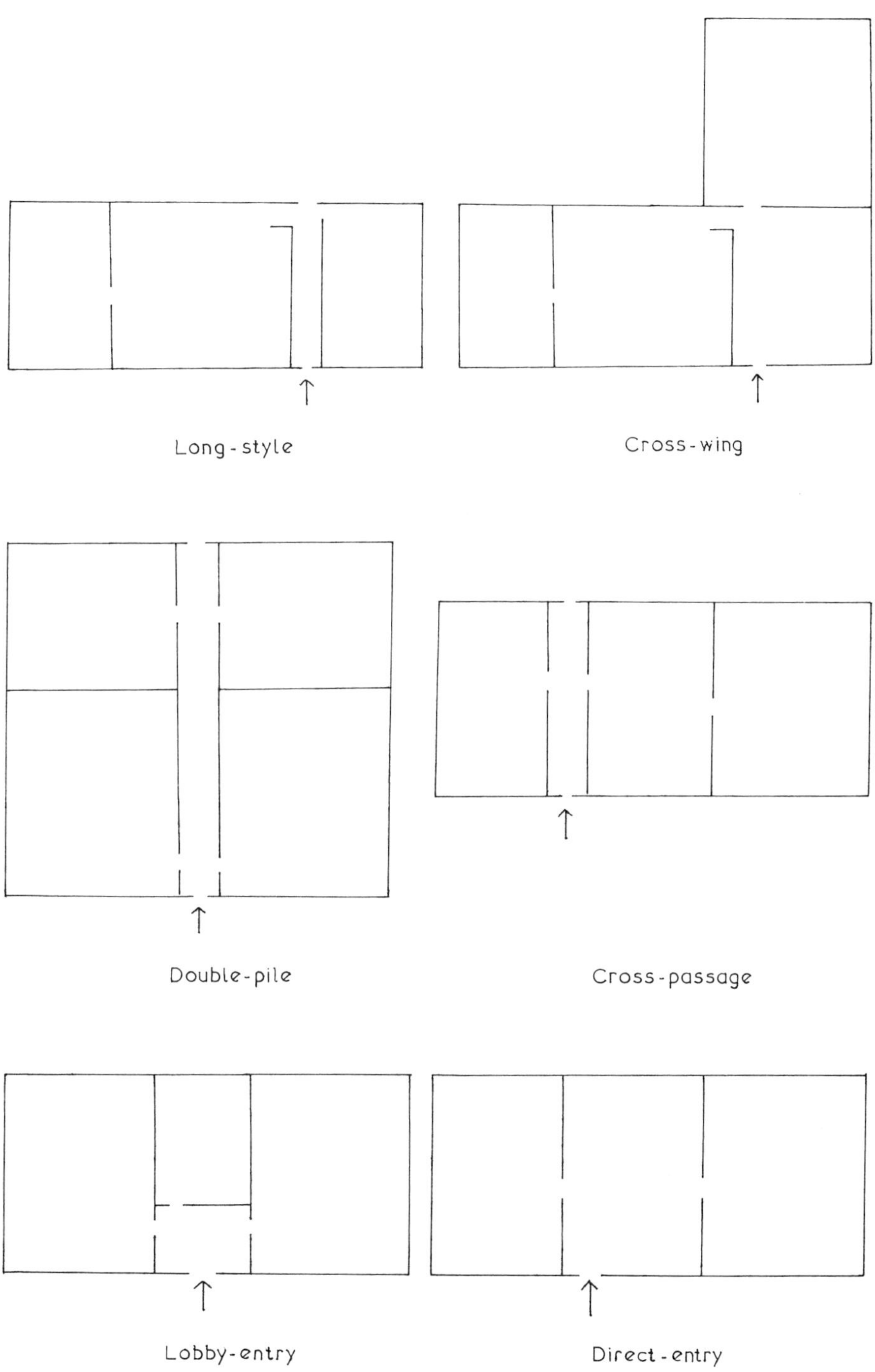

18 *Farmhouse Types*

pitched roof necessary to shed water from the thatch was relatively easy to achieve. Many of the present irregular-shaped old farmhouses are the result of later adapting the original long building, by the construction of an extra wing, or wings, at right angles to the older part. This gave rise to the cross-wing farmhouse which was again often thatched, as the wings were fairly narrow (Fig. 18). It was only towards the end of the eighteenth century that the double-pile farmhouse (more than two rooms deep) became established in Dorset. This much squarer type of house was not usually thatched because of the difficulty in obtaining the desired pitch angle for the roof. It was more convenient to use tiles or slates which required a less steep roof.

In early farmhouses, such as the medieval open hall and the cross-passage long house, a through passage invariably divided the living quarters from the various service rooms. The bedrooms and main living-rooms were always on the ground floor. An example of such a medieval cruck constructed farmhouse stands about half a mile outside the hamlet of Holwell, which is situated near to Sherborne. The building, called Naish Farm, has a hall between the two-storeyed solar end and the now partly altered one-storeyed service end, on the other side of the through passage. When the farmhouse was first built with stone rubble walls in the fifteenth century, the single-storeyed hall was open to the thatched roof but in the sixteenth century the hall was chambered over to provide the upstairs rooms. At the same time, a large open fireplace with an oven was built in the hall. The through passage of the farmhouse still retains parts of its medieval timber-framed partition and also one of the original fifteenth-century doorways. Some brick additions have been made to the house and the steep thatched roof which now covers the farmhouse has hipped ends. The various out-buildings of the small farmyard are not the original ones but it is thought they occupy the same site as those first constructed in the fifteenth century. They therefore illustrate, together with the farm-house, the arrangement of a medieval farmstead.

A thatched farmhouse with a somewhat similar history also survives at Margaret Marsh, near Shaftesbury, in North Dorset. The building, called Higher Farm, was built in the fifteenth century, with stone rubble walls and a thatched roof in the open hall design. The hall was again open to the underside of the thatch and there was probably an open hearth with a smoke hole in the roof. The house was built with a two-storeyed service bay on one side of the hall and a further bay on the opposite side. The hall was chambered over in the sixteenth century and a chimney stack constructed through the thatch. Part of the hall was then made into the through passage. Several of the original roof timbers still support the thatched roof and some are probably of cruck construction.

Moonfleet Farmhouse – Higher Ansty

Another thatched medieval farmhouse may be found on the outskirts of the hamlet of Higher Ansty, about ten miles from Blandford. The building is called Moonfleet, or Lower Farm, although it is now a private residence rather than a farmhouse. The house was originally built in the middle of the sixteenth century of stone rubble and it is likely that some of the material used was brought from nearby Milton Abbey, after the Dissolution of the Monasteries. However, the building has been much extended over the centuries. It was enlarged in the seventeenth century and also during the eighteenth century, when two adjoining medieval cottages were incorporated to make a right-angle wing to the original block. There has recently been some additional alterations and the modernized farmhouse with its annex is now very large. The two-storeyed thatched building contains more than twenty rooms spread throughout its long winged layout. The thatched roof covering the farmhouse has a beautiful raised ridge, with long lines of scallops cut along the under-edge.

One of the main ground floor rooms boasts an exquisite Cyma-Cavetto ceiling structure, consisting of longitudinal and transverse interlocking carved beams. These are rare and represent one of the few surviving coffered ceilings of this type in England. The room also has its original sixteenth-century deep inglenook fireplace, complete with bread oven. The farmhouse possesses its own wishing well. Many such wells exist in Dorset, no doubt due to the wealth of springs and wells which abound in the county. Most wishing wells cherish their own individual mystique as regards the curative powers of their waters, or their ability to determine the future on a mere wish.

Although the particular coffered ceiling structure at Moonfleet is very unusual, another more common type has survived through the centuries in Upton Manor Farmhouse at Loders, near Bridport. This medieval thatched stone-built farmhouse has its original moulded ceiling beams forming a pattern of nine sunken panels on its kitchen ceiling. The farmhouse has a somewhat similar building history to Moonfleet, as Upton Manor Farmhouse was also built in the sixteenth century with rubble walls under a thatched roof. Similarly, the two-storeyed building was extended in the seventeenth century and again in the eighteenth century when a wing was added. A stone with the date 1655 is set in the gable of the extension. The barns and outbuildings associated with the farmhouse were probably once all thatched but tiles have now been substituted on many of them.

Winfrith Fields Farm at Winfrith Newburgh retains an attractive collection of thatched farm outbuildings, many of which date back to the late sixteenth century, including the barn. The walls of the barn were built using courses of graded stone rubble, although various repairs in brick have since been made. The front porch of the barn has a lean-to roof with the original timbering retained on the interior. The thatched roof of the barn is supported by jointed cruck trusses.

A thatched L-shaped outbuilding in the same group also originates from the late sixteenth century. This was constructed with diapered brickwork to form a single-storeyed building but attics were included which were lit by dormer windows in the thatch. This suggests the building may have formerly been used for domestic purposes. There is also a thatched cart-shed with a timber-supported open fronted roof amongst the miscellany of other farm buildings close by. Nowadays, traditional thatched cart-sheds on farms are generally utilized to house modern farm equipment, rather than carts or wagons but the old rustic thatched roofs continue to make such buildings look extremely attractive.

Another large farmstead which has maintained its thatched buildings over several centuries exists at Friar Waddon, just outside of Dorchester on the road to Portesham. There is a mixture of cottages, barns, a stable and a cowshed all roofed with thatch. Some of the buildings were constructed in the sixteenth century but there are also several eighteenth-century buildings in the group. The farmstead is situated by the roadside with pleasant views of the tumuli of Corton Down rising up on the opposite side of the road. The manor of Friar Waddon is very ancient and in the eleventh century it was held by the French nunnery of St Mary, Montevilliers.

The mellowed stone-built two-storeyed thatched cottages at Friar Waddon have gabled ends to their thatches but one, probably built in the late sixteenth century, has a projecting chimney on one of its side walls, as well as a gable wall chimney. The thatched cottage nearest the roadside oddly displays a sixteenth-century mullioned window, with three arched lights, in one of its rooms on the ground floor, although the cottage itself was built in the eighteenth century. The window was doubtless salvaged from another building.

The large eighteenth-century barn also by the roadside has a large tiled porch in the centre and also one on the opposite side of the building. The main roof of the barn has thatched gabled ends and the buttressed mellowed stone walls contain several ventilator slits. The other thatched barns, stable and cowshed at the farmstead are all thought to have been constructed in the eighteenth century. Some of the buildings have raised ridges on their thatched roofs and they are decorated with points.

In the seventeenth and eighteenth centuries, service rooms became an integral part of the farmhouse and they were no longer divided from the main living quarters by a through passage. The entrance to the house was gained either through a lobby or by a direct-entry door. There are many thatched farmhouses of this era in Dorset but a rather unusual one with an extremely large expanse of thatch may be viewed at Waddock Cross, Affpuddle. The building, called Waddock Farm, was built with red brick in the early eighteenth century to make an exceptionally spacious dairy farmhouse under its thatched roof. The large two-storeyed house was constructed with three wings branching out from the main block. A central doorway gave direct entry to the house. Attics and basements were also provided in the building.

In the eighteenth century George Boswell, an expert in irrigation control, lived at Waddock Farm. He worked on the design of the water meadows in the vicinity of Affpuddle and the planned supply of water to them through a series of sluices and water carriers. Water meadows provided controlled grazing facilities for the dairy herds by encouraging rapid grass growth in the spring. George Boswell appears to have disliked Waddock Farm House facing a northerly direction for, in 1797, he altered the house to make its front look to the south. At the same time, other changes were made to enlarge the wings and a porch entrance was made.

Despite the alterations, the northern side of the house still appeared more like the front of the building than the southern side. Today, the farmhouse continues to give the impression that it is built the wrong way around, as the back seems more formal than the front. The impressive main gate to the farmhouse displays large gate piers, with stone ball finials set on their tops. The present thatched roof is constructed of wheat reed, with a pointed raised ridge. The roofs of the wings are hipped and a thatched dormer window provides light to the attic. The farmhouse is occasionally opened to the public around the Easter period to raise funds for charity.

It is perhaps interesting that a search for oil has recently commenced on a site at Waddock Cross and a 'nodding donkey' pump installed at an exploratory drill hole to bring test oil to the surface. Another oil-field at Wytch Farm, near Corfe Castle in Dorset, at present constitutes the largest on-shore oilfield in Britain.

A farmhouse, with a smaller expanse of thatch but of a similar period to Waddock Farm, may be seen in the delightful main village street of Loders, in West Dorset. The two-storeyed building, called Yondover Farm, was originally built in the seventeenth century, with walls of coursed rubble under its thatched roof. The south wing of the house with its gables and thatch was added later, as it displays a stone in the wall with the date 1738 and the initials RB.

A much smaller thatched dairy farmhouse, built in the seventeenth century, survives in the small hamlet of Batcombe on the edge of the Blackmore Vale. The house is known as Church Farmhouse, as it lies within a few hundred yards of the church of St Mary. The farmhouse has a direct-entry central door and consists of two storeys, with the thatch eaves undulating around the upper floor windows. The thatched roof is hipped. Views of the farmhouse were once seen in many homes when it featured in an episode of the 'Survivors' shown on BBC television. The farmhouse has two downstairs rooms, one contains a Minster stone fireplace and fitted window seats. There is also a large inglenook fireplace with oak beams and columnar supports, together with a bread oven. The walls of the farmhouse were built with clunch and rubble.

The nearby church of St Mary at Batcombe rests right under one of the steep hills surrounding the hamlet. Legend relates that in the past, a member of the local Minterne family gambled with the devil that he could jump his horse cleanly over the church from the very steep hill above. This rather unorthodox form of steeplechasing was only partially successful as the pinnacles of the church tower were reputedly knocked off during the attempt. They were replaced in 1906. It sounds as if the gamble with the devil had an unusual influence, as the rider of the horse later asked to be buried half in and half out of the church.

A rather rare sight, a Queen Anne thatched farmhouse may be found at Bovington, just south-west of the army camp. It lies on the road leading to Lawrence of Arabia's cottage at Clouds Hill, when travelling from Wool. Bovington Farmhouse is beautifully proportioned when viewed from the front and consists of two storeys with an attic. It was built in the early eighteenth century of red brick on a rubble plinth but alterations have since been made. Combed wheat reed constitutes the thatch material for the roof and there is a central porch entrance sheltered by a separate little thatch. The white-painted windows give an air of symmetry to the house, as four are positioned each side of the front porch and one immediately above it. There is an additional window in the centre of the thatched roof to serve the attic. A chimney

Bovington Farmhouse – Bovington

stack at each end of the thatched roof adds further uniformity to the house design.

The farming at Bovington Farm is mixed and pumpkins are one of the many crops grown. Recently, the owners claimed they had made the world's largest pumpkin pie which they hoped would win a place in the Guinness Book of Records. The pie, 13 feet 9 inches long and 1 foot 6 inches wide contained more than 100 pumpkins, in addition to the 220 eggs, 50 pounds of flour, 20 pounds of fat and 3 gallons of whipping cream.

East Farm, Osmington, comprises a delightful collection of thatched buildings. It lies on the opposite side of the road to The Sunray Hotel and behind a thatched polygonal-shaped bus shelter. There are three main thatched buildings, the thatched East Farm Lodge stands immediately behind the bus shelter. The thatched East Farm cottage lies adjacent to the lodge. The doorway of the cottage bears a plaque stone, dated 1697 and the building has mullioned windows with hood-moulds.

The main large thatched farmhouse stands next door and forms the most spectacular member of the thatched group. An archway cuts through the centre of the front section of the L-shaped stone thatched building. The beautiful thatch flows over the arch and joins the farmhouse on each side of it, thus making a long continuous stretch of thatch. The raised ridge of the magnificent thatched roof is artistically ornamented with rows of scallops and at intervals very large scallop patterns are introduced. The ridge is also decorated with elaborate traceries of liggers and spars. A weather-cock sits on the top of the ridge and the thatched roof is gable ended.

East Farm – Osmington

East Farm is a dairy farm but an unusual one in some respects. Most dairy farms have their milk collected on a regular daily basis by milk lorries of the Milk Marketing Board, who take it to a centralized plant for processing, pasteurizing and bottling, before distribution to the customer. East Farm shortens the delay which occurs between the cow being milked and the customer drinking the product, by processing their own milk production. The farm then delivers it immediately to their own local customers.

Modern dairy farms are now highly mechanized and machine milking, twice a day, allows a large number of cows to be milked in a short space of time under extremely hygienic conditions. On a national average, a cow produces a yield of 8,000 pints of milk a year but nearly all Dorset dairy farms achieve a figure well above this average. In fact, Dorset constitutes one of the most intensive dairy farming areas in Europe and much of the success is due to the quality and quantity of the grass available for feeding the animals. This is especially so in the north and west of the county where the soil is usually wet due to the underlying clay formations and thus ideal for grass production.

Another dairy farm, with a sizeable thatched roof, stands alongside the minor road linking Herringston with Came, about one and a half miles to the south of Dorchester. Herringston Dairy Farm House consists of a two-storeyed long building, constructed with brick and rubble walls during the earlier part of the nineteenth century. The upper storey is predominantly brick but some of the walls have been

Herringston Farmhouse – near Dorchester

partly rendered. A combed wheat reed thatch covers the farmhouse and the hipped roof has a raised neatly pointed ridge, with square aprons of thatch below the two chimney stacks. The front of the farmhouse has several attractive multi-pane windows. The farm enjoys beautiful views over the wooded countryside and just along the road is the site of the annual Dorchester Agricultural Show, held in September.

The use of brick for the building of farmhouses in Dorset became common during the eighteenth and nineteenth centuries. A good example is Lower Hilton Farm, in the small village of Hilton. The two-storeyed farmhouse is thatched and gabled. It was originally built of brick in the eighteenth century as a two-bay cottage but it was greatly enlarged in the nineteenth century. The extension was constructed of flint, mixed with courses of brick. The farmstead also possesses several thatched outbuildings. The nearby village of Winterborne Houghton also boasts a fine old brick and flint farmhouse at Middle Farm which is thatched and was probably built in the eighteenth century.

Most of the older thatched farmhouses in Dorset may be expected to survive well into the future. Unfortunately, the same cannot be said for the remaining thatched outbuildings on many farms. These are more prone to demolition, or sadly the replacement of their roofs with materials cheaper than thatch. Such farm buildings have always been functional units and new farming methods have made many of them redundant. The replacement of the horse by the tractor has outdated stables and cart-sheds. The modern milking parlour has made the old-fashioned cowhouse obsolete. Barns and granaries have not been needed for their original purposes since the middle of the nineteenth century.

Thatched barns still make a delightful contribution to the Dorset countryside, although they are disappearing at a rather alarming rate due to the huge expense of maintaining their roofs. Farmers incur bills of thousands of pounds in re-thatching even a medium-size barn. The surviving barns now store a great miscellany of things on a farm although, of course, their original purpose was to store grain. The old English word 'bern' meant a storehouse for barley. Traditional barns were built with two doors on directly opposite sides, so that wagons could go straight through after unloading in the middle. Opposing doorways were therefore an essential feature of barn design.

Magnificent tithe barns, some cathedral-like, were built for storing one-tenth of the grain produce of a parish, the value of which was paid in tithes to maintain the church and its incumbent. The compulsory payment of tithes, through good and especially bad times, naturally produced some resentment amongst the farming community. A typical Dorset saying became 'just like the parson's barn', meaning that despite something being already full it could always find room for more.

The lord of the manor sometimes exploited the situation to raise a little extra cash for himself, by not collecting the tithes due from his tenants, but instead receiving a bribe from them. For instance, at the village of Thornford, near Sherborne, it is related that tenants of the manor used to deposit five shillings in a hole in a particular tombstone in the churchyard. This donation exempted them from providing their tithe of produce. Pride in the evasion of the payments of tithes was often echoed in the chorus of an old harvest song, sung by farmers in many a local when relaxed with a glass of cider or ale:

> 'We've cheated the parson, we'll cheat him again,
> For why should the vicar have one in ten?'

The huge monastic tithe barns began to disappear with the Dissolution of the Monasteries and the breaking up of the large ecclesiastical estates. However, the Church of England parson still claimed his tithes in kind for many years to come. This continued until the various Tithe Commutation Acts of 1836 to 1860 were passed which substituted a so-called corn rent, payable in actual money. The system was finally abolished in 1936. The famous great tithe barn at Abbotsbury, built about five centuries ago to house produce from the monastic estates, was once the largest in England, until a substantial part of it became ruined. The barn was part of the Benedictine Monastery of St Peter which was first founded in the eleventh century. Incidentally, an old

Tithe Barn – Abbotsbury

story relates that the last of the abbots was imprisoned and starved to death in the gatehouse leading to the barn.

Strangely, the barn survived when the rest of the monastery was destroyed in 1539 by Henry VIII's Commissioners; the nearby St Catherine's Chapel situated high on the hill also escaped destruction. This may have been because the stone roof of the chapel was too heavy to dismantle and the walls were extremely thick. The barn itself was originally roofed with smooth flat stone slates, very likely quarried in Purbeck. It was only later that it became thatched with Abbotsbury reed and this has helped in its preservation to the present day.

The barn is about 272 feet long and 30 feet wide and it is now used for the storage of Abbotsbury reed, after being cut from the reed beds at the nearby swannery. The present huge beautifully thatched roof of the barn possesses a flat straight ridge and the whole thatch surface is wired-in. The interior of the roof, which supports the thatch, has a cathedral-like look due to the arched appearance created by the curved timber braces and the hammer-beam vaulting.

The walls are supported by a series of three-stage buttresses and when the barn was first built there were two porches and five separate doorways. Just the one porch remains on the surviving part of the barn and near to this there is an octagonal staircase turret. The porches and many doorways of the barn were used to create draughts to blow away the chaff when the grain was winnowed through sieves. The open slit ventilators, or loop-lights, present in the walls admitted a gentle flow of air which reduced the risk of overheating of the stored grain and also allowed daylight to illuminate the working floor. The loop-lights are similar to the arrow slits present in castles and give a splayed interior. In barns, the main object was to gain some protection from high winds and rain without impeding ventilation, whilst in castles loop-lights gave a wide angle view for persons looking outwards.

Ancient tithe barns were built exceptionally large and wide but in general most later barns were constructed with much smaller dimensions. The earlier barns served three main purposes, storage, threshing and granary. Until the introduction of steam operated threshing machines in the nineteenth century, the separation of the corn from the ears was always done by hand, with a flail on the threshing floor of the barn. The threshing floor was the origin of our modern term, threshold. Threshing was a winter's job to be done after the sheaves of corn cut in the summer had been dried. The wooden hand flail was hinged with a leather binding in the centre. One half was held in the hand and the beater arm of the flail was swung to strike repeatedly the ears of corn spread on the threshing floor. Hand threshing was a slow and laborious process. The spent straw was piled for later use as bedding for cattle. The grain after being winnowed was stored in the granary of the barn.

There was a great impetus to barn building in the seventeenth and eighteenth centuries and most in Dorset during this time were built with thatched roofs. The increase in corn production in the eighteenth century required extra storage space and it became the practice to build separate granaries. Some of these were a considerable size and many were thatched. To keep rats and mice at bay, granaries were raised on a series of staddle stones, with mushroom shaped tops. Many of the stones used were fashioned by stonemasons working at Portland. For similar reasons, barns were always provided with an entrance hole in the top of the gable wall for owls. These were encouraged to become resident in the barn for the killing of vermin and thereby protect the grain. To restrict the menace of rats and mice, some granaries were built at first floor level, above a ground floor cart-shed with an open front. The combined granary and cart-shed offered a further advantage that the air circulation below the upper granary floor helped to keep the grain sweet.

When the steam engine developed from the stationary type to the portable in the nineteenth century, the corn was then threshed in the open fields and the need for a long threshing floor in the barn vanished. Barns then became mere storage places. However, those situated in or near villages continued to have a social role to play and they were still used for barn dances and other village functions. The cruciform layout of the old barns was not ideal for modification to other farm uses because of the space wastage; although in theory, buildings between sixteen and twenty feet wide could be converted into milking parlours. With the advent of the combine harvester in this century, the barn found another small useful role as a convenient place to dry the grain, threshed from the corn in the fields by the huge machines. The grain is brought back in an undried condition after harvesting with the combine. Grain driers housed in converted barns are therefore much used after the grain has been cleaned from weed seeds, insects and other debris. Normally up to five per cent of moisture has to be extracted. It is only in exceptionally dry summers that the grain will not need artificial drying. The drying process prevents mould formation on the grain during storage.

The architecture of barns has remained fairly simple through the centuries, although the timbered interiors of many look very impressive. The earliest were often cruck built to support the roof and walls; later ones used a crown post frame, whilst a post and truss construction became popular in the seventeenth and eighteenth centuries (Fig. 19). In Dorset, most barns were thatched with wheat straw grown on the farm, although a few were roofed with water reed when this was available in the immediate locality.

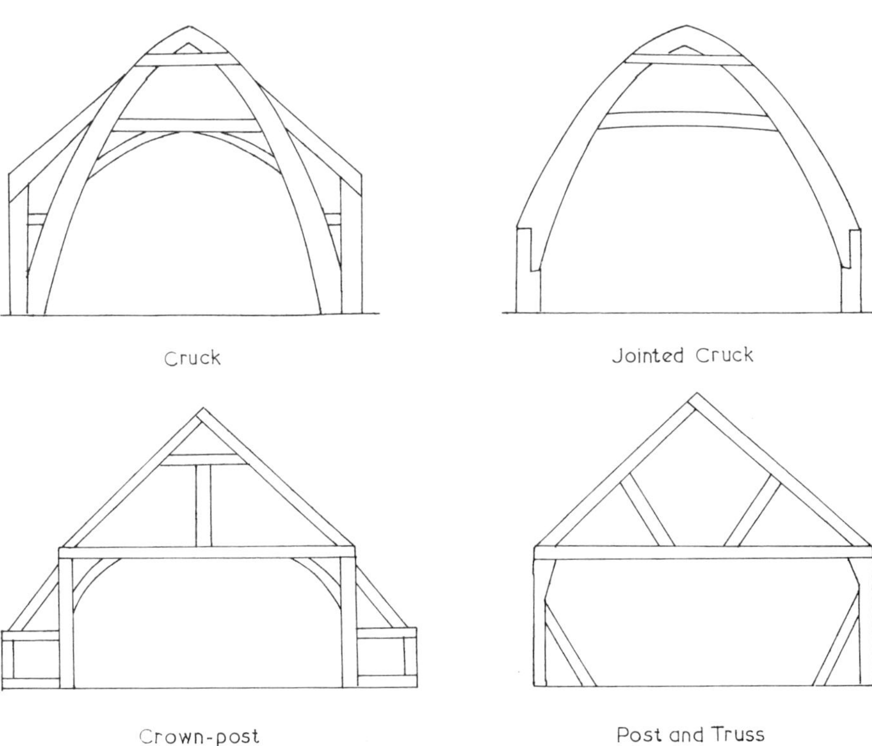

19 *Barn Roof Designs*

A barn dating back to the sixteenth century with a thatched roof supported by a series of jointed cruck trusses spaced ten feet apart, still remains at Hazelbury Bryan. It is situated about fifty yards from the church. The barn has large opposing doorways and the walls were constructed from graded rubble laid in courses. The threshing floor was very likely originally made of timber, laid on a hard dirt floor which had been well rammed down. Another thatched sixteenth-century barn at Wytherstone Farm, Powerstock, has centre arches with curved timbers underneath the thatched roof.

The use of crucks for supporting barn roofs continued in Dorset well into the sixteenth and also the seventeenth centuries. However, most were of jointed or scarfed-cruck construction, as typified in the Hazelbury Bryan barn. Another example may be found at West Stafford in the main street of the village. The barn which was formerly the Squire's barn (the main farm barn to the manor, Stafford House) was built in the seventeenth century. It is now known as the Barton Barn. The jointed cruck construction of the roof with collar beams is a little unusual, as the main oak timbers which support the thatch are free standing on the base walls of the barn and they are held in place solely by the weight of the enormous roof. The walls of the barn are constructed of a mixture of stone and brick with some exposed timbering.

The thatched roof has been magnificently maintained and it constitutes one of the larger thatched roofs in Dorset. It has been recently re-thatched with new ash poles fitted under the thatch to ensure adequate support for the new wheat reed thatch. The porches to the

Barton Barn – West Stafford

barn are also thatched and the ridges of the roofs are flat. The barn has not been employed for farm storage for many years but it has been used as an arts and crafts centre, combined with a shop. This function has recently ceased and the future of the barn has not yet been determined.

A barn built in about 1600, with a beautiful quarter-hipped thatched roof and still utilized for farm purposes, stands at Woodsford Farm, just to the east of West Stafford. The walls of the barn, known as the Long Barn, were constructed with weather-boarding and timber-framing, as was fairly common in Dorset and in most of southern England. The timbered walls were erected on the top of a high brick plinth, with stone footings to protect the wooden walls from the rising damp.

Just about one mile to the east of West Stafford, a fine example of an early eighteenth-century thatched barn may be viewed from the roadside at Lower Lewell Farm. The brick built barn contains eleven separate bays, each lit and ventilated by an individual slit-light. The building has opposing porches, one with a thatched gabled roof whilst the other has a hipped roof. The brick walls of the barn are heavily buttressed and the brickwork carries the initials IR, with the date 1704. The main thatched roof is supported on collar-beam trusses and it is half-hipped at each end. The smaller thatched building standing next door to the barn is a thatched cowshed, probably built in the early seventeenth century. It has now been mainly rebuilt in brick but it was originally constructed of stone.

A very impressive and massive eighteenth-century barn, with a fine

Long Barn – Woodsford Farm, Woodsford

Lower Lewell Barn – near West Knighton

North Barn – Affpuddle

thatched roof, may be viewed next door to the church in the village of Iwerne Courtney (Shroton). The barn is very high and its walls are made of rubble, with ashlar quoins at the doorways and corners. There are slit-lights in the stone walls. The main section of the barn is rectangular in shape but there are two wings projecting to the north at each end. A wide main doorway is centrally positioned between the two wings. On the south side of the barn there is an imposing doorway in the central bay which projects towards the church. The large expanse of thatch covers the entire barn, including the wings, in a continuous sweep. The barn is still used for storage by the nearby farm.

An example of an early nineteenth-century thatched barn may be seen at Affpuddle, on the B3390 road leading to the A35 road. The building, called North Barn and dated 1802, possesses imposing porches and the main thatched roof sweeps down as a catslide to shelter them. The walls of the barn are made of cob, set on a brick base plinth and again there are slit-lights in the walls for ventilation. The hipped thatched roof has a flat ridge. The barn, built about a century later than the one at Lower Lewell Farm, shows that little change in basic barn design had taken place.

The village of Stratton has a fine example of a thatched stone and flint barn with a 1778 datestone over the doorway. A thatched field barn designed and built for a different purpose also survives at Stratton. This is Hog Hill Barn, which typifies a Dorset 'Hill Top Barn' built in about 1800. This small thatched stone and flint barn was constructed to store the feed for cattle, who were kept enclosed in a yard to obtain manure for the upland arable fields nearby. The cattle were housed in a yard attached to the barn. Field barns thus served a different purpose to the larger barns built to thresh and store grain.

Field barns were also erected in areas of newly enclosed land which were some distance from the main farmstead and these again stored hay for cattle. When barns were constructed of cob and cattle were kept near, it became more essential than usual to treat the walls regularly with lime-wash. This deterred the cattle from licking the walls because untreated cob walls over a period of time often developed holes caused by the licking action of the animals.

As the traditional uses for barns have waned, so conversions to make residential homes have gained momentum in recent years. One of many examples in Dorset exists at the village of Tolpuddle, where a thatched barn conversion has been tastefully carried out to retain the outer walls and appearance of the original barn. The building stands alongside the road near the famous Martyrs Tree and memorial seat in the heart of the village.

The thatched barn was built of brick in the early nineteenth century and the high porch entrances may still be viewed at the rear of the building. On the front of the barn visible from the main roadside, the slitted ventilators in the brick walls have been retained. One of the problems of converting barns into residential units is where to place the windows without destroying the aesthetic look of the original barn. One method, as done in the present case, is to retain the slitted ventilators on the side visible from the road whilst the back garden side of the barn, not usually visible from the road, has large windows incorporated to maximize the intake of light. Sometimes, architects favour an alternative method which involves the insertion of small windows just below the eaves level. The residences converted from the barn at Tolpuddle are called West Farm Barn and Central Farm Barn. They are covered with a beautiful thatched roof, with a raised ridge of scallops and points. One end of the combed wheat reed thatch is hipped and the other half-hipped.

7

Thatched Villages of Central Dorset

Without doubt, the most famous and frequently visited thatched cottage in Dorset is the birthplace of Thomas Hardy, at the hamlet of Higher Bockhampton, just outside of Dorchester. Thomas Hardy was born in the cottage in 1840 and about 10,000 people now visit it each year. Unfortunately, this sheer weight of numbers over the years caused some subsidence to the front walls but extensive repairs and strengthening work were carried out in 1981 to rectify the situation. The cottage

Thomas Hardy's Cottage – Bockhampton

belongs to the National Trust, who acquired it in 1947 and the interior may be viewed only by appointment with the tenant. However, the cottage gardens are always open to the public during the summer months, from April to October.

The two-storeyed cottage was built by Thomas Hardy's great-grandfather in 1800, with walls of cob but without dug foundations, as was usual at the time. The cob was protected with the traditional use of a thatched roof but the cob was also shielded with a facing of bricks, making a total wall thickness of about two feet. For this reason, the cottage was obviously of a better class than the average countryman's. The thatched roof is hipped and most likely it has always been thatched with Norfolk reed or combed wheat reed. The ridge on each side of the central chimney stack assumes slightly different levels, which suggests the cottage may have undergone some minor alterations since it was first built. The eaves are cut with eyebrows above the upper multi-pane windows to increase the light inside the bedrooms.

Hardy's grandfather was a stonemason, although he also did a little occasional brandy smuggling. The rather isolated position of the cottage on the edge of Puddletown Heath, with its wild moor (Hardy's 'Egdon') would have been an ideal spot. He used a squint in the porch to watch the lane for excisemen. Hardy's father was a master builder and he worked from a small office in the cottage. This had a barred window at the back facing the heath, through which he used to pay his workmen. Outside his trade, his chief interest was music.

The cottage was fairly spacious and had a kitchen with the traditional inglenook fireplace and bread oven. In addition to the other downstairs accommodation, it had three bedrooms and Thomas Hardy was born in the middle one. The bedroom next door was eventually shared by Hardy's younger sisters, Mary and Kate. The third bedroom was later shared by Thomas Hardy with his younger brother Henry. Kate became a school mistress at Piddlehinton, whilst Henry took up the building trade. Thomas Hardy became articled to an ecclesiastical architect at 39 South Street in Dorchester. He later moved to London to study architecture and so continued the family tradition, until he achieved his greater fame as a novelist and poet.

A granite obelisk now stands just outside the thatched cottage. The inscription states that: Thomas Hardy, OM was born in the adjacent cottage, 2nd June, 1840 and in it wrote *Under the Greenwood Tree* and *Far from the Madding Crowd*. The monument was erected to his memory by a few American admirers in 1931. A track from Hardy's cottage leads down to the wildlife sanctuary and nature trails set in the forty-six acres of Thorncombe Wood, which contains a magnificent collection of trees and bushes, including rhododendrons. The old Roman road that once linked Dorchester to London runs nearby and at night it is still supposedly haunted by the figure of a Roman centurion.

About a mile away hides the hamlet of Lower Bockhampton, where Thomas Hardy first went to school. A delightful view of the many stone and thatched cottages in the hamlet may be gained from the ancient stone bridge at the bottom of the road. One of the thatched cottages near the bridge, over the River Frome, offers the fairly rare sight of a thatched garden wall, although several other better examples may be

Yalbury Cottage Restaurant – Bockhampton

found in Dorset. A short distance up the road from the bridge stands Yalbury Cottage which is now run as a family restaurant. The cottage possesses a fine hipped thatched roof over its brick built walls. An old water pump still survives on the opposite side of the road to the cottage.

The village of Stinsford nestles close by, along the banks of the stream. The churchyard is worth a visit as, below a giant yew tree, the heart of Thomas Hardy lies buried, although his ashes rest in Poets' Corner, Westminster Abbey. He died in 1928. On leaving Stinsford by road to join the A35 to Dorchester, a terrace of former farm cottages covered with a large continuous expanse of thatch, with a catslide end may be spotted. The impressive raised ridge of the thatch is artistically decorated with scallops and points.

The county town of Dorchester has retained few thatched buildings, although at one time it possessed many thatched cottages, especially in the Fordington area and The Grove. There was also a thatched barn called Damer's and until recently a thatched abattoir. However, a thatched building of historical significance has survived in the shape of the Hangman's Cottage, situated at the bottom of Glyde Path Road, in Northernhay. It lies beside the mill stream of the River Frome.

The thatched cottage was built in the early seventeenth century and it was the home of the town's executioner. At this time, the gallows at Dorchester stood near the present junction of Icen Way and South Walks. The condemned prisoner was dragged on a tumbril, or on a

Hangman's Cottage – Dorchester

hurdle, for the journey to the gallows but a stop was usually made at The Bell Inn (long since demolished) to allow the victim a last drink. Later, the gallows was moved to Maumbury Rings, the site of the Roman amphitheatre.

The public executions continued here until the new prison was built during the period 1790 to 1792, near the site of the Hangman's Cottage. The thatched cottage was occupied by the busy hangman at the time of the Bloody Assize, held in Dorchester in 1685 under the notorious Judge Jeffreys. The following quotation and musing typified the Judge's uncompromising approach in dealing with prisoners before their trial:

'The love of fair play and justice is in the very marrow of my bones. What could be fairer than my command at ye start of each case – Bring in ye next prisoner and let us see his rascally face – it is a warning to ye villains to be on their best behaviour and not to waste ye court's time by pleading ye innocence.'

The Bloody Assize at Dorchester resulted in seventy-four men meeting the executioner.

Hangman's Cottage today is an attractive family home, bordered by a neat white picket fence and it has been much extended and modernized over the years. The long thatched building is partly two-storeyed and the smart thatched roof has a straight ridge. The country garden behind the cottage has a dovecote and the stream runs by the side. Thomas Hardy was fascinated by the cottage and used it for a scene in 'The Withered Arm', one of his *Tales from Wessex*. He described Gertrude visiting the hangman, Davies, the night before the execution. He was about to go to bed when she arrived, by ascending a flight of wooden steps fixed against the end of the cottage. She had come to arrange to touch the corpse the next day, immediately after the execution, to 'charm' away the skin affliction on her arm.

The River Piddle rises at the secluded downland village of Alton Pancras, to the north of Dorchester and runs down through the Piddle Valley. It passes a string of picturesque thatched villages and hamlets, all with the name 'Piddle' or 'Puddle' associated with them. There is a Piddletrenthide, Piddlehinton, Puddletown, Tolpuddle, Affpuddle and Turners Puddle. Puddletown was formerly called Piddletown but it adopted officially the name 'Puddle' in preference to 'Piddle' in the 1950s, as it sounded more proprietous. However, unofficially it had been called 'Puddle' for many years before. The villages below Puddletown are also called 'Puddle' rather than 'Piddle'.

At Alton Pancras, there are a number of cob-built, thatched cottages scattered through the village and all enjoy excellent views of the surrounding countryside. Some of the thatched properties are detached, whilst others are terraced. In addition to the cob cottages, there are others with banded walls of brick and flint under their thatched roofs. Such a building was the former village store and post office which was closed in 1977. It has since been improved and modernized to become a private thatched home.

The village of Piddletrenthide was owned by Winchester College from the Reformation until the 1950s but the land was always leased to long term tenants. The village contains several yellow-tinged stone houses, many with thatched roofs and they straggle for about a mile along the deep narrow stretch of the valley. A thatched butcher's shop serves the village and it is attached to some other delightful cottages. The walls of these were constructed from banded brick and flint. The thatched roof of the butcher's shop displays a raised ridge with points and it has a neat quarter hip over the entrance. The playground gates of the village school are of interest, as they were originally made for Westminster Abbey in the sixteenth century. They were later given to Piddletrenthide in 1826, as a present from a former villager who had made his fortune in London.

The next village along the valley, Piddlehinton, was owned by Eton College, again from the Reformation until the 1950s and in former times

Butcher's Shop – Piddletrenthide

it was called Honey Puddle. Similarly to Piddletrenthide, the land had always been leased for farming. There are many beautiful thatched cottages in Piddlehinton and several are detached with raised ridges. Combed wheat reed is the most favoured thatching material found in the Piddle Valley. A large thatched barn survives in the middle of the village and it stands next door to the thatched inn, The Thimble. There is another thatched barn at the south end of the main village street.

An interesting story still lingers that once an old lady lived in one of the thatched cottages in Piddlehinton. The cottage was always kept dark and the door, when knocked, was never answered. Inevitably she was thought to be a witch. At the same time as the old lady lived in the cottage, a hare was thought to haunt the village. One night the squire was riding home when his horse accidentally kicked a hare which ran across its path. Next morning, the old lady was seen in the village walking with a limp. Later, the hare was also seen limping. Both remained lame for the rest of their lives. Rather unusually, the wide belief in witchcraft in Dorset lasted nearly to the end of the nineteenth century. This may have been due to the agricultural nature of the county and the lack of educational advantages through the centuries. Ignorance has often bred fear and superstition.

Puddletown, with the busy main road passing through it, still possesses several old cob-walled thatched cottages. Most have raised ridges, decorated with points rather than mixed scallops and points. In the square, there is a row of nineteenth-century thatched cottages and there is also a Tudor cottage built in 1573. This village was Hardy's Weatherby in *Far from the Madding Crowd* and it was in the porch of the church that Troy spent a night. Hardy knew the village well as he often visited his aunt who lived in a cottage near the mill stream. He also used to play his fiddle in the barn attached to the cottage. Unfortunately, a fire in 1884 destroyed the whole row of thatched cottages that led down to the stream.

The best-known village name along the River Piddle is no doubt Tolpuddle, due to its association with the Tolpuddle Martyrs and their historic influence on the future of the trade union movement. The six farm labourers met together in an attempt to obtain an increase in their wages. They were later arrested and in 1834 sentenced to seven years' transportation for administering illegal oaths while founding a trade union. After many protests, the men were pardoned and allowed to return to England. In 1934 a memorial seat, sheltered by a thatched canopy, was erected in their memory near the old sycamore tree, under which they originally decided to go together to ask for a wage increase. A few hundred yards away, the TUC also built in 1934 six cottages in memory of the Martyrs – George Loveless, James Loveless, Thomas Standfield, John Standfield, James Brine and James Hammett.

Memorial Seat – Tolpuddle

Pixie's Cottage – Tolpuddle

These cottages were not thatched but the cottage where Thomas Standfield lived still remains in the village and it is partly thatched. It stands a short way up the road from The Martyrs Inn and opposite the inn there is a particularly beautiful row of thatched cottages. There are many other delightful thatched cottages along the village street and several have smart raised ridges with scallops and points.

Some of the thatched cob cottages date back to the sixteenth century and the spacious one, standing nearly opposite the memorial seat and village green, is known to have partially exposed roof trusses under the thatch which date to the fourteenth century. The majority of the thatched cottages however are seventeenth century and a few have rustic thatched porches supported by roughly cut timbers. There are also thatched barns in the village, some converted to houses. On the outskirts, near the river, is the Tolpuddle Trout Fishery School, which is a red brick thatched building, also known as Lawrence's Farm.

Just across the stream from Tolpuddle lies Affpuddle and on the ridge to the south Cull-pepper's Dish, the largest natural swallow-hole in Dorset. It measures about one hundred yards across and the conical shaped pit is about forty feet deep. The surrounding terrain is heathland and there are also smaller swallow-holes in the vicinity. There is no doubt they were formed naturally, sometime in the distant past, probably by chalk subsidence and movement of sand in the underlying strata. Trees often grow at the bottom of such pits and in the deep ones the treetops do not reach the level of the ground above.

The village of Affpuddle has several charming thatched cottages and the majority were again built with cob walls in the seventeenth century. Many have since been repaired with brick. The 'Old Barn Cottage', situated next door to the farm, has a very attractive thatched roof and the name suggests it is another conversion. Many barns were built at Affpuddle in the early nineteenth century with thatched roofs and several have been rebuilt or modernized for other uses.

The nearby pretty hamlet of Briantspuddle abounds with white-walled thatched buildings of various ages, ranging from the late fifteenth to the twentieth century. Most are thatched with wheat reed, although there are a few roofed with long straw. The majority of the ridges are raised and decorated with points. The occasional one displays a straw bird perched on the top of its roof. One of the oldest is the cruck cottage, situated in the main street opposite the long symmetrical thatched building with thatched turrets, known as The Ring, a former dairy farm.

The thatched cruck cottage was built in the late fifteenth century of cob but it has been considerably reconstructed with rubble. It was originally built with four cruck trusses under the thatch, to make a medieval house with an open hall of two bays, with a third bay for

The Ring – Briantspuddle

service. The building has endured many alterations and extensions over the centuries to make it into the spacious modern home that now exists.

In contrast, The Ring, on the opposite side of the road, was built by Sir Ernest Debenham in 1919 and it was then called the Bladen or Briantspuddle Dairy. Sir Ernest was the founder of Debenham's stores. However, he invested also in agriculture with a view to increasing productivity by adopting efficient farming methods. He was a great agricultural pioneer and innovator. To test his theories, he ran a model estate of about 6,000 acres around Briantspuddle but the estate was dispersed and sold after his death in 1952.

The thatched Ring was built originally as part of his model dairy complex but it has now been converted into a series of quaint terraced cottage homes. The building was unusually constructed with cavity concrete bricks, with a view to reducing interior condensation. This type of brick was referred to in Chapter 1. The centre section of the dairy was made one storey high but a two-storeyed block was built at each end to complete the design for a symmetrical building. Two ornamental turrets were also built at the ends and each was furnished with a conical bonnet of thatch.

The main street of Briantspuddle still retains an olde-worlde charm, as the new thatched cottages blend unobtrusively with the old. The thatched barn in the centre of the main street has now been converted for use as the Briantspuddle Village Hall and the Bladen Social Club.

Bladen Valley Estate Cottages – Briantspuddle

The barn was constructed in the early nineteenth century, with walls of cob on a brick plinth. It was built with two wide porch entrances and it was roofed with the traditional thatch to protect the cob. The nearby hamlet of Turners Puddle also contains some delightful thatch.

The influence of Sir Ernest Debenham may also be seen in the model estate village he created at Bladen Valley, just a quarter of a mile away from Briantspuddle. The beautiful thatched houses stand each side of the road in a cul-de-sac, with the war memorial at the top. They are neatly spaced apart, some in groups of three, others in twos and there are also detached thatched homes. Wide green verges run along the fronts of the houses. The roofs offer a variety of ornamental thatch designs, some have thatched aprons below windows, others have scalloped ridges and there is a mixture of different roof levels. Most are thatched with combed wheat reed. The overall view of the cul-de-sac hints at the Blaise Hamlet estate of Nash and it has some similarity with the ordered layout of Milton Abbas.

Sir Ernest Debenham had an influence on the provision of some excellent cottages in the nearby village of Milborne St Andrew, where he had established a large milk factory. Many old thatched cottages also remain in the village and the post office has a thatched roof. This is made of wheat reed and the neatly cut raised ridge has ornamental points.

About four miles away lies the large village of Bere Regis. The Regis

Post Office – Milborne St Andrew

originated from the royal connection with King John, who was lord of the manor and often visited it for hunting expeditions during the early thirteenth century. He was succeeded by Simon de Montfort, founder of the English Parliament and eventually by the Turberville family, who retained the manor for the following centuries, until the early eighteenth. The impressive church with its magnificent and unique timber carved roof contains the tombs and memorials to the Turbervilles. It also displays two large iron fire hooks made in about 1600.

These were used to strip burning thatch from cottages and also to form fire breaks on nearby thatched roofs to arrest the spread of fires. The hooks, with chains attached, were originally screwed to the ends of long poles, so that the roof level could be easily reached (Fig. 20). Iron rings were sometimes installed under the eaves of cottages, so that the heavy fire hooks could be pulled up more readily with a chain or rope.

Bere Regis, like several other thatched villages in Dorset, suffered badly from fires during the seventeenth and eighteenth centuries. This has meant that few of the very old buildings in Bere Regis have survived. However, the present thatched post office, with the thatched butcher's shop next door in the main street were built in the early seventeenth century with cob walls, although these have since been

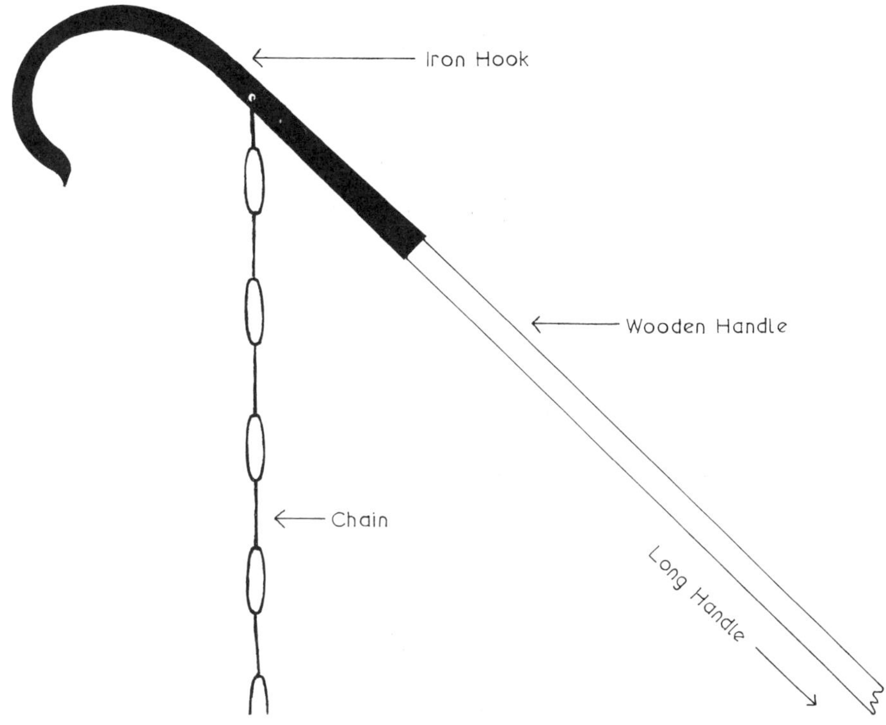

20   *Thatch Fire Hook*

rendered with pebbledash. The present hipped continuous thatched roof over the two shops is made of long straw. There are several other thatched cottages, especially at the eastern end of the village, although at the beginning of this century nearly all the cottages in Bere Regis were thatched. The village has recently regained its former rural peace, as a new bypass diverts the noisy traffic away from the centre.

Just a mile to the east of Bere Regis stands the Iron Age hill-fort of Woodbury Hill. One of the largest fairs in the south of England was formerly held within its ramparts. It was a regular September event for nearly seven hundred years, having first commenced in the thirteenth century but it gradually dwindled in extent and finally ended with a very small fair in 1951. The original fair lasted for five days and each day was known by a different name. There was a Wholesale Day, a Gentle Folks Day, an All Folks Day, a Sheep Fair Day and finally, a Pack and Penny Day. A well-known local saying was that oysters and roast pork came into season on Woodbury Hill Fair Day.

Thomas Hardy featured the fair, which he called Greenhill Fair, in his novel *Far from the Madding Crowd*. A picture exhibited in the County Museum at Dorchester, alongside the Thomas Hardy section, shows the fair with its swings, tents, coconut-shies, roundabouts and

Butcher Shop and Post Office – Bere Regis

Village Street – Milton Abbas

also a few thatched buildings. In the eighteenth century some perma-nent thatched farm cottages and barns were constructed on the site but these have since been demolished.

Many of Dorset's charming thatched villages remain undiscovered by the tourist but a notable exception is the lovely village of Milton Abbas. This attracts many visitors due to its unusual past and its many picturesque thatched cottages, set amidst idyllic surroundings in a wooded valley. Joseph Damer acquired the original Milton Abbas about two hundred years ago and at that time it was a market town with many streets, shops, inns and a brewery. Most of these were gathered on the south side of the Abbey. However, Joseph Damer ordered the buildings to be demolished as he wanted to rebuild his mansion and create a park for himself, where the old town was situated near the Abbey. The monastic buildings escaped destruction and the former Damer mansion built from them is today the famous public school. The thatched house found near the Abbey also escaped being razed to the ground.

The autocratic nature of Joseph Damer was further emphasized when he abolished the grammar school to protect his orchard apples from the boys. The school was moved to Blandford. He also once deliberately opened a sluice-gate to flush out an argumentative lawyer who was opposing his plans. Nevertheless, it took Damer twenty years to acquire all the properties he wanted. Fortunately, Joseph Damer, who became Lord Milton, built a complete new village about a mile away in a steep narrow coombe. It was laid out in 1771–90. It is this splendid wide street of neat thatched cottages that is admired by the many visitors of today. The street, with wide grass verges each side, runs up the hill from an artificial lake created at the bottom. Twenty square thatched cottages, nearly all identical, were built in pairs on each side of the street. Each cottage was divided in order to house two families but many have since been converted to make single detached houses. Originally, a huge chestnut tree grew between each cottage but these were removed in the middle of this century, because their age had made them unsafe. New smaller trees have since been replanted. Each cottage has a back garden that climbs the steep sides of the valley. Many of the cottages still retain their original bread ovens.

In addition to the thatched Hambro Arms in the village, there is also a museum now housed in thatched, eighteenth-century, former stables on the top of the hill. The building, known as the Park Farm Museum, displays rural exhibits to illustrate life on the land in bygone days. In addition to old tools, there are many photographs and documents illustrating the many changes in village life. The museum was formerly located at the bottom of the hill near the pond, together with riding stables. However, this site has been developed to convert the old buildings into several modern thatched cottages which blend in harmony with the rest of the village.

The village of Hilton is close by to Milton Abbas and this small unspoilt place nestles in seclusion at the foot of Bulbarrow Hill. It has many beautiful thatched cottages clustered by the church, with its background of woods and downs. It was formerly part of the Milton Abbey estate, when owned by the wealthy Hambro family. Many of the woodland clumps on the hillside would have been planted as cover to encourage pheasants on the estate. Several of the flint-built cottages in Hilton are thatched with long straw, in contrast to the more commonly used wheat reed at Milton Abbas. The charming single-storeyed cottage, known as Long Thatch, in the heart of the village was built over two hundred years ago and was formerly the old school. It is now a private home.

The village of Cheselbourne hides in a valley just to the south-west of Hilton; several minor roads lead to and from the village, with its narrow curving main street. There is a good sprinkling of thatched cottages, mingling with modern houses, in the village. A variety of wall materials including flint, chalk and brick may be seen blending with the thatch. Wheat reed forms the main thatching material and in former times a pagan custom associated with wheat was held in the surrounding fields. The ceremony known as 'Treading the Wheat', was performed by the girls of the village dressed in white, walking through the fields. The exact reason for the ceremony appears to have been lost in the past.

The Winterborne stream which rises on the slopes of the steep Bulbarrow chalk escarpment in the heart of Dorset gives its name to many villages and hamlets strung along its course, before the stream eventually joins the River Stour. The North Winterborne flows through Winterborne Houghton, Stickland, Clenston, Whitechurch and Kingston before reaching the Winterborne hamlets of Muston, Anderson, Tomson and finally the village of Winterborne Zelston. Many of the houses in these villages and hamlets are thatched.

The Winterborne villages rest in narrow chalk valleys and their apt common name was gained from the intermittent and unreliable nature of the stream which runs through them. It appears mainly in winter time and mostly disappears below the ground surface throughout the summer. There is also another Winterborne chalk stream in Dorset, known as the South Winterborne. This flows, again mostly in the winter, through several villages and hamlets to the south of Dorchester, before it joins the River Frome at West Stafford.

The first village through which the North Winterborne stream travels is Winterborne Houghton. This is a very rural, straggling village but it contains several pretty thatched cottages. Many were built in the eighteenth century with walls of cob, or banded brick and flint, under their thatched roofs. The old rectory garden behind the church still has a thatched wall. The villagers who lived at Houghton were once jokingly known as 'Houghton Owls' because of the unfortunate experience of one of their locals. The story is that he became hopelessly lost at night in the woods and called for help. The only response to his plea was the hooting of owls in the wood, which the poor confused and lost fellow thought were human voices trying to lead him out to safety.

The Winterborne stream from Houghton flows by the side of a winding lane until it reaches the larger village of Winterborne Stickland, about one mile away. This village shelters in a hollow under a tree-clad hill. The way out to the east is fairly steep and the name of Stickland derives from 'Stikel' meaning steep. Many of the cottages in the village are over three hundred years old. Most were built with cob walls under their thatched roofs, but there are also some brick and flint thatched cottages. The village also boasts a thatched inn called 'The Crown'. This is a white-painted, L-shaped building with walls of stone. The thatched roof has a raised pointed ridge and a thatched outbuilding has been retained in the pub's car park.

Many of the thatched cottages possess interesting histories which reflect the various trades and aspects of past village life. One of the thatched cottages known as 'Wheelwrights' is now a private home but, in the past, the three or four-hundred-year-old, cob-built cottage has housed wheelwrights, carpenters, button-makers and has been used as a forge and sawpit. Another interesting thatched building is 'The Old

The Old Malt House – Winterborne Stickland

Malt House' situated just along the road from the rectory. The beautiful thatched roof over the malt-house is decorated with scallops and points. As suggested by the name, the long building constructed of brick and flint about four hundred years ago, was once used as a malt-house. The water for the malting process was obtained by building a dam across the Winterborne stream opposite and diverting the water into storage tanks held in the cellars of 'The Old Malt House'.

The majority of the thatched cottages in Winterborne Stickland are roofed with wheat reed although there are a few thatched with long straw. In addition to the cottages, some with the traditional straw birds perched on their roofs and others with thatched porches, there are several private garages with thatched roofs. Some were purpose built as garages but others are conversions of thatched farm outbuildings present in the village.

Winterborne Clenston lies in a fairly wide section of the chalk valley and it contains many interesting thatched buildings. There are groups of thatched two-storeyed farm cottages with neat pointed raised ridges, nestling close to thatched barns. A large thatched barn also stands by the roadside, built of flint with a brick inlay. The roof has a quarter-hipped end to its thatch. The nearby village of Winterborne Whitechurch has several pretty thatched cottages with brick or rendered walls, whilst the hamlet of Winterborne Muston has a thatched manor house. Winterborne Whitechurch was the birthplace of Samuel Wesley, whose son John became the founder of Methodism. This village also has an unusual field called Round Mead. Local tradition believes it is bewitched and therefore can never be made to yield hay. The reason is thought to be that the field was once reaped on a Sunday and therefore became cursed.

Winterborne Zelston hides down a cul-de-sac and there is a humped-back bridge over the stream in the centre of the picturesque village. There are other bridges further along the stream and the banks bloom with flowers in the summer. The names of some of the thatched cottages hint that water lies close by. There is the beautiful Bridge Cottage with its long thatched roof and porch, with the brook running by its front under the humped-back bridge. The Pond Cottage also stands a little further along the stream and it has an elaborately ornamented raised ridge. The cottage has a splendid catslide roof at one end.

There are many pink or white-washed cottages in the village, most have raised ridges with points but a few exhibit scallops and points. A thatched farm stands in close proximity to the church and an excellent example of a thatched wall, bordering the grounds of a private house, still survives a little way down the road. The thatching of walls was formerly a common practice carried out to protect their tops from the rain and save them from disintegration. This was necessary because

Bridge Cottage – Winterborne Zelston

boundary or farmyard walls were generally built from various unstable mixtures, such as straw and clay or chalk and flints. These were prone to break down under persistently wet or wintry conditions. The fine example of thatch on the wall at Winterborne Zelston is smartly finished with three horizontal liggers, sparred into the thatch along its entire length. At the end of the wall, a raised bonnet of thatch in a conical shape completes the splendid picture.

In the heart of Dorset, between Dorchester and Sherborne, lies one of the county's most well-known villages, Cerne Abbas. The popular attraction which has made the village famous is no doubt the Cerne Giant, carved by removing the turf to expose the white chalk on the steep downs just outside the village. The virile figure is thought very likely to represent the Roman god Hercules and most experts date the 180 foot long giant as 1,800 years old. It is assumed the figure had associations with ancient fertility rites.

The village shelters in the wide valley of the River Cerne and it possesses a large variety of mellowed buildings. Many were built with orange-tinted stone and flint but Georgian brick was also used. A good number of thatched roofs remain and these cover a range of house sizes, from small cottages to substantial homes.

The village stocks are still retained outside the fourteenth-century church in Abbey Street. At the head of this street, beyond the duck

A Thatched Wall – Winterborne Zelston

pond, may be found the remains of the gatehouse and also the guest house of the Benedictine Abbey, which was founded at Cerne Abbas in the late tenth century. The former tithe barn of the Abbey is located at the southern end of the village.

At the bottom end of Abbey Street, in the main thoroughfare, stands the Royal Oak, the thatched pub described in an earlier chapter. Just along the road may be found a former pub called The Old Bell. This also has a thatched roof but it has now become a tea and coffee house. It was built with facing bands of clunch and flint in the seventeenth century. The thatched house adjoining The Old Bell, called Cockers, has an eighteenth-century wing protruding to the rear, making an L-shape.

The Cerne Valley Forge in Duck Street leads to the present craft forge which specializes in ironwork, fire baskets and fire irons, amongst many other items. The Forge Cottage displays scallops and points on the ridge of its attractive thatched roof. There is also a stone with the date 1793 set in the wall and the building formerly served as a village school. Until recently, a thatched butcher's shop stood in Duck Street but it has now been converted into a private home. It is interesting that during the renovation of the roof, roofing felt was laid and battened below the thatch. An unusual marriage of a modern roofing technique with the ancient craft of thatching. Many others of the older thatched cottages in the village have undergone renovation to make them into modern comfortable homes and several possess thatched garages.

Many legends relate to the Cerne Giant and one says he was carved to terrify the villagers of Sydling St Nicholas that lies to the west, on the other side of the hill. Sydling St Nicholas nestles deep in a chalk stream valley, with the hills on either side reaching nearly 700 feet. In numerous places on the surrounding hillsides may be seen the terraced outlines of the ancient Celtic 'lynchet' cultivation system. The long

Cottage in Abbey Street – Cerne Abbas

narrow valley makes the village sprawl and the stream divides as it meanders through it. Because of this, some of the picturesque cottages have to be reached by crossing tiny foot-bridges. There are many different types of thatched cottages, some of yellowstone and flint, others with mixed banding of these materials. Pretty, brick-built, thatched cottages also abound, together with others of cob and chalk ashlar.

As the name of the village suggests, there is a church of St Nicholas and in the past the St Nicholas Fair was an annual village event held on the 6 December. The stone and flint tithe barn, which is well concealed near the churchyard, possessed a thatched roof for most of its lifetime but unfortunately, for many years now, the thatch has been replaced by less attractive corrugated material.

Cattistock, to the west of Sydling St Nicholas, is perhaps most noted for its famous hunt and fox hounds. A former parson founded the hunt after he had established a pack of hounds. However, in addition to the church and nearby pub, the large village contains a fair number of attractive thatched cottages. Nearly all of these are thatched with combed wheat reed. There are many farms in the close vicinity and a few thatched barns built in the seventeenth century still survive. Flint and clunch, obtained from the chalk, were the commonly used wall materials. The nearby village of Chilfrome also contains one or two very attractive thatched cottages.

The River Frome, after leaving Cattistock, runs on to the large village of Maiden Newton. The main stream of the Hooke joins the Frome here and makes it a more sizeable river. There are several thatched cottages in the village and the River Frome then flows on past Notton, which has some pleasing thatch, before reaching the most attractive village of Frampton.

The miscellany of thatched cottages, that line the single side of the long main street of Frampton, adds much charm to this very old village, where many Roman remains, including tessellated pavements, have been found. Until about 1840, there were also cottages on the other side of the road but the lord of the manor decided to demolish them, to enable trees to be planted on the edge of his park estate. The river meanders by on this side of the road behind the bordering wall. The village was formerly associated with the estate of Frampton Court but the huge mansion in the park was demolished during the first half of this century. In the nineteenth century, it was lived in by the dramatist Sheridan and his family who, incidentally, framed the game laws relating to English field sports.

Most of the thatched cottages in Frampton are furnished with combed wheat reed roofs and several have raised ridges with points. A number also possess thatched porches. One or two thatched guest-

Wessex Barn Guest-House – Frampton

houses have sprung up along the main street in recent years and the largest of these is the Wessex Barn Guest-House. A fine expanse of thatch covers the building and it displays dormer windows and a thatched porch. As the name suggests, the building was once a barn, but it later became The Red Lion Coaching Inn and then five thatched tenements when it was sold in the early 1930s.

Another thatched building, with an interesting and varied history, is that opposite the turning to Southover in the village. The thatched building, now in the form of three dwellings with separate porches, was originally constructed as the village schoolroom. It later became the village institute and was once utilized as the local police station.

Southover lies just on the other side of the river to Frampton and adjoins Frampton Park. A picturesque timber-railed humped-back bridge leads to Southover over the River Frome. Beehives are kept in the field near the timber bridge and the nearby Frampton Park has classic stone bridges to remind one of the former wealth of the estate. There are several delightful stone-built wheat reed thatched cottages in Southover. Also, next to Southover Farm stands Southover House and this boasts a huge and impressive area of thatch. The stone-built L-plan house has a straight thatched ridge with gabled ends but there is an extension to the building at a lower level with a hipped thatched roof. The main gate to the grounds has stone finials and the house has a pillared porch. The building overlooks green farmland and the trees of the nearby former estate park.

The Frome wanders on to the village of Stratton, just to the north-

Southover House – Southover, near Frampton

Terrace of Cottages – Charminster

west of Dorchester. The village contains several modern homes due to its nearness of the county town but it has retained many of its old thatched cottages. Most of these have flint coursed walls, under their roofs of combed wheat reed. There are a variety of thatched buildings, including single-storeyed and two-storeyed cottages, some with gabled and others with hipped thatched roofs. There are also thatched farm buildings, as well as an impressive eighteenth-century thatched barn of stone and flint in the centre of the village. Stratton was one of the very last manors in Dorset to retain an open-field arable system, which explains the presence of the many farm buildings in the centre of the village.

Charminster lies even closer to Dorchester and it is located above the southern end of the Cerne River, which joins the Frome below the village. This watery encounter has been made to yield a lush area of water-meadows before the river flows on to Dorchester. On its journey, it passes by a beautifully thatched mill at Burton.

Like Stratton, Charminster possesses many modern houses but the older part of the village has retained several of its delightful thatched cottages. Again, most are thatched with wheat reed. One spacious picturesque home along East Hill Road has a hipped thatched roof and a separate thatched porch shelters the doorway. Nearby in the village, there is a very well-maintained row of thatched cottages, some with walls of banded flint. The neat thatch sweeps up and down around the upper storey windows of the cottages. In the summer, many of the owners adorn the fronts of their cottage walls with hanging baskets and tubs of flowers.

8

Thatched Villages of North Dorset

Several attractive villages stand on the uppermost reaches of the River Stour, Dorset's largest river. The river drains North Dorset and runs over seventy miles from its source at Stourhead, until it ends its journey in the sea at Christchurch. One of these northern villages is Stour Provost and its centre presents a delightful picture with many colour-washed stone cottages spread along its crossroads. Fortunately, two of these roads are cul-de-sacs and this helps the village to escape serious traffic problems. Some of the cottages date from the seventeenth century, when they were built with stone rubble walls under thatched roofs, and a few were made just one storey high with attics below the thatch. There are also several eighteenth-century and early nineteenth-century cottages and again these were constructed with stone and roofed with thatch, but most of them were given two storeys.

One of these thatched cottages, built in the early eighteenth century, later became known as Mundays Cottage. An interesting note in the Parish records dated 17 October 1797, states that 'At a Vestry the Overseers agreed to fit up a house now called Mundays for the benefit of Poor Orphan Children and other poor of the said Parish'. The thatched cottage is now a private home.

Several methods were adopted in Dorset to try and relieve, to some small extent, the misery of the many poor. These ranged from occasional help, such as the vicar giving away every Christmas, a pound of bread, some mince pies and a pint of ale to each individual poor member of the parish, to more substantial, longer term assistance. In the latter case, several so-called 'charity farms' were purchased by donation from various benefactors and the rents obtained from leasing the farms were used to assist the poor. Occasionally, the money was employed to allow a child of a poor family to take up an apprenticeship. A particular craft was sometimes defined, or there may have been a firm stipulation that the boy should not be sent to sea. Most of these 'charity farms' in Dorset have now been sold and the money realized placed in trust for their designated charity.

The village of Fifehead Magdalen lies on the other side of the Stour to Stour Provost and well above the river level. Again the majority of the thatched cottages here were built with stone in the seventeenth century.

The thatched vicarage, about three hundred yards from the church, also originated from this period but it was much enlarged in the eighteenth century. In addition, Fifehead Magdalen claims a thatched property built of stone, as an open hall house, in about 1550. The building is now a modernized two-storeyed home and the present thatched roof displays a smart raised ridge with points. There is one gabled and one hipped end to the roof.

The village of Marnhull is situated to the south of Fifehead Magdalen and about three miles from Sturminster Newton. The Crown Hotel in Marnhull is partly thatched and as mentioned in an earlier chapter, Thomas Hardy called it 'The Pure Drop Inn' of 'Marlott' in his *Tess of the d'Urbervilles*. Many of the thatched cottages in the vicinity of Marnhull are built with local yellow-coloured stone, obtained from the nearby quarries.

A thatched cottage of particular interest, known as Tess Cottage, stands about one mile outside of Marnhull, down a narrow, no-through lane. Tess Cottage is thought by some to be the original Durbeyfields home and to be the birthplace of Tess, Hardy's beautiful but ill-fated heroine. The pretty white-washed thatched cottage may be found by bearing left at the church, upon leaving the village and then travelling for approximately one mile, until a lay-by with a postbox is reached on

Solicitor's Office – Sturminster Newton

the left-hand side of the road. The cottage may be glimpsed from here, as it is situated just across the road, down the lane. It is a private residence and therefore not open to the public.

Sturminster Newton rests on the upper reaches of the River Stour, at the edge of the Blackmore Vale, or Hardy's 'Vale of the Little Dairies'. Thomas Hardy lived in the small bustling market town for two years, while writing *The Return of the Native* and by coincidence it was also the birthplace of the dialect poet William Barnes, who later attended the school near the church. Although Sturminster Newton has always been deeply associated with agriculture, it was once a cloth making centre as well. It also has a seventeenth-century mill, which was restored to full working order in 1981. The watermill produces both wholemeal flour and animal feed and it is leased to a tenant miller.

Sturminster Newton retains many old quaint houses threaded along its streets and several of these are thatched buildings. Cob, stone and brick have all been used over the centuries. Some of the walls exhibit exposed Tudor style timbering, including the thatched building which is now a solicitor's office, situated in the market-place opposite the thatched pub, The White Hart. The thatched solicitor's office has an attractive dormer window in the thatch and the main roof ridge is well decorated with points. On market days, colourful stalls stand outside it in the main street and in the nearby square.

A fine six arch bridge, dating from about 1500, spans the River Stour and leads from Sturminster on the north side, to the charming village of Newton, just the other side of the river to the south. One of the famous Dorset 'Transportation' signs appears on the bridge. It reads as follows:-

DORSET
Any person wilfully INJURING
any part of this COUNTY BRIDGE
WILL BE GUILTY OF FELONY AND
UPON CONVICTION LIABLE TO BE
TRANSPORTED FOR LIFE
BY THE COURT
T FOOKS

These notices, made in cast iron, were fixed on many other bridges in the county but they were not solely directed to vandals who maliciously set out to damage the structure. The warning also applied to any accidental injury to a bridge, such as that caused by an overladen cart. In addition to the transportation sentence, the Act of Parliament under which the notice was erected, also empowered the court to have the offender publicly whipped. Such notices were still being fixed to Dorset's bridges only 150 years ago.

Immediately over the Sturminster Newton Bridge, in Newton, stands the thatched pub called The Bull. Just along the main road from the pub are several other delightful thatched cottages and houses. Their ages generally range from the seventeenth to the nineteenth century but most are Georgian. They make a splendid display, with their well-kept gardens and several have attractive thatched porches.

One of the larger picturesque thatched houses in Newton, known as Barton House, claims a history which traces back to the fifteenth century. In medieval times, the Abbots of Glastonbury owned the house and it was used by the monks. Incidentally, the connection with Glastonbury Abbey was the origin of the word 'minster' in Sturminster Newton. Henry VIII later seized Barton House and gave it to Catherine Parr. Elizabeth I subsequently donated it to Lord Rivers. It is also reputed that the Tolpuddle Martyrs held clandestine meetings in the house and there is evidence that the premises once had a secret room below the thatched roof.

The present beautiful thatched roof has eaves which steeply undulate around the many upstairs windows and these are fitted with leaded lights. A thatched porch shelters the front door by the main road. One end of the roof is gabled but there is also a quarter-hipped end on

Barton House – Newton

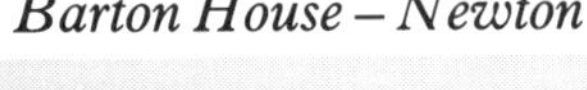

another section of the house. The stone walls under the thatch possess some exposed and elaborate Tudor style timbering.

After leaving Sturminster Newton, the River Stour winds its way downstream to the hamlet of Fiddleford. This boasts a restored mill dating back to 1566 and the house attached to it can trace its origins back to the fourteenth century. The presence of watermills along the river demonstrates that the Stour was used to provide energy, as well as donate beauty to the surrounding countryside.

Fiddleford contains several picturesque cottages and in bygone days the hamlet was much favoured by smugglers as a distribution centre. About a quarter of a mile away from Fiddleford Mill stands a delightful thatched house, known as Little Brook. The beautiful and colourful cottage garden of the house is open to the public, from April to October. The garden was created from a hayfield in 1977 and now displays flowering cherries, spring bulbs, roses and delphiniums.

The River Stour flows on past the villages of Childe Okeford and Shillingstone, although both are set well away from the river, due to its unfortunate reputation for flooding after heavy rain. Hambledon Hill, a neolithic camp and Iron Age hill-fort, towers behind Childe Okeford and magnificent views of the Blackmore Vale may be viewed from its top. There are many good examples of thatch to be found in both Childe Okeford and Shillingstone, with cottage walls built from a variety of constructional materials. This also applies to the other nearby village of Okeford Fitzpaine. A thatched garden wall may be seen in Shillingstone and it is interesting that this village was previously called Shilling Okeford, thus making the third village containing the name Okeford. The 'Shilling' was derived from the Saxon tribal name, 'Eschillingas'.

Okeford Fitzpaine is perhaps the most picturesque of the Okeford villages, with its collection of thatched cottages, farms and well-kept gardens. Several of the thatched cottages are built along a raised walk, above the main road which passes through the village. The walls of some of these show alternating bands of brick and flint.

The old thatched farmhouse, on the opposite side of the road to the raised walk, exhibits a complex mixture of stone, flint, brick and timber-framing in its walls. The timbered section, with brick in-filling, probably dates to the early sixteenth century because the interior of the house was also built with a cross-passage and hall. The stone and flint wings were seventeenth-century additions, when the stone mullioned windows were also incorporated.

To the south of the village rests the Okeford Hill picnic site that extends over an area in excess of nineteen acres. A short walk along the ridgeway from here leads to an area of mixed downland and woodland, with commanding views over the Blackmore Vale.

Another superb view over the Vale may be obtained from Ibberton

Church, which must be one of the most attractively situated in the county. The church stands about halfway up a steep hill and the village itself is located on the northern slopes of Bulbarrow Hill, to the south-west of Okeford Fitzpaine. Few tourists manage to find Ibberton and the small village therefore retains its peace and solitude. The thatched cottages in the village are perched on the hill and most are thatched with wheat reed. Some display timber traceries on their walls.

The villages of Durweston and Stourpaine sit close together to the north-west of Blandford Forum. Both are located in the Stour Valley but on opposite sides of the river. They retain a few thatched cottages, although in the past Durweston contained many more built of brick, flint and stone. There are both pretty single-storeyed and two-storeyed thatched cottages. Many of the villagers, at the beginning of this century, worked on the nearby Portman estate at Bryanston. In those days, a large herd of deer was kept in the grounds of the house, built for Viscount Portman during the latter part of the nineteenth century. The house was converted in 1927 to the famous public school.

The estate workers were formerly allowed to pick up acorns and conkers in the park, for which they were paid two shillings a sack, as winter food for the deer. In those days many of the estate workers also kept bees in their gardens and these were encouraged to build their comb in any suitable container or box. A strange custom, known as 'Telling the Bees', was often carried out by the cottagers when a death occurred in the family. The top of the hive was covered with black crêpe and gently tapped. The bees were then told that grandma or grandfer had passed on. It was believed that if this ritual was not followed then the bees would die, or at least desert the hive.

The neighbouring village of Stourpaine has preserved some neatly thatched cottages and the occasional home may be found which is partly thatched and tiled. Stourpaine nestles between Hambledon Hill and Hod Hill, another of Dorset's major hill-forts.

Groups of villages containing a common name are frequently encountered in Dorset and the name is usually that of the river or stream that runs through them. There are several Caundle villages and hamlets, notably Purse Caundle, Stourton Caundle, Bishops Caundle, Caundle Marsh and Caundle Wake, all located in a small region to the east of Sherborne. The Caundle brook meanders close by on its way to the River Stour. Many of these villages contain delightful mellow stone built cottages, roofed with thatch. In addition, Bishops Caundle possesses one large and beautiful thatched house which dates from the sixteenth century. The thatched house, known as The Orchard, is set in its own extensive grounds on the edge of the village. The interior of the house claims an original plank and muntin wall in the entrance hall and few of these have survived to modern times. Incidentally, it is perhaps of interest that Stourton Caundle in the nineteenth century devised a most admirable motto, 'May we all strive like bees of a hive and never sting each other'.

Another group of three villages, with a common name, are the Iwerne villages. These are situated east of Sturminster Newton and lie along or just off the road from Blandford Forum to Shaftesbury. There is an Iwerne Minster, an Iwerne Courtney (Shroton) and an Iwerne Stepleton. The Iwerne stream rises near to Iwerne Minster and gives its name to the two other villages. Although Iwerne Minster has several charming thatched cottages, Iwerne Courtney possesses a wider array of thatched buildings. In addition to the massive towering thatched barn by the church, there are many thatched cottages. The majority are roofed with wheat reed and ridges decorated with scallops and points are chiefly favoured. The village post office is thatched and a separate bonnet of thatch sits on top of the square bay window at its front.

Iwerne Courtney has two substantial houses built in the eighteenth century, known as Shroton House and Ranston, although neither is thatched. The alternative village name of Shroton arose because the Sheriff held the manor at the time of the Domesday. As mentioned earlier, Shroton derives from Sheriff's town. The town was famous in the past for its Shroton Fair which rivalled that held at Woodbury Hill, near Bere Regis. Shroton Fair is no longer in existence but it survived for many centuries, always being held during the last week of September. Farm produce from the Blackmore Vale was sold at the large fair, together with many horses and cattle.

A village with the charming name of Fontmell Magna also rests along the road from Blandford Forum to Shaftesbury but a little to the north of the Iwerne villages. Fontmell Magna stands at the foot of a chalk escarpment and many springs arise in the area, including the Fontmell Brook which flows directly southwards towards the River Stour. The abundance and purity of the water in the region were once of paramount importance to the brewery that formerly thrived here. It is now dismantled but a potteries industry has arisen in its place. The village also has an early nineteenth-century mill which has now been converted to a craft pottery.

Fontmell Magna offers many attractive thatched cottages and farmhouses, mingling with larger stone-roofed Victorian houses. The many excellent examples of ornamented thatch, in the large and rather sprawling village, shield several buildings which were first erected in the seventeenth century but a few still survive that are a century older. The thatched roofs on these more ancient buildings are supported by cruck trusses and the walls have timber framework. Several of the thatched cottages have just the one storey but most of these have dormer windows peeping through the thatch. Both wheat reed and long straw roofs may be viewed and several display scallops and points.

A range of wall materials may be seen, in addition to a little herring-bone brickwork encased in timber framing. Many of the thatched cottages were originally built of ashlar and stone rubble but sometimes the stone became topped with brickwork when the walls were later heightened to create extra space. For many years, the former village water supply, the old pump house, has had a thatched shelter over it; the conical shaped thatched canopy is supported by stout vertical timbers.

The village of Ashmore lies just to the east of Fontmell Magna. It is also near to Tollard Royal, the place where King John once used the hunting lodge for his excursions on Cranborne Chase. The lodge, called King John's House, can still be viewed from the churchyard. In King John's time, at the end of the twelfth century, the lord of the Chase had the right to hunt game over the whole Chase area. This vast tract of land, populated with deer, was bordered by Wimborne, Blandford Forum, Shaftesbury, Salisbury and Ringwood. It therefore spilled outside of Dorset into Wiltshire and Hampshire.

The Chase village of Ashmore offers a special attraction because its thatched cottages may be viewed across its very large pond which reputedly never dries up. The pond forms a haven for all types of wildfowl and ducks but is unusual as it exists in the centre of Dorset's highest village. In fact, Ashmore stands on chalk over 700 feet above sea level and on clear days the Isle of Wight may even be glimpsed. The pond was no doubt the reason why early pre-Roman settlers favoured the site of the village. When the Domesday Book was compiled it was called Aisemare, meaning 'ash-mere' – the pond where ash trees grow.

The pond varies in depth but is often sixteen feet deep in the centre. The shape is circular and it measures about forty yards in diameter. An annual event, called 'Filly Loo' has been held in the village for many years, no doubt to celebrate the presence of the pond but the exact reason appears to be lost in the past. The festivities, always held on the third Friday evening in June, include Morris Dancers performing at the pond's edge to music played by a band of three to five musicians on a decorated farm-cart; the makeshift bandstand having first been pushed into the pond. The celebrations culminate in a torchlight procession.

The thatched cottages situated near the pond were mostly built in the seventeenth century of one storey but with attics below the thatch. They are thatched with wheat reed and several possess new raised ridges with points. The walls are mainly constructed of alternating bands of flint and stone rubble. In addition, there are other thatched cottages erected in the early nineteenth century but these were constructed with two storeys. Some brickwork was also incorporated in their wall structure, together with the stone and flint.

Cottage by Pond – Ashmore

There have been reports of ghostly figures being seen near the pond in the past. One man claimed that in broad daylight and in a dead sober condition, he saw a procession of horses and men, all cloaked in medieval dress. The horses were saddled with regal splendour and one of the men appeared to be a king. On a different day, a lady confirmed that she had witnessed the same sight.

Sixpenny Handley is another Chase village, located to the east of Ashmore. Its fascinating name came about by the amalgamation of two ancient hundreds in the fourteenth century; namely Saxpena, The Hill of the Saxons and Hanlega, meaning High Pastures. Some of the sign posts in the area amusingly mark the village as '6d Handley'. The 6d symbol, of course, representing the old-fashioned sixpence. The houses in the village were once mainly thatched, until a terrible fire destroyed nearly all of them in 1892. The fire was accidentally started by sparks carried in the wind from a wheelwright's fire, as he was bonding wheels in the village. The sparks flew to the roof of a nearby shed which had been thatched with heather. The thatch was tinder dry and the wind blowing that day soon carried the burning heather, in a shower of sparks, to other thatched roofs. Most of the men of the village were unfortunately away working in the fields on that fateful day and so little could be done to save the destruction of the thatched cottages. About one hundred people were left homeless.

The rebuilt village of Sixpenny Handley therefore contains few really old buildings but the occasional thatched roof may still be spotted in the near locality, towards Gussage St Andrew and Minchington in the same parish. The notorious smuggler Isaac Gulliver was married in the church of Sixpenny Handley in 1768 and the church register records the fact. He married a local landlord's daughter and used the pub as the headquarters for his vast smuggling operations. Poachers also resided in the village. The tombstone by the north wall of the churchyard covers the hollow tomb formerly used by them to hide deer carcasses when they were being chased by the keepers of the Chase.

The village of Pimperne is situated about two miles north-east of Blandford Forum, on the road to Salisbury. During Henry VIII's reign, the main manor here was given by him to Catherine Howard and later to Catherine Parr. In Elizabeth I's reign, it was granted to John Crooke and later to John Ryves. During this period of history, there was a Queen's Walk at Pimperne and a maze. Also, at this time, a thatched Elizabethan farmhouse was built at Pimperne which is now known as The Anvil, the only restaurant between Blandford Forum and Salisbury.

For many years, it was thought that the property was most likely of eighteenth-century origin, built as four separate cob-walled thatched cottages. The four cottages were single-storeyed, with dormer windows in the attics below the thatch. However, during extensive restoration work carried out in 1958 when the cottages were combined, the original roof-line was disclosed and the property in its present integrated form is now thought to represent the actual Elizabethan farmhouse. If this is correct then the farmhouse, together with the manor house, were at that time the only two buildings standing between Blandford Forum and Salisbury.

The beautiful thatched roof on The Anvil is richly decorated with scallops and points. It consists of wheat reed. The name The Anvil came about because of the forge that stands a few yards along the road. The interior of the restaurant and hotel has retained many of its original roughly hewn beams, together with several open fireplaces, complete with their timber bressummers. The pretty front garden has a magnificent weeping willow, no doubt watered by the underground stream which flows beneath the front tarmac. The stream which runs through Pimperne becomes very low in the summer months, just like many others that flow through the villages of North Dorset. However, local farmers suggest that the total quantity of water seems drastically reduced in recent years and hint that this may be due to the heavy extraction of water from boreholes, near Blandford Forum.

The small Cranborne Chase village of Farnham lies close to the road between Blandford Forum and Salisbury. The name of the village formerly became well-known because of its unusual museum, which several years ago displayed the archaeological finds of General Pitt-Rivers. The museum no longer exists and the many exhibits, found in the Cranborne Chase, have been dispersed to the Salisbury Museum in Cathedral Close and the Pitt-Rivers Museum at Oxford. The village of Farnham now attracts fewer visitors, so fewer people now see the long main street sprinkled with thatched cottages. The majority of these white-washed cottages face end-on to the street. Many of the thatched cottages were built in the eighteenth century, with walls of flint, stone rubble or cob. There are also one or two older thatched cottages that may date back to the sixteenth century. As mentioned in an earlier chapter, The Museum Hotel of Farnham is also thatched.

The historic town of Shaftesbury, to the north of Cranborne Chase, has gained recent publicity through the land via the medium of television. Most homes in the country have seen the well-known Hovis bread company advertisement, featuring the boy wearily climbing up one of Shaftesbury's steep hills, known as Gold Hill. The cobbled lane up the picturesque hill is lined with delightful old mellowed houses, including two with thatched roofs. These were built during the seventeenth century with walls of stone rubble. It is possible that the two thatched cottages may have originally been roofed with tiles or stone-slates, rather than thatch. There is evidence that at some stage the walls were heightened so that a steeper pitched roof could be obtained to accommodate the present thatched one over the cottages. The top of Gold Hill gives magnificent views over the Blackmore Vale, as Shaftesbury is Dorset's only hilltop town. For this reason it is much visited and Gold Hill is one of the most commonly photographed locations in Dorset.

The spectacular high stone buttressed wall, on the opposite side of the road to the cottages, was constructed during the late fourteenth or early fifteenth century. It marked the boundary of the land belonging to

Thatch at Gold Hill – Shaftesbury

the Great Abbey which was once the richest in the region. In addition to the Abbey, Shaftesbury also had eleven churches. The old Saxon name of the town was Shaston and this still lives on in the novels of Thomas Hardy. There are other thatched cottages to be found in Shaftesbury besides those on Gold Hill. Several seventeenth-, eighteenth- and early nineteenth-century cottages, built with stone rubble walls under their thatched roofs, are dispersed along various other streets of the town.

The village of Motcombe, just to the north of Shaftesbury, also has several eighteenth-century thatched cottages, again most of them constructed with stone rubble walls. Several show neat raised ridges on their gabled roofs and most of the cottages in the centre of the village hide behind long front gardens. The base of an old preaching cross remains near the church. These crosses were formerly erected on sites for worship before a church was built.

Another village in North Dorset, Bradford Abbas, has gained a little limelight in the past by advertisements based on some of its inhabitants. As long ago as 1934, British Movietone News made a documentary film depicting country village life and selected several of the older residents of Bradford Abbas to feature in it. 'The Lads of the Village', as they became known, had ages in the range of eighty-one to ninety. Most of the 'lads' possessed long white beards, wore hats, carried sticks and the leader of the group of five was a gentleman called Thomas Coombs. Later the Dorchester brewery, Eldridge Pope, decided to renew the theme and used pictures of the 'lads', each with a pint of beer in front of him, in their advertisements. The local village pub, The Rose and Crown, has an original photograph of the 'lads' hanging in the bar. The Rose and Crown was formerly used as a rest-house for the monks of Sherborne Abbey, in the fifteenth century. The Abbots owned the village and hence the word Abbas in the village name.

The pub is not thatched but there are some beautiful thatched cottages nearby. A straw fox and a perched straw bird may be spotted on one of the thatched roofs. Many of the pretty cottages were built with yellow-tinged Ham stone, obtained from the quarries a short distance over the border in Somerset. There is a delightful row of old thatched cottages in North Street and some of these have thatched porches. Just outside Bradford Abbas, on the road to Yetminster, a small stone-built thatched field barn still survives and stores animal feedstuff.

Another village to the south of Bradford Abbas also derives its name from an earlier religious connection. This is the small settlement of Hermitage which was an Augustinian hermitage until the fifteenth century. The village has several thatched cottages, mingling with farmhouses close to the church.

9

Thatched Villages of South Dorset

The Isle of Portland constitutes the most southerly region of Dorset. The huge mass of almost treeless limestone rises up to about five hundred feet above the sea at its highest point. Thomas Hardy called Portland 'The Gibraltar of Wessex' and it also became his 'Isle of Slingers', no doubt due to the former reputation of its inhabitants for their prowess with the sling, using ammunition gathered from the nearby Chesil Beach. The pebbles vary in size from several inches across at Portland, to fine shingle at the other end of the eighteen-mile long beach at West Bay. Fishermen used to claim they knew their whereabouts on the beach at night by feeling the size of the pebbles.

In his novel, *The Well Beloved*, the heroine Thomas Hardy named Avice, lived in a thatched cottage. The cottage, known as Avice's Cottage, still stands but it has been converted, together with an adjacent cottage, to form the Portland Museum. The two cottages, 217 Wakeham and Avice's were built of stone in 1640. The buildings stand on the corner of Church Ope Road, near The Pennsylvania Castle Hotel, at the top of the path that leads down to the island's only peaceful cove and beach. This lies about half-way along the east coast of the island. The museum was opened in 1930, after the cottages had been renovated and converted for this specific purpose by public subscription. The cottages and their grounds were donated to Portland by Dr Marie Stopes who lived on the island for many years. The museum exhibits local relics, including many fossils and giant ammonites found in the old quarries of Portland. The original light-turning mechanism installed in Portland Lighthouse is also featured, together with many items associated with the former harsh convict prison on the island. Convict labour from the prison was largely responsible for the building of the massive breakwaters that enclose the naval harbour. The work was carried out between 1894 and 1905.

The present thatched roof on the museum has a flat ridge and the whole surface is wired-in with netting. Hardly any thatched roofs now remain on Portland but at one time there were a fair number, despite the island's exposed position and the likelihood of gale force winds. However, as in Cornwall, the thatched roofs were not usually found in village locations facing south westwards, where they would have been

Museum and Avice's Cottage – Wakeham, Portland

exposed to the severest of the weather. In fact, the locations of the villages on Portland were first dictated by the need for fresh water and most were clustered around wells. This is shown in many of their present names, such as Fortuneswell, Maidenwell, Chiswell and Southwell.

At one time, the Chesil Beach formed the only link between the island and the mainland but the Fleet Lagoon was bridged in the nineteenth century to join Portland with Wyke Regis and the suburbs of the seaside town of Weymouth. The rather uninspiring village of Chickerell is situated about three miles to the west of Weymouth but it contains several thatched cottages built in the early nineteenth century. There are also some that date back to the seventeenth century and one of these has stone mullioned windows. The old thatched cottages are mostly built with stone rubble walls.

The more appealing village of Radipole lies east of Chickerell and about two miles to the north of Weymouth. The River Wey, from which Weymouth takes its name, has an outflow at Radipole and forms the well-known lake. In 1983 a new information centre was opened for the Royal Society for the Protection of Birds on the edge of Radipole Lake. The single-storeyed building was furnished with a thatched roof, so that it would blend well with its natural waterside surroundings. The hipped thatched roof is topped with a raised ridge cut with ornamental points. The new building forms part of the general improvement plan to allow visitors to the lake to enjoy more easily the bird sanctuary and scenery to be found there.

There are other thatched buildings to be seen in the heart of Radipole village. Some have impressive elevations of Portland stone under their thatched roofs of Radipole reed, cut from the local reed beds. A thatched shelter and a separate thatched garage may also be spotted in the grounds of one of the larger thatched residences. The pretty thatched houses are mainly single-storeyed but with dormer window attics below their main thatched roofs. A narrow winding road twists between the thatched cottages in the village and the eaves of the thatch

Information centre (RSPB) – Radipole Lake

are sometimes threatened by passing lorries. One cottage in particular is perilously close to the bend of the road. This picturesque cottage, known as Letterbox Cottage, is thought to be about three hundred and fifty years old. The long thatched detached building boasts three staircases and two inglenook fireplaces and this suggests it was originally in the form of two or three separate cottages.

The village of Preston is now nearly linked to Weymouth and Melcombe Regis, due to the expanding suburbs of the seaside town. There are many modern houses in Preston but a few old thatched roof cottages still survive to mingle with the new. However, there is something much older in Preston because the stone foundations of a small Romano-Celtic temple are preserved on Jordan Hill.

Thatched Manor Farm, with its thatched porch may be found just along the main street of the village and behind it lays a modern holiday park. Some delightful gabled roof thatched cottages may be seen alongside Preston Post Office, which itself is also thatched. The outbuilding of the post office is not thatched although it is thought that it was formerly covered with reed.

Most of the thatched cottages were probably built during the eighteenth century and all possess beautiful orange-tinged stone walls. Preston Post Office bears a scratch stone at its side with the date 1715 but over the door a plate states the date 1747. The latter is probably a marriage plate. The fixing of these was once quite common. The stone walls of the post office are about two feet thick and the interior still guards its original brick-lined and domed bread oven. Such domed ovens are now quite unique.

The main roof of the post office is thatched with wheat reed and it bears a splendid raised ridge. This is elaborately ornamented with points and a large scallop-like shape, terminating in a point. The whole ridge is richly decorated with liggers, spars and cross-slats. Similarly ornamented ridges may be seen on several other thatched roofs in Dorset, all obviously bear the artistic mark of the same thatcher.

Sutton Poyntz snuggles close to Preston on the outskirts of Weymouth. Without doubt, this village is one of South Dorset's most outstanding beauty spots, with its enchanting thatched cottages and willow trees overhanging the peaceful duck pond. The surrounding hills shelter the village and several springs gush out of them, culminating in the beautiful springhead, with the old thatched cottages by its side.

Both old and relatively new thatched cottages mix happily together in Sutton Poyntz. One of the delightful thatched cottages in the centre is named Bellamy Cottage and what is now the thatched garage of the cottage was formerly used, over one hundred years ago, by the village blacksmith. Some of the thatched cottages in the village were built in

Post Office – Preston, near Weymouth

Cottage by Waterside – Sutton Poyntz

Cottage – Sutton Poyntz

Terrace of Cottages – Sutton Poyntz

the 1930s with grey Portland stone rubble under their thatched roofs. It is perhaps of interest that the architect of these twentieth-century thatched village properties also designed the New Victoria Cinema in London. Some thatched cottages on the hillside were built around the same period with brick and their south-facing location gives them excellent views of the sea at nearby Bowleaze Cove.

Thomas Hardy called Sutton Poyntz 'Overcombe' in his novel *The Trumpet Major* and frequently featured the village in his story. Sutton Poyntz rests in a lovely hollow in the Downs and on the side of one hillside about a mile away may be seen the giant figure of a horse and rider. This depiction of King George III on his charger was carved in 1808 by removing the turf from the hillside until the chalk of the subsoil was exposed. The figure, known as the Osmington White Horse, measures 323 feet high and 280 feet long.

The rear of the horse faces Weymouth and local legend suggests this was because the monarch turned his back on the town and he was never to return. King George III had earlier patronized Weymouth for many years and even swam in the sea there. He also frequently visited the village of Upwey, to the north of Weymouth, to sample the water from the romantic wishing well at the far end of the village. Incidentally, the gold cup he drank from at the well eventually became the original Gold Cup, presented by his successors, for the winner of the famous Royal Ascot horse-race. Upwey has preserved several of its thatched stone cottages, mainly built in the eighteenth and early nineteenth centuries.

The village of Osmington nestles amongst the Downs close to Sutton Poyntz. Its pretty thatched stone cottages and farms were built several centuries ago, in what was then a quiet dell. Some date from the seventeenth century but others were constructed later, in the late eighteenth or early nineteenth centuries. Most are thatched with wheat reed and one or two possess conical shaped thatched roof porches. As mentioned in an earlier chapter, a thatched bus shelter stands by the roadside outside the magnificently thatched East Farm.

The nearby hamlet of Osmington Mills also has some quaint thatched cottages, in addition to the eye-catching Smugglers Inn with its thatched roof. Constable spent his honeymoon at the vicarage in Osmington, as a guest of Archdeacon John Fisher. Whilst visiting Osmington Mills, he painted a picture of a distant view of Weymouth Bay. This now hangs in the National Gallery. A good vantage point to enjoy the view towards Weymouth is from the path leading down to the seashore. A delightful white painted stone-walled thatched cottage borders the stony path and a stream runs nearby on its journey to the sea. The thatched cottage stands only about a hundred yards away from Smugglers Inn and the same stream passes through the grounds of the pub.

A little inland from the coast, to the north-east of Osmington, may be found several other lovely villages. The small village of Owermoigne has many charming thatched cottages near the church. The majority of these were built in the eighteenth or nineteenth centuries with walls of cob or stone rubble below their thatched roofs. However, a couple of picture postcard thatched cottages by the stream are thought to date back to the late seventeenth century and the reign of William and Mary. However, Owermoigne is perhaps better known for its Moigne Court, situated a short distance away to the north of the village. This is a thirteenth-century moated house but it is roofed with slates.

Winfrith Newburgh is well known because of the Atomic Energy Establishment, located nearby on Winfrith Heath. Nevertheless, the village has managed to preserve much of its former charm and this includes many old but tastefully modernized thatched cottages. Most were originally built of cob but brick and stone rubble were also used. One of the thatched cottages is known to contain an intriguing concealed passage behind a bookcase, which leads to the present study of the house. The neighbouring village of East Knighton also has some quality thatched homes, including some modern built ones furnished with thatched roofs. Some have separate little bonnets of thatch shielding their bow windows.

To the east of Winfrith, across the heath, may be found the small village of Coombe Keynes. An ancient church, parts of which date back to the thirteenth century, is situated half-way up the hill on the south side. There are also several old thatched cottages and converted farm buildings and these range in ages from the seventeenth to the nineteenth centuries, when they were mostly constructed of cob. Nearby is the small triangular green.

The twin villages of East and West Lulworth lie to the south of Coombe Keynes. West Lulworth is especially popular with holiday visitors because of its proximity to the well-known Lulworth Cove. The beautiful circular cove, surrounded by its cliffs but open to the sea through a gap, was formerly much used by smugglers. It is the same cove that Thomas Hardy called Lulstead Cove and from which Troy swam out in *Far From the Madding Crowd*. Lulworth Cove was formed by the sea forcing its way through a narrow limestone fault and scouring out the soft chalk of the cliff.

Geological faults have given rise to many interesting phenomena along this stretch of coastline. For instance, there are many stories of old sailors knowing where to obtain fresh water from undersea springs. In some of these, the fresh water flowed out of the seabed in such copious quantities that the salt water was diluted enough, in the immediate vicinity of the spring, to enable the sailors to fill their casks from it. One such spring bubbles up fresh water into the sea just off the coast from Swanage. The location is between Old Harry Rocks and Ocean Bay. The fresh water originates from the large accumulations of it in the chalk layers on the mainland. A geological fault extends from the chalk and eventually reaches the seabed where the water gushes out.

The local land-owning Weld family, during the second half of the eighteenth century, constructed a park at East Lulworth to surround their home, Lulworth Castle and a Roman Catholic chapel they had just built. Incidentally, this chapel was the first new Roman Catholic church to have been built legally since the Reformation; King George III gave special permission to the Weld family. The creation of the park involved the demolition of part of the old village of East Lulworth and the building of new thatched estate cottages a short distance away. However, the new estate was not laid out in any formal pattern as was frequently done in such cases by other great landowners. Many of the cottages are now thatched with long straw, although combed wheat reed is also seen.

A vast area of land, including the coastal strip from near Lulworth Cove to Kimmeridge Bay to the east, is a restricted zone when the Army firing range is in use. However, Kimmeridge Bay just outside the zone may be safely visited at any time as long as the low cliffs of crumbling shale are left well alone, despite the attraction of their fossils. The Romans used the bituminous shale from the cliffs to make coins and jewellery in the form of armlets and rings. Today, 'nodding donkeys' of British Petroleum, blended well into the landscape, are constantly pumping crude oil from the underlying strata at the relatively shallow depth of 1,800 feet. The rate of oil production has been about 100,000 gallons a week since 1961, although production has now fallen from its peak. The cliffs offer a haven for wildlife and the shallow clear waters of Kimmeridge Bay conceal a wealth of marine life.

The village of Kimmeridge stands about one mile inland, at a height of three hundred feet above the sea. The cottages are built of grey limestone, some with weathered stone slate roofs but many with thatched roofs. Most of the thatched nineteenth-century cottages were originally built for miners who were to work the shale deposits as a source of solid fuel, known as 'Blackstone' or 'Kimmeridge Coal'. This existed as a two-foot thick band amongst the various other shales at Kimmeridge. Although the fuel had previously shown some merit, the proposed scheme in the nineteenth century proved impractical, due to the high sulphur content of the shale giving it a very pungent smell. It also emitted an oily smoke when burned.

Kimmeridge's sub-post office and general stores was built as a single-storeyed cottage with a thatched roof in the late eighteenth century. The stone-walled building is rather unusual, for a relatively simple thatched cottage, as the interior displays a plaster barrel-vaulted ceiling. Another attraction of Kimmeridge is the Clavel Tower, raised in 1831 by the owner of Smedmore House. The tower stands about one mile outside the village on the promontory above Kimmeridge Bay. It was probably erected as a folly, or lookout tower but it is now unsafe for visitors to enter.

The road from Kimmeridge leads north-eastwards to the village of Church Knowle and then on to Corfe Castle, in the heart of the Isle of Purbeck. However, like Portland, Purbeck is not a true isle. It gained its name because its southern and eastern perimeters are surrounded by sea, whilst to the north it is cut off by Poole Harbour and the rivers flowing through Wareham. There is another stream, known as Luckford Lake, to the west, furthermore, the only remaining land links near East Lulworth are low-lying. In the past these would have been very boggy and difficult to cross in the winter.

The unspoilt village of Church Knowle was formerly much associated with the chalk quarries which can still be seen on the Purbeck hillside to the north-west. The chalk was mainly used for making roads. The few old cottages and farmhouses in the village are nearly all built of Purbeck limestone, which is also quarried locally, but the roofs are more varied. Several have very heavy stone slab roofs supported by substantial roof timbers and thick walls. In contrast, thatched roofs may also be seen and these require only the lightest of support timbers. Long straw is the favoured thatching material and several of the buildings have quaint little stone porches guarding their entrances. It may seem surprising that thatched roofs are seen at all in such a predominantly stone rich area as Purbeck. The reason may be that it proved easier and cheaper to build such roofs because of the advantage of the weight factor of straw against stone. Also, the wheat grown in the Purbeck area provided a local source of thatching straw.

The spectacular ruin of Corfe Castle guards the narrow gap etched by the River Corfe in the Purbeck Hills. The village lies at the foot of the remains of the former Norman castle perched on the top of a steep conical hill, with its violent history of murder, torture, intrigue and treachery. Its sad history started even before the Normans constructed the castle, as in the year 978 the site was just a Saxon hunting lodge on the hill when young King Edward was murdered with a dagger in the back, at the instigation of his stepmother, Elfrida. She relished the throne for her own son, who later gained the rather apt name of Ethelred the Unready.

The body of the assassinated King was secretly hidden in the village of Corfe and subsequently buried quietly at Wareham. Later, there were many reports of supernatural manifestations taking place at his tomb and in 980 his body was removed with great ceremony to the Abbey at Shaftesbury. Edward was declared a saint and martyr.

Later, after the Normans had built the castle, King John used the fortress as a prison and starved to death in its dungeons twenty-two French nobles who had been audacious enough to support his nephew's attempt to claim the throne. Many other unfortunates, including the hermit Peter of Pomfret who foolishly forecast the downfall of King John were also imprisoned before meeting grisly fates at the hands of the executioners. In later years, successive monarchs resided at the castle and extended its fortifications. Lady Bankes held the castle for the Crown during the Civil War in the seventeenth century but its three-year long gallant resistance to Parliamentary forces was ended by the treachery of one of the defenders. Afterwards, the order to destroy the castle met only with partial success. Mines and explosives shattered many of the walls but the robustness of the stone construction saved it from being razed to the ground. The great towers were displaced but still left standing.

Some of the stone from the ruined castle was used to build houses in the village and nearly all the cottages are built with the local Purbeck stone. Most have heavy stone roofs but a good sprinkling of thatched roofs may also be seen. The mixture of mellowed stone and thatch gives the village an air of peace and charm, despite the grim towering ruins of the castle and the many visitors it attracts. Several of the old cottages have stones engraved in geometrical designs over their doorways, the former work of the Purbeck Marblers. These men quarried a special type of limestone found in Purbeck and when polished it gained the sheen of marble. In medieval times, the marble was used to decorate churches and cathedrals but today Purbeck marble is only quarried in limited quantities for restoration work. Most of the cottages that are thatched are done with wheat reed and some display elegant ridges cut with scallops. A few are roofed with an unusual combination of thatch and heavy stone slates. The latter material is sometimes employed on the area immediately below a dormer window in the thatched roof, the stone slates running down to the eaves. One such cottage bears the delightful name Wayfaring Cottage.

Several of the thatched cottages around Corfe Castle have no doubt been lived in by workers involved in Purbeck's main industry, the production of ball clay. In former times, the clay was dug out of the ground by the use of a curved spade, called a tubal. This shaped the clay into nine inch square balls, each weighing thirty to thirty-five pounds. The clay is still a vital ingredient of ceramic products and most famous pottery manufacturers in Staffordshire and Poole use the ball clay. In fact, Purbeck still supplies about fifteen to twenty per cent of the United Kingdom's present output of the product. Nowadays, the clay is dug out with pneumatic spades, along with giant excavators and scrapers.

The Blue Pool, one of Dorset's famous beauty spots, just outside of

Wayfaring Cottage – Corfe Castle

Corfe Castle, at Furzebrook, is an old clay pit dug in the nineteenth century which has become filled with water. Heathland surrounds the pool but in the immediate vicinity of it, a woodland of lovely Scots pine and silver birch thrives. The colour of the Blue Pool varies from hour to hour, changing from shades of turquoise and blue. The colour of the water is due to the diffraction of light from colloidal particles of clay suspended in the water. The pool therefore appears blue even on cloudy days, as the colour is not dependent on directly reflected sunlight. Despite its beauty, the pool supports no vegetable or animal life and it is over thirty feet deep. In the past, clay from the pool was supplied to Minton, Wedgwood, Royal Worcester and most other leading pottery manufacturers. Nowadays, many visitors toss coins into the water and these are collected regularly for distribution to charity.

Studland Bay lies to the east in Purbeck and the unspoilt village of Studland hides amongst woodland, away from the beach. Studland still harbours several of its old stone-walled thatched cottages, mingling with others furnished with weathered stone roofs. There are also red brick houses in the locality. The substantially built Norman church is unusual in the fact that it is pure Norman, without the additions of another period. On the southern side of Studland Bay, the well-known Old Harry Rocks arise from the sea. The crumbling chalk stack of Old Harry's Wife still stands by his side but it is believed there was once a total of three rocks; the third being Old Harry's daughter but this has long since disappeared. The name Old Harry derives from a nickname for the devil.

The village of Wool shelters well inland from the Purbeck coast to the west of Wareham and to the north of Lulworth. The old part of the village retains many of its pretty thatched cottages. As well as the picturesque cottage orné near the church, mentioned in Chapter 5, there are many other beautiful cottages with a variety of ornamented ridges and some cottages possess thatched porches. Both long straw and combed wheat reed roofs may be seen. Wool also offers a thatched tea-room and even a thatched hairdresser's shop.

Further west along the Frome Valley from Wool rests the peaceful village of Moreton, on the edge of the heath. The most prominent and unusual thatched building in the village is the lofty post office, situated just above the river near the ford. The gabled thatched roof of combed wheat reed climbs especially high over the front of the building, which also serves as the village shop. A house adjoins the post office and the

Post Office – Moreton

thatched roof on this section is ornamented with points along its raised ridge. The combined building dates from the late eighteenth century, although the post office end was added in Victorian times. The walls were constructed with brick below the thatch and there is a mixture of new and old fancy brickwork.

A very appealing cul-de-sac of thatched cottages runs to the left of the post office. Many of these were built with walls of cob and they range in age from the late seventeenth to the nineteenth century. The majority are single-storeyed but with attics below their thatched roofs which undulate neatly around the upper windows. There is a terrace of thatched cottages with raised ridges and points, but there are also individual thatched homes on the opposite side of the road.

Many visitors come to Moreton to pay homage to the legendary Lawrence of Arabia, who was buried in the cemetery situated on the opposite side of the road to the church of St Nicholas. Winston Churchill was among the many distinguished mourners at the funeral and he later paid his own tribute to Lawrence by saying 'We shall never see his like again'. Lawrence was tragically killed after a motor cycle crash during May 1935. The accident occurred near his tiny cottage home, known as Clouds Hill, situated on the heath a short distance away to the north-east of Moreton. It is thought he was killed after swerving to avoid two cyclists but the exact facts stay a mystery. After being taken to the Military Hospital that then existed at nearby Bovington Camp, Lawrence remained in a coma for six days before his death.

Lawrence's cottage home was a woodman's or gamekeeper's cottage when he bought it in 1925. It is now cared for by the National Trust and it remains virtually as it was when he lived in it. It therefore contains his furniture, personal belongings and other relics. The philosophic Greek inscription over the door means 'Nothing Matters'. The fascinating brick cottage has a tiled roof but there is a thatched wooden outbuilding in the grounds. This is thatched with combed wheat reed and the building also possesses a thatched verandah on one side. Unfortunately, the roof is tree shaded and the thatch has deteriorated due to moss formation on its surface. One wonders if Lawrence kept his fateful motor cycle in this thatched outbuilding. Since his death there have been several reports of people claiming they have not only seen the ghostly figure of Lawrence in Arab dress but have heard before dawn the sound of his motor cycle, a Brough Superior, along the nearby road. In 1983, a commemorative tree was officially planted near the cottage to mark the spot where he crashed.

The attractive tiny hamlet of Whitcombe is located to the west of Moreton and just south-east of Dorchester, off the main road to Broadmayne. The original village of Whitcombe was burned down

Group of Cottages – Whitcombe, near Dorchester

during the plague. Present-day Whitcombe consists of a farmhouse, a farmyard, a small ancient redundant church and an exquisite group of thatched cottages. These were built, either in the late seventeenth century or perhaps the early eighteenth century, with walls of cob and also stone rubble. There are three cottages arranged in pairs and a single detached one; recently all have been beautifully re-thatched. Most are gabled with dormer attic windows below the undulations of their thatch. The thatched cottages make a perfect setting for the church, parts of which date back to the twelfth century. This is the church where William Barnes once preached and the building has been restored as a memorial to him. Amongst its treasures, it cherishes a late thirteenth-century wall painting of St Christopher.

The expanding village of Broadmayne is about one mile away and a sprinkling of old thatched cottages has been preserved, despite the building of many modern homes. Very few cottages built before the eighteenth century are found outside the area of the old village, as the open field system of agriculture survived here until 1811. Most of the thatched cottages have stone rubble walls but cob and brick were also used. Unfortunately, several of the old thatched buildings have been demolished in this century, including a thatched cob barn that formerly stood near the centre of the village.

The charming village of West Stafford is also near to Whitcombe, on the south-east side of Dorchester. West Stafford harbours an extremely wide variety of thatched buildings. These include a fine example of a massive thatched barn, the thatched pub called the Wise Man, many thatched cottages and even a thatched bus shelter on the opposite side of the road to the pub. One of the thatched cottages, along the winding street, displays a thatched apron roof, in which a raised layer of thatch extends three-quarters the way down the roof surface. There are therefore three separate and distinct layers of thatch – the raised ridge, the thatched apron and the lower thatch area above the eaves. The bottom edge of the apron is cut with ornamental shapes.

The church occupies the centre of the village and it was here that Tess and Angel Clare were probably married in Hardy's imagination in *Tess of the d'Urbervilles*. One of the weirs of the large area of water-meadows just outside the village, was the tragic spot where Eustacia and Damon

Bus Shelter – West Stafford

Cottage with Thatched Apron Roof Layer – West Stafford

drowned in another of Hardy's novels, *The Return of the Native*. It is in this region of West Stafford that the South Winterborne stream joins the River Frome.

The South Winterborne has its true source to the west of Dorchester, at Bridehead in Little Bredy. The trickle of water emanating from here is boosted to a more significant extent just to the west of Winterbourne Abbas. A spring breaks near the site of the Devil's Nine Stones that stand near the roadside. This prehistoric stone circle is now a National Monument. The nine stones gained their name as they were thought in former times to represent the devil, his wife and children. There have been many other stories told about the stones, including one that they were once unfortunate children turned to stone as a punishment for playing games on the Sabbath.

The brook from the Devil's Nine Stones flows on through Winterbourne Abbas, Winterbourne Steepleton, Winterborne St Martin, Winterborne Monkton, Winterborne Herringston and Winterborne Came before reaching West Stafford. Several of these villages and hamlets along its course have kept their thatched cottages.

A Thatched Gabled End – Little Bredy

'Eyebrow' Windows – Little Bredy

Latticed Window Cottage – Little Bredy

Although the stream first breaks at Bridehead, it passes over several other springs in addition to the first major one to the west of Winterbourne Abbas and all these add to the volume of water flow through the winter. The stream nearly dries up during the summer. In recent years, the South Winterborne has occasionally surfaced from springs below its true source and one possible explanation of this may be the increased extraction of water from boreholes near the primary source.

The village of Little Bredy hides in a deep wooded valley beneath the downs and it is close to many tumuli and stone circles. It presents a tranquil scene with its old picturesque thatched cottages, thatched rectory and thatched village hall that was formerly the school. Lovely grounds adjoin the church which is one of the very few Dorset rural churches built with a spire. Below the church, the village has a great house, called Bridehead, built in about 1830. The artificial lake in front of the house was created from the spring water which rises to form the source of the River Bride and also the start of the South Winterborne stream. The lake is both beautiful and secluded; it attracts many wildfowl.

The little River Bride meanders by a variety of thatched cottages in the village, nearly all thatched with combed wheat reed and built of stone. Some are two-storeyed with hipped thatched roofs and often their country gardens have tiny foot-bridges at the bottom to cross the stream. One enchanting small detached thatched cottage, with white painted lattice windows, never fails to attract the attention of photographers. The upstairs windows below the thatch give an air of symmetry, as they are placed centrally above the lower windows, with the doorway positioned at the extreme end of the cottage. The chimney stack arises through the thatched ridge in a central position, above the middle line between the lattice windows, to complete the symmetrical pattern. The quaint cottage gives the impression of a delightful doll's house.

As mentioned, the South Winterborne stream from Bridehead first flows through Winterbourne Abbas and then Winterbourne Steepleton. It is perhaps interesting that these two villages have the letter 'u' included in the spelling of their names, all the other Winterbornes in Dorset are spelt without the 'u'. Winterbourne Abbas and Winterbourne Steepleton shelter close together under high downs and many of the old cottages have stone rubble or flints in their walls. Some display bands of flint and stone. Unfortunately, most of the thatched roofs in Winterbourne Abbas have disappeared over the years but the more peaceful village of Winterbourne Steepleton has retained many of its thatched cottages. Some of these are thought to date back to the sixteenth century and a few possess mullioned windows.

The cottages, thatched with combed wheat reed, make a restful picture with the stream flowing by the roadside in front of them and filling a pond a short distance down the road. The road outside the village to the south-east is lined with conifers and hard woods. The manor house stands in the heart of the village, along the curving roadside by the thatched cottages but the church is set back from the road. As the name Winterbourne Steepleton may suggest, the fourteenth-century church possesses a steeple and like Little Bredy, it is one of the few stone spires to be found in the county. Most Dorset churches possess towers. The village was formerly sometimes known as Steepleton.

The next village along the chalk valley, Winterborne St Martin is now usually called Martinstown, especially by the local population. The main street is spacious and several thatched roofs still survive along it. The stream again follows the course of the road and most gardens of the houses are reached by crossing a variety of tiny foot-bridges. Many of the old thatched cottages are built with stone walls.

One pleasant well-maintained thatched cottage, on the outskirts of the village, bears the name 'The Old Shepherd's Cottage'. This was formerly two cottages and the name suggests that one, or both, were once a home for shepherds tending the many flocks of sheep which were bred in the locality. Sheep still graze on the slopes of Maiden Castle, the famous prehistoric stronghold that lies just to the south-east.

Winterborne St Martin was until the early part of this century, the venue for an annual fair where many sheep were assembled. Gypsies also did an appreciable amount of horse trading at the same fair. Gypsies have always been adept at keeping horses 'sound' and they place much faith in plant medicines, both for their animals and themselves. In Dorset, gypsy families may still be seen in the market towns selling sprigs of heather. Their forebears were much in demand for such matters as wart charming and fortune telling.

The South Winterborne flows through Winterborne Monkton before reaching Winterborne Herringston and Winterborne Came. As mentioned earlier, Winterborne Herringston contains a thatched farmhouse, whilst Winterborne Came conceals the picturesque thatched rectory formerly lived in by William Barnes. Incidentally, the farmhouse situated close to Came House was also thatched, until a few years ago, when the roof was replaced with tiles. In the past, about a quarter of a mile to the west of Came Church, there was a neighbouring village called Winterborne Farringdon but historians think its population was wiped-out by the plague several hundred years ago. The site of the deserted medieval village still reveals evidence where the buildings once stood, including the church.

Thatched Villages of East Dorset

A chalk stream named the Tarrant, flows southwards along a ten-mile stretch of valley, situated to the east of Blandford Forum, before it joins the River Stour at Spetisbury. The Tarrant gives its name to eight villages and hamlets strung along its winding course; these are Tarrant Gunville, Tarrant Hinton, Tarrant Launceston, Tarrant Monkton, Tarrant Rawston, Tarrant Rushton, Tarrant Keyneston and Tarrant Crawford. Several harbour picturesque thatched cottages, set in the quiet downland scenery of the green valley they all share. There are many ancient long and round barrows as well in the immediate neighbourhood. The peace of the valley was temporarily shattered in World War II, when an airfield was built at Tarrant Rushton and the road leading to Witchampton was closed. The airfield was much used and it played an important role when Normandy was invaded on D-Day in 1944.

Tarrant Hinton stands on the main A354 Blandford Forum to Salisbury road, towards the head of the valley. The village expanded at the beginning of the nineteenth century when many brick and flint banded cottages were built. This was due to the earlier construction in 1755 of the Great Western Turnpike road (now the A354). The church of St Mary nestles amongst some older thatched cottages situated along a quieter lane. Several of these were constructed with cob during the eighteenth century and most have white-washed walls. Incidentally, the splendid church contains a superb sixteenth-century Easter sepulchre.

Excavations carried out, about a mile outside the village, exposed the presence of an extensive Roman settlement. Some of the finds from the site are now exhibited in the Priest's House Museum in nearby Wimborne Minster. This museum, specializing in local history, was opened in 1962 but originally it was one of four similar Priests' houses, built during the sixteenth century in the town 'to serve the cure of Wimborne'. The museum building is the only one of the four to survive. Wimborne Minster itself preserves two or three thatched cottages, gathered along its main streets. One of these, known as Turnpike Cottage, stands in a prominent position along Leigh Road. A charming thatched roof covers the single-storeyed white-washed cottage and the door at the rear opens onto a verandah, framed with two ornamental arches. The thatched roof has a raised pointed ridge. Despite the busy traffic along the main shopping road, a tranquil cottage garden and a botanical art studio are hidden away in the grounds behind the thatched cottage.

Tarrant Monkton, a little further down the valley from Tarrant Hinton must be one of Dorset's most peaceful villages, as it is located well away from any main traffic route. The village, set amidst the fields, has a ford and also a packhorse bridge. In the past, this took considerable horse traffic, as it lay along the main route to London from Weymouth.

Tarrant Monkton is built on both sides of the stream and nearly all the cottages are beautifully thatched, some with long straw and others with combed wheat reed. In addition, many of the white and colour-washed cottages have thatched porches, supported by rustic timbers. A large number of the thatched cottages are clustered around the flint and stone-walled Church of All Saints. Most of the cob-walled cottages were built during the eighteenth century.

As with many English villages, the social life of Tarrant Monkton centres around the local inn, The Langton Arms. This is thatched with

Group of Cottages – Tarrant Monkton

combed wheat reed and it has a neat raised ridge, with scallops and points. The building dates back to the seventeenth century, when it was built as a small cottage pub, with brick walls inlaid with bands of flint. The premises have since been expanded to include a thatched skittle alley and a restaurant, the latter without a thatched roof.

In complete contrast to the tranquillity of Tarrant Monkton, the village of Tarrant Keyneston has had its peace disturbed by the fast traffic which now speeds through it, on its way to and from Blandford Forum. The village is unfortunately clustered around a busy cross-roads, with the main road both wide and straight and this encourages traffic to go through at speed.

The red brick village pub, quaintly named The True Lovers' Knot, stands at the crossroads. Although it is not thatched, a delightful thatched house may be found a few yards away, with perched straw birds on its roof. The beautifully thatched village shop and post office may be seen just the other side of the crossroads from the pub.

Tarrant Keyneston is located very close to Badbury Rings, one of the great Wessex circular hill-forts of the Iron Age. Also nearby is another earthworks, known as Buzbury Rings, whose enclosures were probably formerly used more for the herding of cattle than for defence purposes.

Marigold Cottage – Spetisbury

Badbury Rings, with its huge triple earthworks, was obviously built to gain protection from hostile forces and to achieve good observation of the surrounding countryside. The outer slopes now give excellent viewing facilities for the point-to-point races held regularly over the countryside immediately below.

The Tarrant stream ends at Spetisbury where it joins the River Stour, just to the north of the village. Spetisbury itself is close to yet another Iron Age hill-fort, known as Spetisbury Rings, or sometimes as Crawford Castle. Many skeletons, some with broken skulls, were found here when the Somerset and Dorset Railway was cut through in the last century. The skeletons were thought to be the remains of the casualties left after a Roman attack around AD 100.

The village of Spetisbury contains many pleasing examples of ornamental thatched buildings along its main road. The thatched tea-room, known as Marigold Cottage, displays scallops on its ridge and it also possesses a thatched porch. The cottage was built around 1525. A sign to the left of the entrance door confirms this, as it proudly states:

This cottage has stood through the following reigns

Henry VIII	George II
Mary I	George III
Elizabeth I	George IV
James I	William IV
Charles I	Queen Victoria
Cromwell Protectorate	Edward VII
Charles II	George V
James II	Edward VIII
William III	George VI
Queen Anne	Elizabeth II

George I

This long list of England's rulers gives a better realization of the passage of time and the true age of the building, than a mere statement that the cottage is sixteenth century. Just along the road there is a thatched Tudor timber-framed building, in the form of a terrace of three cottages, all with individual thatched porches. The main thatched roof of the terrace is ornamented with scallops and points and the back thatch takes the shape of a catslide. On the opposite side of the road, a thatched guest-house exhibits a straw bird perched on the neat pointed ridge of its thatched roof. The house has two thatched porches.

The River Stour, after leaving Spetisbury, flows under the medieval Crawford Bridge with its nine low arches, to reach the village of Shapwick. The Romans built a road through here to link the nearby

Badbury Rings with Dorchester. Thatched cottages still survive in Shapwick, together with the stump of the village cross which marks where the great evangelist, John Wesley, once preached. The local pub, The Anchor Inn, was originally thatched, with dormer windows in its roof but the building has now been much altered and the thatch replaced by a modern roof.

The name Shapwick derives from a Saxon word meaning 'sheep village'. An amusing story of one of its shepherds, who tended the flocks on the downs about three hundred years ago, illustrates the fact that few villagers in those days ever had the opportunity to travel, or gain any experience outside the immediate confines of their own village. One day, the shepherd suddenly stumbled upon a large live crab that had fallen from a travelling fishmonger's cart. He was terrified at the sight and immediately rushed off to warn the other villagers. They returned to view it with caution and all thought the Devil must have assumed this frightening form, as none of them had witnessed such a creature before. Later, the fishmonger returned and the mystery was solved amidst much relief and laughter. The unfortunate villagers had to endure the scorn of the inhabitants of the surrounding region for many years to come because of their simple and ignorant fear of the so-called Shapwick monster.

The next village along the Stour valley is Sturminster Marshall, on the south bank of the river. Although much modern building work has taken place to make it fairly sizeable, the original village centre by the church still preserves a long line of pretty thatched cottages. These were recently restored after a fire severely damaged the thatched terrace in 1976. There are seven cottages under the long continuous stretch of thatch and the terrace follows the curve of the road. The rear of the cottages are especially picturesque, with the thatch undulating around the many upper floor windows of the long terraced row. A good sprinkling of other thatched properties may be found close by and several are thatched with long straw. A few possess thatched porches.

Whitemill Bridge spans the river just outside Sturminster Marshall. This is reputed to be the oldest bridge in Dorset and it still rests on its original eight-hundred-year-old oak piles. The Norman style stone bridge has eight arches which are ribbed with an alternating mixture of limestone and sandstone.

Corfe Mullen is also on the south side of the river, a little further along the Stour Valley and there are several splendid examples of thatched cottages remaining in the locality. Quite a few have timber-framed walls whilst the others are of cob construction. Most were built during the eighteenth and nineteenth centuries but one or two survive from the late sixteenth century. It is thought that some of the original wattle-and-daub panels are still preserved in the partition walls inside these older cottages. Long straw is the favoured thatching material. There are several other interesting buildings in Corfe Mullen, although they are not thatched. These include a thirteenth-century church, a seventeenth-century manor house and an eighteenth-century mill house, now converted to a tea-room.

Closer to Wimborne Minster, along the Stour Valley, lies the village of Pamphill. There is a large green at Pamphill, with an unusual but fine avenue of oaks across it, leading to the church. Just below the green may be found the village inn, together with several charming thatched cottages. Many were built in the seventeenth century, with timber-framed walls and brick below their thatched roofs.

As well as the thatched cottages, there are many other interesting buildings located in or near Pamphill. One side of the green claims the school and almshouses, built of brick in 1698, whilst the stone-slated manor house of about the same period stands on the opposite side. About a mile away, the great house and estate of Kingston Lacy dominates the scene. The house was built during 1663 to 1665 for the Bankes family, who had previously lived in Corfe Castle. In 1981, the house was bequested to the National Trust. Incidentally, a magnificent avenue of beech trees stretches for two miles from the lodge gate of Kingston Lacy to the foot of Badbury Rings. The trees, planted over one hundred years ago, form a natural cathedral arch over the road and the total number of trees is supposed to be three hundred and sixty-five, one for each day of the year.

The village of Witchampton hides in seclusion to the north of Wimborne Minster, by the little River Allen which eventually meets the River Stour at Canford Bridge, after wandering through the town of Wimborne Minster. Witchampton must be regarded as one of Dorset's loveliest villages, with its many delightful thatched cottages, many of timber-framed construction with brick in-fillings. The present village was built around 1765, having been moved from its original site, due to the demands of Crichel House, when it was enlarged to create a Palladian palace within its own park.

A little water well lies on the outskirts of Witchampton and a small humped-back bridge leads to the winding road climbing around the church, standing on a knoll, in the heart of the village. Many thatched cottages surround the church and most are thatched with long straw, with rich decorative ridges of scallops and points. Several have thatched rustic porches and nearly all the cottages have well-kept picturesque gardens, filled with a host of flowers throughout the summer months.

Just above the church, further up the hill, may be found the post office and general stores but the building is not thatched. The tranquillity of the village may be partly responsible for the reputation of the church for its long serving rectors. In the last century, John Glyn Carr

A Long Straw Thatched Cottage – Witchampton

was incumbent for sixty-seven years, while Robert Willis served for fifty-five years in the preceding century.

The ancient game of chess must have been known to some of the local inhabitants, because a unique and priceless treasure was discovered during excavations in a field at Witchampton. This unearthed the oldest set of chessmen ever to be found in England. The individual pieces are now kept in the British Museum and they measure about five inches high. They were carved from whalebone and are thought to have been made in Saxon England. The game of chess was probably first played in India, during the early part of the seventh century but it took many hundreds of years before it spread across Europe. It had certainly reached Britain by the early eleventh century, although its popularity was not truly established until a little later.

The small and rather scattered hamlet of Manswood rests on the

Ornamental Thatch and Timber Framed Cottage – Witchampton

A Long Stretch of Thatch – Manswood

nearby Crichel estate. The hamlet boasts several attractive detached cottages which are thatched with long straw. Manswood also claims the longest continuous stretch of thatch to be found in England. This measures one hundred and twenty yards in length and covers a terrace of eleven cottages, a post office and general stores, making a total of twelve buildings in the long row. The official name of the terrace is The Buildings and its long thatched main roof consists of long straw. One end of the thatch is gabled, whilst the opposite end is half-hipped.

The terrace was constructed with cob walls, just over two hundred years ago but small brick-built extensions, with slated roofs, have since been added at the rear of the cottages. The fronts of the cottages have individual tiled porches. There are a series of entrance gaps through the terrace, linking the front gardens with the rear, every two houses along the row. The post box set in the wall bears the letters VR, denoting it dates back to Queen Victoria's reign and such boxes are now becoming quite rare. The Buildings may be found on the Witchampton road at the outskirts of Manswood. Alternatively, the long thatched terrace may be reached from the centre of the hamlet by following the footpath marked with a wooden sign-post, indicating the direction of the post office. The path leads alongside open farmland and makes an attractive short walk.

The small village of Chettle lies in a valley by Cranborne Chase, to the north of Witchampton and Manswood and it possesses several pretty cob-walled thatched cottages. Many were built in the seventeenth century, with single storeys and attics and some had dormer windows incorporated in the thatch. Other cottages were constructed at the same time with brick or stone walls and there are also several houses with tiled roofs. An unusually wide variety of building materials was therefore used, considering the relatively small size of the village.

The tiny church at Chettle stands in the grounds of Chettle House. This fine red brick manor house, with its rounded corners and stone dressings, was built between 1710 and 1720 by the Bastards of Bland-ford and designed by Thomas Archer. It was originally the home of George Chafin who held the important post of Ranger of Cranborne Chase. His son became known as the sporting parson, as he still hunted when well over the age of eighty. The house has now been converted into flats but the exterior still delights the eye as an outstanding example of English Baroque.

Wimborne St Giles borders on Cranborne Chase and it has belonged to the Earls of Shaftesbury since the fifteenth century. Their ancestral home, St Giles House, is a beautiful Elizabethan mansion, set in a magnificent park and fine gardens. During its history, it has been visited by kings, cabinet ministers, philosophers and musicians, including Handel. The church in the village is early Georgian and it is unusual because it is attached to some impressive almshouses, built earlier in

1624. A few hundred yards away stands the old mill house also of the same period as the almshouses.

The weathered village stocks, now provided with a roof over them, are preserved by the side of the wide stretch of green, opposite the church. The stocks made of oak, with iron hasp and staple, are thought to date from the eighteenth century. A most unusual sign-post also stands nearby indicating the directions to Blandford and Salisbury. A painted picture of St Giles, nursing a hind, is fixed on the top of the post and at the base is a seat.

Many of the houses in the charming village were built with red brick in the seventeenth century but there are also eighteenth- and nineteenth-century cottages, laid out in spacious fashion. Many of the pretty cottages display thatched roofs and these are mainly located along the quiet road a short distance away from the church and green. Some are thatched with long straw and a pair of perched straw birds may be spotted on the ridge of the occasional cottage. There are also lofty trees to add further beauty to the rustic scene. Nearby, in former times, stood the hollow Remedy Oak, where Edward VI reputedly cured the sick by touching it 'for the King's Evil'.

The village of Cranborne is only three miles away, towards the Hampshire border. Several thatched cottages mingle with the many other attractive buildings in the centre. Without doubt, the most splendid of these is the former royal hunting lodge, converted into the present magnificent Cranborne Manor, during the reign of James I. Spacious gardens adjoin the mansion and these are opened to the public at various times during the summer months. There is also a garden nursery.

The village of Bloxworth is situated to the south-west of Wimborne Minster just off the A35, between Bere Regis and Poole. This quiet sprawling village, sheltered from the main road by woodland, was formerly well known for its unusual rector, known as 'the fighting parson'. His name John Morton was later to become famous when he became Archbishop of Canterbury and Henry VII's Chancellor. His tempestuous nature gained him a reputation as a fighter and a very able statesman but also that of a ruthless manipulator of power.

Bloxworth is scattered around several crossroads and although many of its old red brick thatched cottages have been demolished to make way for new, many still survive. A few have thatched porches, with their main thatched roofs decorated with points on their raised ridges. The village also claims a bus shelter, neatly thatched with long straw. Bloxworth House stands a short way from the village centre and this fine brick-built manor house, recently restored, dates from the early seventeenth century. It also possesses several interesting and impressive brick-built outbuildings, including stables and a brew-house.

Morden is located just to the east of Bloxworth and this peaceful unspoilt village has left relatively untouched, its many old thatched cottages strung along its quiet lanes. Many of these were built with cob in the late eighteenth century. There are also thatched farmhouses and the surrounding farmland at Morden has been used as a popular venue for point-to-point races for many years.

Lytchett Minster is fairly close by but this village is much larger and busier, as it sits just off the main A35 road on the outskirts of Poole. The unusual name of Lytchett refers to the strip lynchets which were once worked on behalf of its former monastic proprietors. Lytchett Minster boasts two well-known pubs, the thatched Bakers Arms, described in Chapter 4 and St Peter's Finger. The latter name derives from 'St Peter ad Vincula', a term of medieval significance relating to land tenure. The manor court was formerly held in the pub on the 1 August each year. Afterwards, some common ground for sheep and cattle grazing became available to the villagers for a limited period. Rents and rates due from carters were also collected in the pub and this custom continued until just a few years ago. A terrace of cob-walled thatched cottages stands near St Peter's Finger and there are other thatched properties in the locality. Most were built in the late eighteenth or early nineteenth century and several had their cob walls faced with bricks.

The delicate task of Dorset button-making used to be carried out in many of the thatched cottages in Lytchett Minster. This was formerly a thriving cottage industry which gave employment to hundreds of women and girls in East Dorset during the eighteenth and early nineteenth centuries. The boom subsided when machine-made buttons came on the market in about 1850. However, there was a small scale revival of the old hand method at Lytchett Minster between about 1900 and 1910. The present antique shop in the village, called 'The Button Shop', was used as a warehouse for them. Many of the poor were given the task of button-making in return for soup and this practice continued until 1914. This work took place in the thatched local mission hall but the building has since been demolished.

Each hand-made button was fashioned on an iron ring. The ring was first tightly stitched around with linen thread and the edge smoothed with a wood or bone instrument called a 'slicker'. Next the button was 'layered' to create the final form by stitching across the circumference of the ring. There were several popular design patterns, known by the names Old Dorset, Crosswheel, Honeycomb, Carolos, Yarrow and Hightops. They were made in a wide variety of sizes, ranging from the smallest, called mites, to the largest, called outsizes. In between, there were birdseyes, jams and waistcoats.

Water reeds were formerly cultivated in a small area of ground near Lytchett Minster and these were harvested regularly by the local reed cutter. No doubt, the reeds were then used to thatch some of the cottages in the locality. The reeds are no longer cut, due to the death of the reed cutter a few years ago and so combed wheat reed is now much more commonly encountered as the local thatching material. Long straw is also used.

The town of Christchurch is in the most easterly part of Dorset, on the shores of the harbour sheltered by Hengistbury Head and it lies between the River Stour and the River Avon. The two rivers meet in the town, before they flow into Christchurch Harbour. Very few thatched buildings survive in the town but one of them has claims to be probably the oldest thatched house in Dorset. This is the Old Court House, situated in the main street, near the Kings Arms Hotel and only a few yards away from the ruins of the Norman castle and the twelfth-century Constable's House.

The Old Court House dates back to the twelfth century and it is of timber-framed construction, with brick in-fillings. The front of the building has now been pebble-dashed and plastered. The gabled front is highly ornamented with wood and the roof is thatched with water reed, which has now weathered to a dark rich brown. The ridge is decorated with points. The ancient building is where the court-leets were formerly held. The building has now become a perfumery shop and its quaint look attracts the cameras of the many tourists who come to the town to visit Christchurch Priory.

The court-leet was a special type of court of record, held by the lord of the manor on an annual or sometimes a half-yearly basis. In Norman times, the court-leet became the main judicial and local government court. The court-leet employed many local officials such as ale-tasters, meat inspectors and bread-weight checkers. The public thus gained some protection, under the auspices of the court, from any unscrupulous traders. In addition, officials carried out surveys and safety checks on properties and with thatched houses, this particularly involved verifying that chimney flues were clean and free from obstructions. This was known as chimney-peeping and it was done to reduce the potential fire risk, especially when many thatched buildings were in close proximity to one another, in a town or large village.

The fire risk was always present as the majority of cottagers in Dorset, even until the late nineteenth century, cooked their meals over large open fires in their homes. A 'cottrell', adjustable to the height of the fire, hung in the chimney with a 'brandish' attached to it. The kettle, frying pan, saucepan or griddle plate was then placed on the 'brandish'. All the pots and pans were made of heavy gauge metal to withstand the direct heat of the flames.

The great priory church at Christchurch was started in the eleventh century and legend relates that the original site selected was on St

Catherine's Hill, about two miles away from the harbour. However, it is reputed that at the end of each working day, all the building materials were mysteriously moved down the steep hill during the night to the present site. This occurred many times and to avoid further frustrations it was decided that it would be simpler to construct the church in the position where the materials were found each morning.

During the building of the church, an extra workman appeared each day to assist but no one knew where he came from. He never spoke and required no payment for his toil. A little later, a carpenter accidentally cut one of the huge important timber beams for the church too short. However, a miracle seemingly occurred during the night, as the following morning the beam was found to be exactly the right length. It was then recognized in awe that the mysterious stranger who had been helping them must have been Christ himself, so the priory and the town were both renamed Christ's Church. Its previous name had been Twineham, with the Saxon meaning 'between the waters'. The miraculous beam in the church became a focus for pilgrimage and it may still be seen in the wall, high above the choir.

It is perhaps of interest that the priory records note that in the fifteenth century, the incumbent was paid a remuneration of 10 shillings a year, plus twenty-one gallons of best quality beer each week. At today's beer prices, this would make the overall salary quite palatable.

An unexpected old thatched cottage may be discovered near the green at Christchurch. It appears entirely out of place because it has become nearly completely surrounded by tall modern flats and other buildings. The thatched cottage has a raised ridge with points. It seems a shame that the twentieth-century planners decided to overwhelm it with high density building and destroy its views. It will be interesting to observe how long it can survive in its present cramped environment.

11

Thatched Villages of West Dorset

In the extreme western corner of Dorset, the coastal town of Lyme Regis owes its regal name to Edward I, who granted Lyme its first Royal Charter in 1284. This allowed Lyme to add Regis to its name. The town gained much prominence in 1685 when the Duke of Monmouth landed, in his attempt to seize the Crown of England from James II. The rebellion ended in disaster at the Battle of Sedgemoor and Monmouth was later executed on the block, after five attempts had been made to sever his head. Twelve of his men were hanged in chains on the beach where the landing had taken place and the spot is now known as Monmouth Beach.

Monmouth's father, Charles II, had earlier in the seventeenth century been hotly pursued by Parliamentary forces in the locality of Lyme Regis. He had intended to escape to France from the town. On one occasion, he took refuge in a thatched farmhouse, known as Elsdon's Farm, near Monkton Wyld, a small village just to the north of Lyme Regis. The little stone-built seventeenth-century thatched farmhouse still stands, about a half a mile off the A35, near the Dorset and Devon border. A commemorative tablet on the wall of the two-storeyed thatched building states that Charles II stayed here on the 22 September 1651.

In the eighteenth and nineteenth centuries, Lyme Regis became a fashionable seaside resort and Princess Victoria, later to become Queen, sailed from the harbour. Other famous visitors were William III, the elder and younger William Pitt, Jane Austen and James McNeill Whistler, who painted 'The Master Smith' and 'The Little Rose', whilst staying in Lyme Regis. Lord Lister, the pioneer of antiseptic surgery lived in the town and Mary Anning was another well-known former resident. She unearthed many of the fossils in the area, including the first complete skeleton of a pterodactyl on the cliffs. The largest and best of her fossil discoveries are now exhibited in London's Museum of Natural History. This includes the amazing thirty foot icthyosaurus fossil.

The social respectability of the resort encouraged many rich Victorians to spend their holidays in thatched cottages that were built on the sea front. Two of these buildings remain along the Marine Parade, with their colour-washed walls contrasting with the deeper hues of their thatched roofs. They were built during the first half of the nineteenth century, with weather-boarded walls and tall imposing semicircular bow-windows reaching to the thatched eaves level. A most unusual feature of their thatched roofs are the brackets and boarding fixed immediately below the eaves to support and protect the thatch over-hang. The temperate climate, enjoyed by Lyme Regis throughout the winter months, has ensured that the thatched roofs are not tested too severely by harsh weather conditions. In addition, the building of the famous Cobb in the fourteenth century, to form an artificial harbour, has given some protection to the town from the south-westerly gales.

Incidentally in 1980, the town was temporarily transformed back to Victorian times, when *The French Lieutenant's Woman*, based on John Fowles' novel, was filmed at Lyme Regis. Although not used in the film, the most commonly photographed thatched building in the town is the beautiful and unusual Umbrella Cottage, with its cusped eaves and this has been described in detail in Chapter 5.

About two miles along the coast at the mouth of the River Char, nestles the former fishing village of Charmouth, which has now become a busy holiday resort and a favourite place to hunt fossils. Over the years the latter practice has resulted in considerable damage to the cliffs. The main street ascends a steep hill and several interesting thatched build-ings are scattered along it. The miscellany includes a thatched hotel, a thatched guest-house, a thatched restaurant and a number of thatched cottages. The majority are thatched with combed wheat reed and several have ridges richly decorated with scallops and points. A few of the stone-walled thatched buildings were built during the seventeenth century but Charmouth retains many Georgian and Regency houses, with neat bow-windows.

The Charmouth House Hotel, near the top of the hill, embraces a collection of thatched buildings, now all joined together under the same continuous thatched roof. The complex shape of the two-storeyed building means that some extremities of the roof have thatched gabled ends, whilst others are hipped. The attractive white-painted hotel carries a neat pointed ridge on its main thatched roof. Perhaps surpri-singly, the small thatched bonnets sheltering the doorways of the premises are of imitation thatch material. A smart guest-house, known as The Cottage, stands a little way down the road. It has pink-washed walls below its thatched roof and this is furnished with a ridge of scallops and points. A thatched bay window adds further charm to the building, together with a series of pretty upper windows complete with shutters and hanging baskets spaced between them. Again perhaps unexpectedly, only the front of the building bears a thatched roof. Slates cover the rear elevation.

The Cottage – Charmouth

The oldest building along the main street is the former inn, known as The Queens Armes Hotel. Although not thatched, it claims a most interesting history, as it was originally named after Catherine of Aragon, who briefly stayed there in 1501, just after it was built. Another illustrious visitor was Charles II, who stopped there in 1651, whilst waiting without success for the Lyme Regis skipper, Stephen Limbry, to sail him to France and thereby escape his many pursuers. A few yards down the road stands an old stone-built thatched cottage called The Lilac. This displays an ornamental straw bird on its pointed ridge. On the opposite side of the road to this cottage and The Queens Armes, is an attractive thatched house which boasts a two-storeyed bay window that extends upwards to the thatched eaves level. Nearby are several cottages fitted with corrugated roofing materials and these were obviously formerly thatched.

The A35 road from Charmouth leads to Chideock, after first passing through the small village, strung along the roadside, called Morcombe-lake. The latter hides a particularly impressive thatched house on its western outskirts, set back a little from the main road. The wheat reed thatch curves tidily around the upper windows of the building. Mor-combelake enjoys wide fame due to the excellence of its Dorset Knobs. These small hand-produced chunky biscuits were first made about one hundred and fifty years ago by a farmer's wife. She served them, with early morning tea, to the farm workers before they commenced their milking. The knob biscuits were later sold in nearby stores and labourers took them into the fields to eat with the local Blue Vinney cheese. The Dorset knob biscuits were made from home grown wheat and baked in ovens heated with faggots of wood cut from the hedgerows. The present small bakery at Morcombelake was started up later by the son of the founder and it still carries on the tradition of biscuit manufacture.

The pretty village of Chideock shelters in a small valley, protected by hills on three sides. The fourth and south side slopes gently down to the sea, at the hamlet of Seatown. Chideock contains a host of thatched buildings and many have walls of the local yellow sandstone but cob-walled thatched cottages are also present. Nearly all the buildings are thatched with combed wheat reed and many have thatched porches. Unfortunately, the main street is the A35 and the village is therefore always busy with traffic. It is not uncommon for the occasional thatched building to be damaged by a careering heavy lorry, after descending the steep Chideock hill.

Several picturesque thatched hotels and guest-houses welcome the many holidaymakers who stay during the summer months. One of

Cottages in Main Street – Chideock

An Outshut End Thatched Cottage – Chideock

Seventeenth-century Cottage Chimneys – Chideock

these, The Chideock House Hotel was originally built in the fifteenth century, with yellow-tinged stone below its thatched roof. It has been much extended since then and the present thatched gabled roof, decorated with scallops and points, has raised parapets trapping the ends of the thatch. A beautiful vine climbs the front wall of the hotel. The building has a fascinating history, as it was the headquarters of the Roundhead Army in their local campaign against the Royalists in 1645. Earlier, the trial of the Chideock Martyrs took place in its main hall. These were five Catholic priests who refused to conform to the new Established Church and were later savagely killed.

There are also several seventeenth-century guest-houses, with thatched roofs, sprinkled along the main street. The aptly named Seventeenth-century Cottage Chimneys has a magnificent lateral chimney, as well as gable chimneys towering above its thatch. The house also has a large rustic thatched porch at its side and an attractive thatched canopy shelters the quaint guest-house sign in the front garden. The Clock Hotel and restaurant, a little further along the road, is particularly appealingly thatched and is topped with a raised ridge of scallops and points. Also, along the main street, The Thatch Cottage, now a guest-house, was obviously built as a cottage home in the seventeenth century before its conversion to its present use. It stands at the end of a terrace, opposite to The George Inn, also with its thatched roof as described in Chapter 4.

Several of the thatched cottages in Chideock have staddle stones strung along their front gardens to create an enchanting ornamental effect. Some of the most beautiful and unusual thatched cottages are to be found just off the main road, along Duck Street and Mill Lane that lead down to Seatown. One called Swiss Cottage displays an especially beautiful undulating thatched roof and large brick chimneys. It was built with the local yellow-tinged stone in about 1700. The strangely shaped Anvil Cottage, which stands nearby, has its thatched roof richly decorated with prominent tufts and peaks.

As mentioned, most of the thatched roofs in Chideock are made from wheat reed but in the past wheat straw was also used for other intriguing purposes. The local Chideock cider was made from a recipe which included wheat straw and it was made in presses of oak, elm and iron. It was considered potent enough 'to make 'ee zing and dance and tangle up thy lags'. Wheat was also used to make the old country dish known as 'furmity'. This consisted of a mixture of wheat, raisins and currants, with flour as a thickening agent. The mixture was slowly boiled, then sweetened with sugar before being eaten with a spoon as a porridge.

The peaceful village of Symondsbury hides away from the A35 road between Chideock and Bridport. It is sheltered by two rounded hills and the River Simene meanders before joining the River Brit at

Bridport. Nearly all the buildings in Symondsbury are again of the local yellow-tinged sandstone and many are roofed with thatch, although some are constructed with stone roofs. The thatched cottages include a very pretty terrace, situated a short distance along the road from the over four-hundred-year-old thatched pub, The Ilchester Arms, described in Chapter 4. The local post office is not thatched but the house attached to it carries a thatched roof. Just opposite are two attractive thatched terraces.

The nearby seventeenth-century manor house has been converted to a college but its huge thatched stone barn of the same date has been preserved and still borders the road by the main gate. A ladder-like series of liggers straddles the roof from the eaves to the ridge to secure the thatch. A century ago, the manor door would have been knocked at Christmas time by the Symondsbury 'mummers'. These strolling players went from house to house performing plays, the lines of which had strong associations with the ancient crusaders and the Holy Wars. The players would be dressed in paper and tinsel and one would represent Father Christmas. The village was also once renowned for its dancers and talented band of musicians.

In the past, an unusual tradition was followed in Symondsbury when one of its parishioners died. It was carried out not only to inform the villagers that a bereavement had occurred but also to tell them the age and sex of the deceased. The message was passed on by a series of tolls on the church bell. Four tolls were given for the death of a man, three for a woman and two for a child. This was followed by a number of slow tolls, to indicate the exact age of the person.

The town of Bridport contains hardly any thatched buildings but there is one most unusual exception. This is the bottling store of J. C. and R. H. Palmer's Old Brewery at West Bay Road. The eighteenth-century building, probably a former mill, has four separate elevations of reed thatch, arranged as two gabled pairs in an M-shape and the walls have raised parapets to enclose the ends of the thatch. The ridge of the thatch is straight and undecorated. The brewery is the only thatched one remaining in the country and possibly also in Europe.

In addition, the brewery possesses one of the few surviving undershot water-wheels in England which still work. The gigantic eighteen-foot diameter metal water-wheel weighs over five-and-a-half tons and it has been recently restored. Since 1879, it has been used to provide the power to pump millions of gallons of spring water into the brewery, for use in the beer and mineral water production. The brewery also preserves an ancient vertical steam engine. Both this and the water-wheel are now kept as reserve power units for the modern pumps, in the event of an electricity cut or other power failure. At one time, there were many other thatched buildings in Bridport and perhaps the best known

J. C. and R. H. Palmer's Old Brewery – Bridport

of these was the former charity brew-house. This large thatched
building was later converted into a school, known as Miss Grundy's
Infant School. Unfortunately, a serious fire engulfed the thatched roof
in 1906 and despite the frantic efforts of the firemen to pull the burning
thatch away, the building was destroyed.

The village of Burton Bradstock shelters behind the coast ridge, to
the south-east of Bridport and the Chesil Beach commences here and
extends fifteen miles eastwards to Portland. Until 1958, Burton Bradstock was owned by the Pitt-Rivers family but the National Trust now
own the land around the beach and its access to the cliffs. The
picturesque village of mainly thatch and stone is perhaps at its most
lovely near the fifteenth-century church. Many thatched cottages line
the series of quiet lanes that conglomerate in this older part of the
village. Most of the pretty two-storeyed cottages are thatched with
wheat reed and many have thatched porches. Several of these mellow
stone-walled cottages have a profusion of roses and clematis climbing
over them, to add further charm to their delightful appearances. The
village also offers two thatched pubs, The Dove and The Three
Horseshoes and both of these have been described in Chapter 4.

Another beautiful village, quite close to Bridport, is Loders. It is
situated on the site of a priory founded by the Benedictines about nine
hundred years ago. Nothing now remains of the priory but the monks

who, when they first came, were thought to have brought the art of cider-making to Dorset. Present day Loders has a splendid main street, running along the close-sided valley and many pretty thatched cottages, built with yellow-tinged stone, flank each side of it. The occasional catslide thatched roof may be seen and several of the cottages have raised parapets at their gabled ends to trap the thatch. Many of the cottages trace their histories back to the seventeenth and eighteenth centuries. Several thatched farmhouses may also be found in the near locality and fortunately the lanes at Loders escape any main traffic stream.

A further quiet unchanged village is Powerstock, the neighbouring one to Loders. It is centred on a network of peaceful hilly lanes and village life revolves around the church of St Mary, where five of the lanes meet. The Three Horseshoes Inn stands close by. Kenneth Allsop, the well-known television personality and author lived in the area and is now buried at Powerstock. The many surrounding hills and woods form a picturesque landscape to the good sprinkling of stone thatched cottages to be found in the village. Some of the older ones date back to the seventeenth century and possess stone-mullioned windows. However, many of the attractive houses in the centre were built in Victorian times, with local materials and they are generously spaced apart. The houses, which are thatched, are roofed with combed wheat reed. Eggardon Hill, with its eight-hundred-foot high stark hill-fort, covering twenty acres, overlooks the village and nearby is the extensive nature reserve maintained at Powerstock Common. Thomas Hardy thought the neighbouring countryside ideal for the setting of his novel, *Far from the Madding Crowd*.

The pretty and secluded village of Litton Cheney hides in the Bride Valley to the south-east of Powerstock and contains a wide variety of thatched buildings. A sparkling stream runs by some of the eye-catching cottages. Many are thatched and one displays the date 1707. There are both thatched detached and terraced cottages and a few have creeper-clad walls, adding to the sense of rural calm. The village still retains a quaint thatched bus shelter and there is also a thatched wall and a thatched barn to be admired. The latter two may be found at Baglake Farm, on the edge of the village. The thatched stone wall borders the roadside by the farm and the thatched stone-built barn, with its slitted ventilators, stands close by. The barn roof is thatched with combed wheat reed and it has one gabled and one quarter-hipped end. A weather-cock sits on the top of the barn.

There are many farms in the area and one of these at nearby Higher Kingston Russell, is the only one still producing traditional Dorset Blue Vinney cheese in large commercial quantities. It manufactures over a thousand pounds weight a week of this much sought after cheese delicacy, made to a closely guarded and secret recipe. One wonders if the spies Gordon Lonsdale and Harry Houghton ever discussed the secret of the blue-veined cheese when they were using the thatched village inn, The Crown, at Puncknowle, as one of their regular meeting places.

Puncknowle (pronounced 'punnol') is situated by the Bridport to Abbotsbury coast road and contains many neat thatched stone cottages, as well as the inn with its pleasant quarter-hipped thatched roof. The village shelters behind a circular hill, known as The Knoll, about six hundred feet above sea-level. Puncknowle therefore faces to the north and misses some sunshine. However, its thatched roofs gain welcome protection from the south-westerly gales.

Incidentally, Colonel Henry Shrapnel was a former resident and his invention of the fragmentation shell first burst upon the world as a fearful weapon during the Peninsular War. The Colonel died in 1842. At the turn of this century, Puncknowle, like most other villages in Dorset, possessed many residents who were craftsmen. They worked to meet the various needs of the village and to make it virtually self-sufficient. In 1903, Puncknowle's population included two thatchers, a hurdle-maker, a blacksmith, a wheelwright, a beehive-maker, a dress-maker as well as a rabbit dealer, three fish dealers, a shopkeeper, a gardener and various farmers.

The very attractive village of Abbotsbury lures many summertime visitors to enjoy its famous swannery and sub-tropical gardens, with its peacocks and many rare plants. The gardens are now all that remain of Abbotsbury Castle which was built in the eighteenth century and used to look out to sea from its cliff-top site. In 1913, fire tore through the former property of the Earls of Ilchester and left it gutted. The remnants were later demolished.

The huge thatched tithe barn at Abbotsbury has been described in detail in Chapter 6 but the village itself offers a fine array of thatched cottages. As mentioned earlier, many are thatched with the durable water reed cut from the local reed beds at the swannery. A few have walls incorporating various pieces of stone salvaged from the abbey ruins and these stones are whiter than the more common stones used, which have an orange tint. In fact, one of the most striking features of Abbotsbury is the wonderful abundance of buildings constructed with this mellowed orange-coloured stone.

Abbotsbury rests in a valley near the coast and mainly consists of one long street, flanked by many of the stone-walled thatched cottages. The majority of these may be found at the west end of the village. A raised walkway adds further charm to the street and amongst the many delightful ancient terraced cottages stands a thatched dwelling originating from a medieval long house. Several of the lanes branching off from

Terrace of Cottages – Abbotsbury

the village were former medieval trade tracks and one of these, called Hands Lane, harbours a small single-storeyed building, with a half-hipped thatched roof, which used to be a basket maker's workshop. In addition, Abbotsbury now boasts a thatched craft workshop, a thatched antique shop, a thatched pottery, a thatched grocery shop and even a thatched veterinary surgery.

In the past, fishing played an important role in the life of the villagers. At Abbotsbury Beach, many farm workers formerly toiled with seine nets to catch mackerel during the long summer evenings. This was done by first casting out a gigantic net, from a boat rowed a few hundred yards off shore, in a semicircle. A gang of men would then slowly haul the net into the shore. At the same time, the ends of the net, hanging vertically in the water, were gradually drawn together to enclose the fish and on a good evening, thousands of fish might be caught. This method of fishing was possible due to the deeply shelving nature of the beach but it is now rarely carried out, unless a particularly enormous shoal of fish is reported very close to the shore.

An old Mayday tradition was formerly carried out at Abbotsbury to ensure good luck for the fishing harvest. In the morning, crown-shaped garlands, made from wild and garden flowers, were taken from house to house by the children. The garlands were then blessed and carried down to the boats, for fixing to the bows. In the afternoon, sports and general merrymaking took place and in the evening, the boats were sailed out to sea. The garlands were then scattered with prayers for the sea harvest. It is thought that the last occasion this ceremony took place was about sixty years ago.

The nearby village of Portesham also once had strong links with the sea as Admiral Sir Thomas Masterman Hardy, Nelson's flag captain at Trafalgar lived in the manor house, called Portesham House. The village remains unspoilt, with its peaceful green and many old stone cottages, a few roofed with thatch. Even the telephone box is painted green at the request of the villagers to blend with the surrounding scenery. A few modern houses with thatched roofs may also be seen and Elworth, on the south-west fringe of Portesham, contains a small grouping of thatched buildings. Nearly all the thatched roofs again consist of combed wheat reed.

Many attractive thatched villages may be found in the heart of West Dorset, well away from the coastal belt. One of the most picturesque is Melbury Osmond, about twelve miles to the north-west of Dorchester and seven miles to the south of Yeovil, just off the A37. The winding minor road travels up and down hill, before it leads to the idyllic-

A Cottage Group – Melbury Osmond

looking village, set amongst wooded countryside, in a fertile valley. There are beautiful groups of thatched cottages, set at various angles to one another, upon the southern slope of the valley, with a sparkling stream and a ford at the bottom. Several of the thatched cottages were built in the seventeenth century and the occasional one may be seen with quaint bulging walls. Most are thatched with combed wheat reed and built with walls of stone.

Thomas Hardy's mother, Jemima Swetman was born at Melbury Osmond and she was also married in its church on December 22, 1839. The thatched house, which stands at the northern end of the footpath through the churchyard, is reputedly the former home of Hardy's mother. Later, she is thought to have greatly influenced her son, Thomas, with her intense love of the countryside. He, of course, was born in the much more famous thatched cottage, at Higher Bockhampton.

Many of the thatched cottages in Melbury Osmond, between the church and ford, possess rustic thatched porches and the occasional one may be spotted with stone mullioned windows. One large thatched house harbours a thatched barn at its rear. The pretty thatched school cottage, built with stone and brick, stands next to the old school, now converted into a private house. The latter has a slated roof and it still retains the school bell, set in the wall above the doorway.

The other side of the ford leads to Melbury Park and it is possible to walk through this wooded deer park to the village of Evershot, which lies under two miles away to the south. This quiet village is one of the highest in Dorset and the main street contains many pleasant stone-built cottages and shops, in addition to the church and inn. Many of the buildings open their front doors on to a raised walkway and several have stone mullioned windows. There are thatched cottages at both ends of the main street but the majority are gathered at West Hill, near the church. Again, nearly all are thatched with combed wheat reed and many of the cottages are arranged in neat terraces, with raised pointed ridges. The local pub is not thatched but it has a thatched building immediately next door.

Rampisham, Wraxall and Chantmarle all lie to the south of Evershot and possess many picture postcard thatched buildings. For example, Rampisham Post Office has a well-patched rather curious looking thatched roof and the stone built picturesque building has a large tall thatched porch guarding its entrance. The upper-storey dormer windows have small individual tufted thatched bonnets shielding them from the weather. The main roof ridge is flat and it is decorated with liggers and cross-slats. The post office stands by a clear stream and ford, with a wild natural stretch of green shaded by some beautiful tall trees at its front. Just outside the post office is a junction where three

Post Office – Rampisham

country roads meet. A fine example of a Jacobean manor house may be found a short way up one of them and about a mile away, a Roman tessellated pavement was unearthed at the end of the eighteenth century. Strangely, the local pub is called The Tigers Head, a most unusual name for a remote country licensed house.

Several thatched cottages and farm buildings stand in the rather remote countryside around Rampisham. Nearby Wraxall, in particular, offers a good collection of old thatched farm cottages. The majority can be readily seen when motoring from Higher Wraxall and down through Lower Wraxall, on the way to Cattistock. Most are simple cottages built with stone rubble or ashlar and roofed with wheat reed. Metford Mill, at Lower Wraxall, is especially lovely and its walls are made of a mixture of stone and banded flint beneath its thatched roof. At nearby Chantmarle, there are a small group of beautiful and more elaborately thatched cottages, built of flint and brick. The beauty of one charming thatched roof, with its richly ornamented and pointed raised ridge, is further enhanced by the unusual massive chimney projecting from its gable wall. Close by in the valley the scene is dominated by the magnificent early seventeenth-century manor house of Chantmarle, constructed entirely of Ham Hill stone. This fine house is now used as a police training college.

The pretty village of Stoke Abbott lies to the west, near Beaminster. It is surrounded by rather tortuous tunnel-like lanes and also some hills. One of these hills, to the north-east known as Gerrard's, is densely covered with beech trees and drovers were formerly thought to have used such clumps as landmarks, as they journeyed across the country-side. The main street of Stoke Abbott is very narrow and it contains many picturesque honey-coloured stone houses. Several trace their origins back to the early seventeenth century and a high percentage of the buildings are thatched. The thatched post office stands at the end of a tidy terrace of thatched cottages and the occasional cottage door has a thatched canopy to protect it. One thatched house, built in the middle of the eighteenth century, boasts a five-bay ashlar front and also mullioned windows. The seventeenth-century thatched village pub,

An Ornamental Thatched Cottage – Chantmarle, near Evershot

The New Inn, has been described in detail in Chapter 4. Whilst on the subject of liquid refreshment, it may be of interest to know that Stoke Abbott has an excellent spring water and to prove its purity it has even been supplied to quench the thirst of MPs in the House of Commons.

An incident that occurred at Stoke Abbott, about one hundred and twenty-five years ago, may have had an influence on Thomas Hardy and some of his more melancholy thoughts in his writings. The fateful happening was a murder in the village and the later execution of the condemned man at a public hanging at Dorchester, on the 10 August 1858. Thomas Hardy watched the scene through a telescope and he was much affected by the experience. Fortunately, Thomas Hardy witnessed many more pleasurable scenes from the seat of his bicycle. He was very fond of cycling and often pedalled fifty miles a day around the Dorset countryside. Incidentally, Stoke Abbott claims a lesser known poet as its rector in the late eighteenth century. He was William Crowe, whose best acclaimed work was the poem called 'Lewesdon Hill'.

The name Melplash is very familiar in the southern counties of England because it is associated with the sizeable and popular agricultural show which is held annually in August in West Dorset. In fact, the show is now sited at Bridport because it has outgrown its original venue. The village of Melplash lies to the south-east of Stoke Abbott, on the road from Beaminster to Bridport. It was in the bar of the thatched village inn, called The Half Moon, that a sporting challenge between two farmers on the relative skills of their farming sons led to the origins of the annual show. The Half Moon is only partly thatched and it has been much extended since it was first built in the eighteenth century, with a mixture of stone and cob. The pub claims a ghost and many sightings have been reported of the shadowy figure, who apparently enjoys gazing out of the window.

Melplash Court, a honey-coloured Tudor building, stands outside the village and was originally the home of Sir Thomas More, Sheriff of Dorset when Henry VIII was on the throne. An amusing story relates that the Sheriff, when rather merry after a few drinks, decided to release all the prisoners from Dorchester Gaol. He later had cause to regret his decision and to appease the King and the Lord Treasurer, called Paulet, he had to agree to the marriage of his daughter and heiress to the latter gentleman. The Paulet family, by this arrangement, gained control of Melplash Court.

Several thatched cottages may be viewed in the surrounding countryside and also a very large number of fruit orchards. These supply many apples for cider making, not only to commercial outlets in Dorset but also to neighbouring counties. At the beginning of this century, cider in Dorset was usually made by first reducing the apples to a pulp in a hand-operated grinding mill, before the resulting 'pomace' was pressed through filtration mats often made from straw or horsehair. The filtrate was then allowed to undergo its fermentation process in barrels. These were often stored in thatched outbuildings on the farm.

21   *Sketch Map of Dorset*

Bibliography

BILLETT, M. G., Thatching and Thatched Buildings (Robert Hale, 1979)

BROWN, R. J., English Farmhouses (Robert Hale, 1982)

BRUNSKILL, R. W., Illustrated Handbook of Vernacular Architecture (Faber and Faber, 1978)

GANT, R., Dorset Villages (Robert Hale, 1980)

HYMAS, M., Dorset Folklore (Books of Wessex, Taunton 1981)

NEWMAN, J., PEVSNER, N., The Buildings of England. Dorset (Penguin Books, 1972)

OSWALD, A., Country Houses of Dorset (Country Life Ltd., 1959)

ROYAL COMMISSION ON HISTORICAL MONUMENTS (ENGLAND)., County of Dorset. Volumes I to V (1970 and various dates)

WIGHTMAN, R., Portrait of Dorset (Robert Hale, 1977)

Other Edited Books and Publications:

Better Pubs in Dorset (Better Pubs, Red Cross House. Crediton, 1975/6)

Dorset County Guide (British Publishing Company, Gloucester, 1983)

Piddle Valley Book of Country Life (Hutchinson, 1980)

Shell Guide to England (Michael Joseph and Rainbird, 1970)

Sunday Times Book of the Countryside (Macdonald, 1980)

Index

Abbotsbury, 31–2, 87, 114–6, 206–8; reed, 31–2, 44, 115, 206
Affpuddle, 109, 121, 127, 131
Agricultural wages, 19
Ale wife, 80
Allsop, Kenneth, 205
Almer, 80–1
Almshouses, 20
Alton Pancras, 127–8
Anchor Inn (Shapwick), The, 188
Anderson Manor, 65
Anning, Mary, 197
Ansty, Higher, 107
Anvil Restaurant (Pimperne), The, 157–8
Arable farms, 104
Ascot Gold Cup, 168
Ashmore, 155–6
Athelhampton House, 61–4
Avice's Cottage (Portland), 161

Badbury Rings, 186–7, 189
Baglake Farm (Litton Cheney), 205
Bakers Arms (Lytchett Minster), The, 83–4, 194
Ball clay, 172–3
Bankes family, 77, 172, 189
Barley Mow (Colehill), The, 78–9
Barnes, William, 100–1, 150, 176
Barns, 19, 114–22, 129, 131, 132–3, 140, 144, 145, 147, 160, 205
Barton Barn (West Stafford), 118
Barton House (Newton), 151
Batcombe, 110
Bearded tit, 33

Beating the Bounds, 51
Bellamy Cottage (Sutton Poyntz), 164
Bere Regis, 65, 133–6
Biddle, 38
Bishops Caundle, 153
Black Death, The, 16
Blackmore Vale, 12, 21, 86, 150, 152, 154, 158
Blacksmiths, 74
Blackstone, 170
Bladen, 132–3
Blaise Castle Estate, 91, 133
Bloody Assize, The, 127
Bloxworth, 193
Blue Pool, The, 172–3
Blue Vinney, Dorset, 205
Bockhampton, 123, 125
Boswell, George, 109
Bottle (Marshwood), The, 81
Bovington Farmhouse, 110–1
Bowleaze Cove, 168
Brace of Pheasants (Plush), The, 77–8
Bradford Abbas, 159–60
Brewsters Sessions, 80
Briantspuddle, 131
Bridehead, 179, 181
Bridport, 84, 203–4, 212
Bridport Arms Hotel (West Bay), The, 84
Brighton, 92
British Petroleum, 170
Broadmayne, 176
Bronze Age, 12
Broomhill, 78
Bryan, Guy de, 53–4
Bryanston, 153

Buildings (Manswood), The, 192
Bull (Newton), The, 83, 151
Burton, 147
Burton Bradstock, 73–4, 204
Bus shelters (thatched), 20, 111, 177, 193
Butler, John, 54
Button-making, Dorset, 194
Buzbury Rings, 186

Came Rectory, 100–1
Carp, English, 59
Carr, John Glyn, 189
Cart-sheds, 108, 116
Castle Inn (West Lulworth), The, 88
Cattistock, 144
Caundle Marsh, 153
Caundle Wake, 153
Ceres, 29
Cerne Abbas, 68–9, 76, 141–3
Chafin, George, 192
Chaldon Herring, 71
Chalk ashlar, 23–4
Chalk belts, 21
Chantmarle, 210–1
Charity farms, 148
Charlborough House, 95–6
Charles II, King, 74, 77, 197, 199
Charminster, 146–7
Charmouth, 198–9
Cheselbourne, 138
Chesil Beach, 31, 161, 162, 204
Chess, Game of, 190
Chettle, 192
Chickerell, 162
Chideock, 84, 199–202; Martyrs, 202
Chideock House Hotel, The, 202
Childe Okeford, 82, 152
Chilfrome, 144
Chimneys, 46–7
Chiswell, 162
Christchurch, 195–6
Church Farmhouse (Batcombe), 110
Churchill, Winston, 175
Church Knowle, 171

Clavel Tower, 171
Clock Hotel (Chideock), The, 202
Clouds Hill, 110, 175
Coach and posting houses, 84
Cob, 22–3, 121, 124
Coffered ceilings, 107
Colehill, 78
Combed wheat reed, 29–30, 38, 39, 43, 129
Combing long straw, 39
Compton House, 97–8
Concrete bricks, 26, 132
Constable, 168
Coombe Keynes, 169
Copses, 34–5
Corfe Castle, 77, 95, 171–3
Corfe Mullen, 188–9
Corn dollies, 28–9
Corscombe, 79–80
Cost of thatch, 38
Cottage (Charmouth), The, 198–9
Cottage Orné, 91–103
Cottage types, 22–3
Council for Small Industries in Rural Areas, 37
Court-leet, 195
Cranborne, 193; Chase, 21, 73, 89, 155, 192
Crawford Castle, 187
Crichel Estate, 192
Crowe, William, 212
Crown Hotel (Marnhull), The, 87, 149
Crown-post roof, 117
Crown (Puncknowle), The, 206
Crown (Winterborne Stickland), The, 139
Cruck, 106, 117–8, 131
Cull-pepper's Dish, 131
Cusped eaves, 93–4, 98–9
Cyma-Cavetto ceiling, 107

Dairy farms, 104, 112
Damer, Joseph, 17, 68, 137
Debenham, Ernest, 132–3
Demeter, 29
Devil's Nine Stones, 179
Dorchester, 12, 126–7, 135, 212

Dorset Knobs, 199–200
Double-pile house, 41, 106
Dove (Burton Bradstock), The, 73, 204
Drax Estate, 95–6
Drovers, 79, 211
Durweston, 153

East Chaldon, 71
East Farm (Osmington), 50, 111–2
East Knighton, 169
Eaves types, 94
Eggardon Hill, 205
Eldridge Pope, 160
Elsdon's Farm, 197
Elworth, 208
Enclosures (Land), 16–7, 104
Evershot, 209
Eyebrow windows, 39

Far from the Madding Crowd, 124, 129, 135, 169, 205
Farmhouses, 104–13
Farnham, 89, 158
Fiddleford, 152
Fifehead Magdalen, 148–9
Filly Loo, 155
Fire hooks, 134–5
Fire risk, 13, 20, 45, 47, 63, 134, 157, 195
Fisher, Archdeacon, 168
Flail threshing, 116
Fleet, The, 31
Flints, 24
Fontmell Magna, 154–5
Fortuneswell, 162
Fowles, John, 198
Fox (Corscombe), The, 79–80
Frampton, 144–5
French Peter, 71
Friar Waddon, 108–9
Fulford family, 61
Furmity, 202
Furzebrook, 173
Furzehill, 72

Garnett, Edward, 71
Gaunt's House, 93
Geological faults, 169–70
George Inn (Chideock), The, 84–5, 202
Gerard family, 66
Ghosts, 62, 65–6, 69, 73, 85, 88, 94–5, 125, 156, 175, 212
Gibraltar of Wessex, The, 161
Goathill, 94–5
Godmanstone, 74
Gold Hill (Shaftesbury), 158–9
Grain driers, 117
Granaries, 116
Great Western Turnpike, 184
Gulliver, Isaac, 72, 157
Gussage St Andrew, 157
Gypsies, 182–3

Half Moon (Melplash), The, 212
Hambledon Hill, 152
Hambro Arms (Milton Abbas), The, 88–9, 137
Hambro family, 88, 138
Ham Hill limestone, 25, 76, 98, 160, 210
Hammoon, 25, 56–9
Hangman's Cottage (Dorchester), 126–7
Hardy, Thomas, 65, 82, 100, 101, 123–6, 150, 159, 161, 209, 212; see also individual novel titles
Hazel, 34
Hazelbury Bryan, 118
Hermitage, 160
Herringston Farmhouse, 112–3
Higher Farm (Margaret Marsh), 106
Hilton, 113, 138
Hinton Martell, 93
Hod Hill, 153
Hog Hill Barn (Stratton), 121
Holt, 26, 93
Holwell, 106
Honey Puddle, 129
Hospices, 69
Hurdlemakers, 34–5

Ibberton, 152–3
Ice Age, 11
Ilchester Arms (Symondsbury),
    The, 87, 203
Ilchester, Earls of, 54, 80, 87
Industrial Revolution, 52, 100
Insurance, 20, 45
Iron Age, 12
Iron hooks, 36, 41
Isis, 29
Isle of Slingers, 161
Iwerne Courtney, 99, 121, 154
Iwerne Minster, 154
Iwerne Stepleton, 154

John, King, 155, 172
Jordan Hill, 164
Judge Jeffreys, 65, 127

Kimmeridge, 170–1
Kings Arms (Stoborough), The,
    77
Kings Arms (Wareham), The, 85
Kingston Lacy, 189
Kingston Russell, Higher, 205–6
Kinson, 72

Ladders for thatching, 38
Langton Arms (Tarrant
    Monkton), The, 185–6
Latour, Pierre, 71
Lawrence of Arabia, 110, 175
Lawrence's Farm (Tolpuddle),
    131
Leggett, 38, 41
Letterbox Cottage (Radipole), 164
Liggers, 36, 38, 44, 203
Limbry, Stephen, 199
Limewash, 24
Littlebredy, 179–182
Little Brook (Fiddleford), 152
Little Toller Farm, 61
Litton Cheney, 205
Loders, 107, 110, 204–5
Lodges, 92–9
Lodmoor, 32–3
London clay, 26
Long Barn (Woodsford), 119

Long barrows, 12
Longbredy, 12
Long Burton, 86
Long straw, 29, 39–40, 43, 45,
    50, 189
Loop-lights, 115–6
Lower Hilton Farm, 113
Lower Lewell Farm, 119–20
Luckford Lake, 171
Lulworth Castle, 87, 170
Lulworth Cove, 88, 169
Lulworth, East, 87–8, 169, 170;
    West, 87–8, 169
Lyme Regis, 18, 98, 197–8
Lynde, de la, 86
Lytchett Minster, 83, 194

Maiden Castle, 12, 182
Maiden Newton, 144
Maidenwell, 162
Manor houses, 51–67
Manswood, 190–2
Map of Dorset, 14–15;
    chapter areas, 213
Margaret Marsh, 106
Marigold Cottage (Spetisbury),
    186–7
Maris Huntsman wheat, 31
Marnhull, 87, 149
Marsh reeds, 19, 31–3, 41, 43,
    194–5
Marshwood, 81; Vale, 21, 69
Martinstown, 61, 182
Martyn family, 61–2
Maumbury Rings, 127
Melbury Osmond, 208–9
Melbury Park, 209
Melcombe Regis, 164
Melplash, 212
Metford Mill, 210
Middle Farm (Winterborne
    Houghton), 113
Milborne St Andrew, 133–4
Milk stands, 20
Milton Abbas, 17, 68, 88, 136–8
Minchington, 157
Mohuns, de, 56
Moigne Court, 169

Monkton Wyld, 197
Monmouth, Duke of, 197
Moonfleet Farmhouse (Ansty),
    107
Morcombelake, 199–200
Morden, 96, 194
Moreton, 174–5
Morris Dancers, 82, 155
Morton, John, 193
Motcombe, 159
Mummers, 203
Mundays Cottage (Stour Provost),
    148
Museum Hotel (Farnham), The,
    89–90, 158

Naish Farm (Holwell), 106
Nash, John, 91–2, 133
Nether Compton, 97
New Inn (Stoke Abbott), The, 82,
    212
Newton, 83, 150–1
New Victoria Cinema (London),
    168
Norfolk reed, 33, 40–1, 60
Normans, 13
North Barn (Affpuddle), 120–1
Notton, 144

Ocean Bay, 170
Okeford Fitzpaine, 152
Old Bell (Cerne Abbas), The, 142
Old Court House (Christchurch),
    The, 195
Old Harry Rocks, 170, 173–4
Old Malt House (Winterborne
    Stickland), 139–40
Old Shepherd's Cottage
    (Martinstown), 182
Old Thatch (Uddens Cross), The,
    88–90
Osmington, 111–2, 168;
    White Horse, 168
Osmington Mills, 69, 71, 168
O'Toole, Peter, 80
Owermoigne, 169
Oxford, 158

Palmer's Old Brewery, 203–4
Pamphill, 189
Park Farm Museum (Milton
    Abbas), 137
Peninsular Coast Path, 70
Peter of Pomfret, 172
Phragmites communis, 31, 33, 40
Piddlehinton, 75–6, 127, 128–9
Piddle, River, 127
Piddletrenthide, 127, 128
Pimperne, 12, 157–8
Pitt-Rivers, General, 89–90, 158,
    204
Plank and muntin, 153
Plush, 77–8
Population of Dorset, 18
Portesham, 25, 208
Portland, 161–2; stone, 11, 25,
    163, 168
Portman Estate, 153
Post and truss, 117
Post-chaise houses, 84
Powerstock, 118, 205
Preaching crosses, 159, 188
Preston, 50, 164–5
Priest's House Museum, 184
Pubs (thatched), 68–90
'Pudding' stones, 25
Puddletown, 62, 127, 129
Puncknowle, 206
Purbeck, 21, 171, 172; limestone,
    11, 25, 54, 56, 171; marble,
    172
Puritan Act (1612), 79
Purse Caundle, 94, 153

**Queen Charlotte's Cottage
    (Kew)**, 91
Queens Armes Hotel
    (Charmouth), The, 199

Radipole, 163–4; reed, 32, 41,
    72, 163
Rampisham, 209–10
Reaper and binder, 27
Red Post, The, 64–5
Red Standard wheat, 31
Reed-comber, 30

Reed-cutter, 33
Reed warbler, 33
Regency Cottage (Wool), 102–3
Remedy Oak, 193
Return of the Native, The, 150, 179
Reymes, Colonel, 66
Rick finials, 28
Ricks, Corn, 27–9, 30
Ring (Briantspuddle), The, 131–2
Romans, 12
Roof types, 41–2; barns, 117–8;
    ridges, 46, 47–9
Rose and Crown (Bradford
    Abbas), The, 160
Rose and Crown (Long Burton),
    The, 86–7
Round barrows, 12
Round Mead, 140
Royal Lodge, The, 91–2
Royal Oak (Cerne Abbas), The,
    76–7, 142
Royal Society for the Protection of
    Birds, 163
Rye straw, 13, 26

**Sailor's Return (East Chaldon),
    The,** 71–2
Salisbury Museum, 158
Samways family, 61
Saxons, 12–3
Scallops, 49–50
Schools, 20, 204
Sea Life Centre, 33
Seine nets, 207
Seventeenth-century Cottage
    Chimneys (Chideock), 201–2
Shaftesbury, 158–9, 171
Shapwick, 187–8
Shave Cross Inn (near Bridport),
    The, 69
Sheep, 79
Sheridan, 144
Shillingstone, 152
Shrapnel, Colonel, 206
Shroton, 99, 121, 154
Sidmouth, 92
Sixpenny Handley, 156–7
Slates, 18

Slats, 36, 50
Smiths Arms (Godmanstone),
    The, 74–5
Smugglers, 71–2
Smugglers Haunt (Tricketts
    Cross), The, 73
Smugglers Inn (Osmington
    Mills), The, 69–71, 168
Southover, 145–6
Southwell, 162
Spar hook, 35
Spars, 34–6
Spetisbury, 186–7
Stables, 62–4
Staddle stones, 27, 202
Stafford, Sir Humphrey, 54
Stanfield, Thomas, 131
Steepleton, 182
Stinsford, 126
Stoborough, 77
Stocks Inn (Furzehill), The, 72
Stoke Abbott, 81, 211–2
Stone Age, 11–2
Stopes, Marie, 161
Stourpaine, 153
Stour Provost, 148
Stour, River, 148
Stourton Caundle, 153–4
St Peter's Finger (Lytchett
    Minster), 194
Strangeways family, 54
Stratton, 121, 145, 147
Straw pheasants, 46
Studland, 173
Sturminster Marshall, 188
Sturminster Newton, 83, 85, 100,
    149–51
Sutton Poyntz, 164, 166–8
Swanage, 71, 170
Sways, 36, 38
Swetman, Jemima, 209
Sydling St Nicholas, 143–4
Symondsbury, 87, 202–3

Tales from Wessex, 127
Tarrant Crawford, 184
Tarrant Gunville, 184
Tarrant Hinton, 184

Tarrant Keyneston, 184, 186
Tarrant Launceston, 184
Tarrant Monkton, 184, 185
Tarrant Rawston, 184
Tarrant Rushton, 184
Telling the bees, 153
Tess Cottage (Marnhull), 149–50
Tess of the d'Urbervilles, 30, 65–6, 87, 149, 177
Thatched House (Kinson), The, 72–3
Thatchers, 27, 35–50
Thatch sewing, 38
Thimble (Piddlehinton), The, 75–6, 129
Thorncombe Wood, 124
Thornford, 114
Three Horseshoes (Burton Bradstock), The, 74, 204
Threshing, 29, 116, 118
Threshing machines, 37, 116
Tigers Head (Rampisham), The, 210
Tilly Whim, 71
Tithes, 114
Tollard Royal, 155
Toller Fratrum, 60–1
Toller Whelme, 41, 59–60
Tolpuddle, 121–2, 127, 129–31; Martyrs, 129–31, 151
Transportation notices, 150
Trenchard family, 56
Tricketts Cross, 73
Trumpet Major, The, 168
Turberville family, 65–6, 134
Turners Puddle, 127, 133
Turnpike Act (1663), 84
Turnpike Cottage (Wimborne Minster), 184–5
Two on a Tower, 95

Uddens Cross, 88–90
Umbrella Cottage (Lyme Regis), 98–9, 198
Under the Greenwood Tree, 124
Union (Childe Okeford), The, 82–3

Upton Manor Farmhouse (Loders), 107–8
Upwey, 168

Waddock Cross, 109–10
Waddon, 66–7
Walls, 24–5, 113; thatched, 125, 140–2, 152, 205
Wareham, 11, 85, 171
Water meadows, 109, 147, 177
Wayfaring Cottage (Corfe Castle), 172–3
Weld Arms (East Lulworth), The, 87–8
Weld family, 87, 170
Well Beloved, The, 161
Wesley, John, 140, 188
Wessex Barn (Frampton), 145
West Bay, 84, 161
West Stafford, 47, 82–3, 118, 119, 138, 177–9
Weymouth, 68, 162–3, 168
Wheat straw, 12, 26–7, 30–1, 138, 202
Wheelwrights (Winterborne Stickland), 139
Whitcombe, 100–1, 175–6
White Hart (Sturminster Newton), The, 85, 150
White Hart (Yetminster), The, 85–6
Whitemill Bridge, 188
Wight, Isle of, 92
Willis, Robert, 190
Wimborne Minster, 68, 72, 184–5
Wimborne St Giles, 192–3
Winfrith Fields Farm, 108
Winfrith Newburgh, 108, 169
Winterborne Anderson, 65, 138
Winterborne Came, 100–1, 179, 183
Winterborne Clenston, 138, 140
Winterborne Farringdon, 183
Winterborne Herringston, 179
Winterborne Houghton, 113, 138–9
Winterborne Kingston, 138

Winterborne Muston, 64–5, 138, 140
Winterborne Stickland, 43, 138, 139–40
Winterborne St Martin, 61, 179, 182
Winterborne Tomson, 138
Winterborne Whitechurch, 138, 140
Winterborne Zelston, 138, 140–1
Winterbourne Abbas, 12, 179, 181, 182
Winterbourne Steepleton, 179, 182
Wire-netting, 44–5
Wise Man Inn (West Stafford), 82–3
Wishing Wells, 107, 168
Witchampton, 17, 184, 189–191
Witches, 28, 129

Woodbury Hill, 135, 154
Woodsford, 53; Castle, 25, 53–6; Farm, 119
Wool, 102, 174
Woolbridge Manor House, 65–6
Worlds End (Almer), The, 80–1, 96
Wraxall, 209, 210
Wynford, Lord, 61
Wytch Farm, 110
Wytherstone Farm (Powerstock), 118

Yalbury Cottage (Bockhampton), 125–6
Yealms, 39
Yeomen farmers, 16
Yetminster, 85
Yondover Farm (Loders), 110